LEARNING TO LEARN®

THINKING SKILLS FOR THE 21ST CENTURY

SEVENTH EDITION

MARCIA HEIMAN & JOSHUA SLOMIANKO

RECOMMENDED FOR NATIONAL DISSEMINATION BY THE U.S. DEPARTMENT OF EDUCATION

This is the seventh edition of the Learning to Learn® college textbook. This book is an updated version of the previous LTL textbooks, published under the titles *Applications of Learning Theory* (1984), *Methods of Inquiry* (1986 & 1988), *Success in College and Beyond* (1992 & 1995) and *This End Up: A Guide to College Success* (1997).

To Mildred Kelly, Devorah Orrenstein,
Paul Moses, Reg Hannaford, Yehudda Malul,
Sherman David Spector, Dale M. Brethower,
Eddy M. Zemach, and Yeshayahu Leibowitz

Our teachers,
who have dedicated their lives to keeping
the dream and possibility of learning
alive in their students.

**If you give a man a fish, you feed him for a day.
If you teach a man to fish, you feed him for a lifetime.**

Anonymous

**What is the use of knowing? Why, to be able to choose
the line of greatest advantage instead of yielding in the direction
of least resistance.**

George Bernard Shaw

A note from Kathy Braxton

Learning to Learn, Inc.

Box 38-1351
Cambridge, MA 02238-1351
800-288-4465/Fax: 617-441-3920

Dear Friends:

Welcome to Learning to Learn®. Having worked with LTL for almost 30 years, I'm happy to have the opportunity to introduce the 7th edition of the LTL college textbook to new LTL students and instructors.

I want you to feel comfortable as you start to use LTL. The skills in this system will come easily to you, because they're all built on natural learning skills – the skills you use every day without thinking about them. Every time you cross a street in traffic, or find a bargain at the supermarket, you're asking yourself questions about what's in front of you – *Where's there a break in the traffic? Which brand is least expensive?* But you probably drop these questioning skills when you learn in school. Like most students, you try to memorize and memorize, until learning is just a chore.

LTL will bring back the feeling of excitement about learning new things that you had when you were first learning about the world, before school and tests. You'll build on your natural questioning skills, and "translate" back and forth between what you *see* and what you *think* about – the verbal and visual parts of learning. You'll even feel that you've "beat the system" by *predicting exam questions* – and you'll actually learn more in a deeper way.

If you're a new LTL instructor, I'm sure you'll be as excited as I always am when I teach LTL to find how easy it can be to help students discover their natural talents, to find out how gifted they are. Please feel welcome to call me at any time if you have questions or concerns about how to help your students get the most out of LTL.

Regards,

Kathryn Braxton

Kathryn Braxton,
Director of Training

TABLE OF CONTENTS

SUPPLEMENTS

Toll-free telephone consulting

Call us at 800-28-THINK (800-288-4465) if you have any questions about teaching Learning to Learn®

Instructor's manual

Complete package of information, including: Step-by-step instructions for teaching this course; sample course syllabi for 1-, 2-, and 3-credit courses; student handouts; and transparency masters.

Controlled study

Learning to Learn® has been recommended for national dissemination by the U.S. Department of Education as the *only* freshman seminar program which controlled, externally validated studies show has a significant, long-term impact on college students' *grades across the curriculum* and *retention through graduation*. We will help you conduct your own study *comparing LTL's impact on your students to the effect of any freshman seminar program you have used in the past.*

Learning to Learn® video

A 2-hour video which can be used (1) to train faculty new to Learning to Learn® and (2) as an instructional support in the classroom.

Motivational video

A video of interviews with past LTL students who describe the impact LTL has had on their academic and personal success.

Customized syllabus

On request, we will prepare a *free, customized syllabus* to help you adjust this course to your students' needs, the length of your course, and special freshman-related events on your campus.

LTL National Scholarship Award

Winners of this award will receive $1000 in tuition expense reimbursement. See page 182 for details.

ABOUT THE AUTHORS

Marcia Heiman, Ph.D.

Marcia Heiman is Chief Executive Officer of Learning to Learn, Inc., a consulting and publishing firm in Cambridge, Massachusetts. The firm provides Learning to Learn® (LTL) seminars and materials for educators and business persons.

Dr. Heiman has developed and researched the effectiveness of LTL for 30 years. She served as director of college learning centers at a number of colleges and universities, including the University of Wisconsin-Madison, the University of New Hampshire, Roxbury Community College, and Boston College. She has tested the impact of LTL on her own students. LTL's controlled studies showing measurable changes in learning have been externally validated by the U.S. Department of Education. The Department has recommended LTL for national dissemination; it is now used at colleges and universities throughout the nation.

Dr. Heiman holds a Bachelor of Arts from New York University, a Masters in Research in Instruction from the Harvard Graduate School of Education, and a doctorate in Behavioral Sciences from the University of Michigan.

Joshua Slomianko

Joshua Slomianko is Chief Operating Officer of Learning to Learn, Inc. Mr. Slomianko has a wide-ranging background, which includes being part of a research team in immunology at the Medical School of Hadassah Hospital in Jerusalem; directing the blood bank at Misgabladach Hospital; working with television news visuals for the Israeli Broadcasting Authorities; and doing graduate work in philosophy at the Hebrew University in Jerusalem.

Since 1979, Mr. Slomianko has been the co-developer of LTL. In this work he has made the disparate strategies in LTL a coherent whole system and discovered new strategies which strengthen LTL; written LTL instructional materials; and conducted LTL training seminars.

Mr. Slomianko holds a Bachelor of Arts in philosophy and has done graduate work in philosophy at the Hebrew University in Jerusalem. He also received training in the biological sciences at the Hadassah Medical School of Jerusalem.

Dr. Heiman and Mr. Slomianko are also the developers of the National Education Association's *Building Thinking Skills* series; the editors of *Thinking Skills Instruction: Concepts and Techniques,* the authors of *Learning to Learn® – Critical Thinking Skills for the Quality Workforce;* and the developers of *Learning to Learn®,* an interactive video course which IBM has made available to its entire workforce worldwide.

ACKNOWLEDGMENTS

We dedicated this book to the teachers – elementary through graduate school – who were most influential in shaping and encouraging our progress as students. But of course there were others. In the mid-1960's, S. Alan Cohen, then of Mobilization for Youth (a pilot poverty program in New York City), now of the University of San Francisco, provided inspiration and a sense that important changes could be made through education. Sid Groffman, then of Manhattan's Center for Perceptual Development, now in private practice in Redbank, NJ, suggested that the answer lay in a systematic approach to learning. Sidney Aaronson, then of New York University, now of Brooklyn College, and Jeanne Chall of the Harvard Graduate School of Education provided encouragement and opportunity. At about the same time, Donald E.P. Smith, at the University of Michigan, gathered together a group of graduate students with varied backgrounds and asked them to study what they felt they needed to know, and to learn from each other. At the center of this group was Dale M. Brethower, who helped the group focus on a non-deficit-based model of learning: to look at the learning behaviors of successful learners. Carl Semmelroth, Bob Morasky, Dick Olds, Ray Cabot, John Shtogren, Hal Weidner, Rowena Wilhelm, Tim Walters, and Roy Moxley – it was a wonderful time, and a very special group of people. Long hours over dark beer after Friday staff meetings; trying out new ideas, testing them out on each other and on students. Then there were the students: a thousand students each year, first at Michigan, later at the Universities of Wisconsin and New Hampshire. The dedication of professional staff – Pat Rosenberg at the University of Wisconsin, Rick Beebe at the University of New Hampshire. And undergraduate student staff – most importantly, Kathy Braxton and Arnold Sapenter at Wisconsin, Leo Lozada, Celeste Reid, John Anderson and David Litchfield Smith at New Hampshire. All of these people shared and helped make possible an emerging dream: That we could bring a kind of intellectual democracy to higher education, erasing years of educational deficits in students who came to college from non-traditional backgrounds, while stimulating the intellectual curiosity of students who had always done well in school, but had not stopped to think about what they were learning. That we could bring to these varied students a learning system which would not "track" students by "ability" or experience, but enable them to learn *how* to learn, using the same critical academic skills. The Special Services grant at Boston College and Roxbury Community College allowed us to focus on and solve the more resistant learning problems of non-traditional students. The professional staff leading this effort – Pat Williams, Ann Clenott Ide, Lesola Morgan, Dan Bunch, and Don McCrary – helped find solutions to the more difficult problems of academic motivation among disadvantaged learners. Page Kohlhepp, former Administrative Assistant at Boston College's Learning to Learn Program, gave unstintingly of her caring and intelligent support. These people all helped bring Learning to Learn® to its present form, where it helps students from different backgrounds and educational experiences attain their academic potential.

* * *

Perhaps most of all we would like to thank our parents, Sam and Cele Heiman, and Avraham and Tova Slomianko, for instilling in us a strong sense of idealism, the courage to stand by our beliefs, and the feeling that we could make a difference.

Chapter 1:
STARTING OUT

COLLEGE
– *YOUR FUTURE OF POSSIBILITIES*

Going to college marks the beginning of a significant and exciting change in your life – whether you're just out of high school or an adult returning to school. New doors are opening to you. There is an aura of promise and opportunity. It certainly feels like you're standing on an important threshold – where at last you'll find the means and conditions to realize your hopes and dreams – and your place in that future.

At times these "grand" feelings may seem out of proportion and overblown – but they are good and appropriate. Still, you may have other feelings as well: doubt in your ability, fears that you will fail others who depend on you. Those are also natural and appropriate feelings. Although the potential of the future seems unlimited, your doubts about your ability and worthiness can destroy your high spirits. To try to ignore these feelings of insecurity is futile. Even if you could hide these feelings from yourself, you'd miss the important message they carry. Your fears and doubts say, "I'm not prepared. I may fail." *Being aware of these feelings is like recognizing signs of danger – they'll help you take preventive action. Use these warning signs to prepare yourself, to ensure that your dreams, however daring, will become realities.*

In this chapter we'll start you on your way. We'll begin by introducing you to **Learning to Learn**® – which forms the basis of this book. Using LTL, you'll learn to develop your **natural thinking skills**. You'll use LTL both for **improving academic skills** and for making needed **personal and social changes** in your life. Next we'll take a look at two areas you'll need to address as you begin college – **choosing courses** and **finding and using campus resources**. Finally, our **Reaching for the Top Self-Assessment** will help you get a picture of who you are now, as you enter this new world.

WHY IS COLLEGE IMPORTANT?

Some of the key reasons why college is important:

◆ ***More choices.*** The world of the 21st century will offer a wide variety of career choices. We can only begin to imagine the exciting choices that will be available with rapidly expanding technology. And with the continuing revolution in electronic communications, there will be freedom to work from many different locations. The cartoon of a person lying on a beach while working at the "office" is rapidly becoming a reality for many people.

But these choices are only available to people with skills – and with college degrees.

◆ ***Making the most of your talents.*** In the same way that you don't know what the future will bring in career choices, you don't know *yourself* well enough to assess your place in that world. Your talents can only be discovered – and developed – with a college education.

◆ ***Standard of living.*** As the chart below shows, a college degree can significantly increase your financial income and opportunities.

Education and Income

Studies show a strong relationship between education and lifetime earnings. This relationship is clear in the chart below:

Level of Education	Average Annual Income*
Master's degree	$43,032
Bachelor's degree	$35,900
Some college	$27,705
High school graduate	$23,410
Some high school	$18,012

What do these figures mean to you? They mean that as a college graduate you would earn an average of **$60,000** more than high school graduates for *every five years you are in the workforce* – and this trend will probably accelerate. In 40 years of employment, your lifetime earnings as a college graduate would be about **$480,000 more** than as a high school graduate.

---

* The information in this chart was adapted from the U.S. Department of Commerce, Bureau of the Census, Current Population Reports, Series P-60, *Money Income of Households, Families, and Persons in the United States: 1992,* reported in the *Digest of Educational Statistics, 1994,* published by the National Center for Education Statistics, U.S. Department of Education, Office of Educational Research and Improvement.

QUESTIONS ABOUT GOING TO COLLEGE

I don't remember much of what I learned in high school. Besides, the way I see it, a lot of information is useless in real life. So what's the point of college – especially a liberal arts degree?

There are two answers to that question.

1. *Job-related skills.* Whatever content you study in college, you'll acquire important skills which are valued by employers in today's fast-changing economy: For example, you'll learn to plan; to organize information; to weigh the pros and cons of different situations and different approaches to a problem; to analyze and use new ideas. You'll also learn how to *perform under pressure* – a skill of value to you, and to every potential employer.

2. *The value of lifelong learning.* For the most part, high school courses do not make you think – and they do not require much commitment to the information presented. In college, you'll get the chance to become intellectually and emotionally involved in what you're learning. This can enrich your life and stimulate your interests in ways that help you discover new aspects of life. Bear in mind that learning can do more for you than you think. Learning can be an important, lifelong process.

I can see that college is important in the long run. But in the short term, it's expensive. How can I afford college on limited funds?
    There are many routes to finance a college education. We'll give you a guided tour of financial aid possibilities in Chapter 12.

I never did very well in school. Won't college just be more of the same?
Or:

I did okay in high school, but I understand there's a lot more homework in college. How will I get everything done?
    What you lacked before was an effective way to harness your skills. In this course you'll acquire a method – Learning to Learn® – which will enable you to succeed academically with ease and confidence.

    Turn to the next page, and we'll tell you more about that.

THINKING SKILLS FOR THE 21st CENTURY
SUCCEEDING WITH LEARNING TO LEARN®

What can you really do to ensure your success in college? For starters, you have to find the right entry point for your efforts. Taking Learning to Learn® (LTL) as a freshman gives you the opportunity to become a successful learner, able to achieve your goals, and to be an active problem-solver – in college, your later career, and in your daily activities.

What's so special about LTL? LTL provides students with thinking skills that result in significant, long-term effects on students' academic success and retention in college. For more than 20 years, the U.S. Department of Education's Joint Dissemination Review/Program Effectiveness Panel examined the effectiveness of programs at all levels of education. More than 700 educational programs were investigated. The panel found that LTL is the **only** college-level program that:

◆ impacts on both average and non-traditional students;

◆ significantly improves college students' *grade point averages* and *retention* through graduation;

◆ does not require subject-matter tutoring.

Until recently, most colleges conducted only a brief orientation session for new students. Now a great many colleges offer a semester-long freshman orientation course – a class that helps students recognize the importance of the transition from high school to college. Increasing the time spent on freshman year issues is a great boost to new college students.

But more than the extra time is needed. A maximally effective freshman orientation program will present a methodology which has been shown to produce desired results – higher grades in courses across the curriculum and higher college graduation rates.

Student Voices

Steve Caggiano

The Learning to Learn class has meant a lot to me, both academically and personally. As a result of LTL, I'm currently doing my best academic work – even though I had more extra-curricular work than ever, having the lead in Hair *this semester.*

Although I didn't know that LTL could help with personal problems, skills from LTL have also helped me deal with many problems outside the classroom, especially the most disturbing emotional crisis of my life, which I had to face this semester. By generating questions, breaking the problem into parts, setting up and trying certain plans of action, and setting problem-solving goals along the way, I've avoided a lot of potential trauma.

HOW IS LEARNING TO LEARN®
DIFFERENT FROM ALL OTHER
FRESHMAN ORIENTATION PROGRAMS?

Above all, success in college means *learning* well. The centerpiece of most student success programs is their learning improvement strategies. Most programs present *traditional study skills methods* – like those you had in high school.

Traditional study skills were designed by educators from practices which seemed to work well in the classroom. These old-fashioned study skills have limited effectiveness – and some are even detrimental to learning. For example, studies show that skills promoting only short-term memory may actually interfere with learning for meaning.

By contrast, Learning to Learn® is based on basic research on how learning occurs. All of the LTL skills stem from research on strategies of successful learners – research done at the University of Michigan in the late 1960s. Even the organization of the exercises in this book reflects research in the psychology of learning: Most student success books contain a *collection* of skills. By contrast, the skills in this book build on each other in a sequence – and are interrelated as a *system* of learning – which will result in *long-term changes* in how you learn.

What do we mean by long-term results?

Learning to Learn® has significant, long-term impacts on college students' grade point averages and retention through graduation. The studies validated by the U.S. Department of Education showed that:

◆ For students at 2-year colleges, there is a 40% improvement in retention through graduation as compared with another intervention.

◆ For students at 4-year colleges, the improvement in retention is 20%.

◆ The same results would be found if these studies were done in another setting. For example, the LTL studies at 2-year colleges showed that 40% improvement in graduation rates would be found at 999 out of 1000 2-year colleges using LTL. And the LTL studies at 4-year colleges showed that 97 out of 100 students taking LTL would have significantly higher grades at 4-year colleges. [1]

---

[1] For detailed information on the LTL studies – including federally validated LTL studies – write to Learning to Learn®, P.O. Box 38-1351, Cambridge, MA 02238. For information on LTL's status as an Exemplary Program, contact your state's representative of the National Diffusion Network. The telephone numbers of state NDN contacts are listed on the Internet under the U.S. Department of Education's Teachers' Guide site (http://www.ed.gov/pubs/TeachersGuide/pt19g.html).

◆ These improvements resulted from LTL, not other factors: LTL and non-LTL students in the studies were equivalent on many measures, including race, sex, age, number and types of courses taken, previous academic achievement, college entrance exam scores, and motivation to take the course.

Some colleges adopting LTL have done their own studies – and had similar results. For example,

◆ At Shorter College, retention in the sophomore year improved by 38% when Shorter's freshman seminar changed from *Becoming a Master Student* to *Learning to Learn*.

◆ At the State University of New York at Buffalo, a 3-year federally funded study showed that LTL has long-term effects on students' retention, improved academic work, and increased personal confidence.

Thousands of students have benefited from LTL. You can, too.

WHY "THINKING SKILLS FOR THE 21ST CENTURY?"

What and how you learn have wider consequences – beyond college.

We're living in an era of a global economy. The U.S. Department of Labor and the American Society for Training and Development (ASTD) conducted a study of over 6,000 large and small businesses to determine skills needed for 21st century employees. The study shows that large and small companies valued knowing how to learn as the most fundamental skill for the next century:

> *"Learning to learn... knowing how to learn – is the most basic of all skills because it is the key that unlocks future success. Equipped with this skill, an individual can achieve competency in all other basic workplace skills."* [2]

Subsequently, ASTD worked with the developers of LTL to create a version of the LTL program for business and industry. Because of the increased demand on corporate learning, many corporations are now interested in having their workers trained in LTL.

This means that students trained in LTL not only benefit from higher graduation rates, with better grades and skills. They also have an "edge" in the workplace – and in *entering* a workplace that is guided by the principles of a learning organization.

---

[2] Anthony P. Carnevale, et al., *Workplace Basics: the Skills Employers Want*, pp. 8-9, 1988: Washington, D.C. American Society for Society for Training and Development and the U.S. Department of Labor, prepared under Grant No. 99-6-0705-75-079-02 under Title IV, part D, of the Joint Training and Partnership Act of 1982.

THINKING STRATEGIES
OF SUCCESSFUL STUDENTS

Why are the LTL skills so effective?

Most learning improvement systems are based on a version of the medical model: They diagnose – attempt to find out what's wrong – and offer solutions based on their diagnosis. But there are many ways to do something badly, and only a few ways of doing it right. So it's not fruitful to apply the model of diagnosis and remediation – that was so successful in medicine – to education.

With the medical model approach, there are endless options for intervention. And many learning improvement programs try to cover all those possibilities. This approach doesn't work well for college learners: Most diagnosis-and-remediation learning improvement programs show only a year's gain in a year's time. No college student has time for this kind of slow-acting remedy.

By contrast, LTL is based on research on the *learning and thinking* strategies *of successful learners.* It was found that successful students use four major thinking strategies. They

◆ ask questions of new material presented in lectures or books – thinking about which questions the material answers, and which it does not;
◆ break up large tasks and complex ideas into smaller parts;
◆ are goal-directed; direct their study to meet their instructors' objectives; and
◆ take feedback, testing themselves informally to see how much they're learning.

These are *natural* learning skills. They are used on a daily basis throughout life. For example, a boy who has just made a base hit asks himself a series of *questions:* Can he steal the next base? Is the pitcher thinking about the next batter? How fast is the first baseman? By thinking about these questions, he breaks up a complex task into *smaller parts.* His behavior is *goal-directed:* He wants to get to second. And he takes *feedback:* If the pitcher checks him out, he'll stay close to first.

You'll learn how to use these strategies in a mindful way throughout this book, using the *Four LTL Thinking Tools.*

If these are natural learning skills people use every day,
why do so many people fail in school?

From a very early age, we are taught that learning in school is different from other kinds of learning, and that it requires special skills not used in other parts of life. We are taught to look only for the "right" answers, and we memorize in order to produce those answers on exams.

Using natural thinking skills is seldom rewarded in elementary and high school. In fact, students who look for creative solutions are often misunderstood.

With LTL, you'll learn to use your *natural thinking skills* more effectively, both in and out of school. And you'll be able to attain goals that seemed out of reach.

How will these natural thinking skills
affect my performance in college?

We'll refer to the *Four LTL Thinking Tools* throughout this book. In this course, you'll learn concrete skills that are based on these thinking tools; we'll show you how to apply these skills to your content course work.

◆ *Questioning* the material from books and lecture notes brings academic study closer to your experience in "real" life. When you ask *questions* and make *guesses*, you'll tell yourself, "I disagree/agree with this," or "This reminds me of..." You'll think ahead: "Is this topic leading to...?" You'll become a more active learner, bring to the table what you've learned elsewhere – not just waiting for a table of answers. *And* you'll predict your exam questions.

◆ *Breaking up material into smaller parts* will allow you to manage your time better – and deal with issues in a modular way.

◆ *Being goal-directed* – directing your studying to meet your (and your instructors') objectives – will help you find important facts and ideas in your class notes and textbooks.

◆ *Taking feedback:* Combined with the questioning methods, working through small learning tasks will help you test yourself – so that you can *assess your learning progress* before your instructors do. This frequent self-assessment will enable you to make important changes in your performance.

At first, LTL may seem like a collection of separate skills. But when you begin to apply the skills, experiment with different combinations of our methods, and adapt them to your needs, you'll begin to see LTL as a *system* of writing *questions*, breaking up complex tasks and ideas into *smaller parts*, setting *learning goals,* looking for *feedback* on your completion of these goals – and evaluating the process you went through.

Meeting Academic and Personal Goals

In this book you'll learn methods of questioning the world around you, both in and out of school – methods that will improve your learning and thinking. You'll also learn how to shape parts of your life that need improvement. You'll develop a consistent approach to problem solving in both academic and non-academic areas of your life, and you'll solve problems creatively.

College is primarily about learning. We'll begin by exploring issues related to how people learn – including the concept of learning styles. We'll show you how to apply the LTL academic skills to your content courses. We'll present unique LTL methods for taking notes, reading, managing your time, taking tests, and writing research papers. This book is very *interactive,* with lots of exercises to practice the new skills you'll be learning. The skills you'll learn in these areas are all based on the *Four LTL Thinking Tools.*

But succeeding in college also means finding solutions to personal and social problems. Several features of this book will help you integrate what you're learning into both your academic and your personal life:

◆ *Empower Yourself:* These segments will help you use specific LTL skills to solve problems and sort through issues in the non-academic parts of your daily life.

◆ *Student Voices:* These passages contain personal stories of students like you who have taken LTL. You'll read about students you can identify with – recent high school grads, adults returning to school, students with a wide range of backgrounds – who have used LTL to succeed in college and beyond.

◆ *Reaching For The Top:* At the end of this chapter we've included an inventory where you can assess yourself in a number of areas related to college life. You can chart how close to the top you are now by filling in the *Reaching for the Top* bar graph. At the end of Chapter 12, there's another form of this inventory, with another bar graph. You can score yourself and compare the two bar graphs to see the gains you've made – how close you are to where you want to be.

◆ *Life Skills Issues:* In addition to the LTL academic system, we'll present life skills issues, including values; relationships with others; being an adult or a commuting student; reducing stress; taking care of yourself physically; financial matters; and career planning. LTL thinking tools are shown throughout these sections. You'll learn how to apply the *Four LTL Thinking Tools* to solve personal and social problems in these areas.

◆ *Internet Exercises:* We'll introduce you to the World Wide Web, show you how to do research using the web, and provide some Internet exercises to help you feel comfortable with this new form of electronic communication.

◆ *LTL Games:* At the end of most chapters we've included a classroom game to make key points in the chapter more vivid.

◆ *LTL National Scholarship Award:* Winners of this award will receive $1000 in tuition expense reimbursement. See page 182 for details.

CHOOSING COURSES

SURVIVING AN UNSTRUCTURED CURRICULUM

Most colleges have a fairly unstructured curriculum. You'll have more academic choices than you've ever had. You'll be able to take most of the courses you choose, and you might be able to sign up for as many courses as you wish. When you learn how to "work the system," this wide range of academic choices can be fun. In the beginning, having too many choices can be stressful and unnerving. There's a good reason for this: You can make serious mistakes. You're like a visitor from Russia in an American supermarket: There are so many choices that it's confusing.

Here's how to avoid the dangers of an unstructured curriculum:

1. *Don't sign up for too many courses.* Particularly at 2-year urban colleges, students are often anxious to complete a degree in order to re-enter the workforce more competitively. For that reason, they may be tempted to sign up for more credit hours than they can handle. Think twice about your course load. Many new students find that the work load of several courses is too heavy to carry; they drop many of their courses; and because they began by trying to do homework in *all* of the courses, they never really catch up in the courses they keep. In general, don't take more than 4–5 courses each term.

2. *Use the advisor assigned to you when you choose courses for your first year at college.* Your advisor will be able to help you take a balanced curriculum that builds on your interests, skills, and needs. Having a good foundation your first year at college is important: The kinds and numbers of courses you take in your first year can spell success or failure for your career as a college student.

3. *If you did poorly in math, build a basis of good learning skills before you take technical, math-based courses.* Allow yourself to make learning progress step-by-step. Don't take math-based courses – like chemistry – until you've adapted LTL skills to courses whose material is more familiar to you.

FINDING AND USING CAMPUS RESOURCES

In Your Words:

Finding and Using Campus Resources

Part of adjusting to college involves knowing where to look for help – *before* emergencies arise. Working with another student, use a campus map to locate key campus resources. Write their locations and a problem that might be solved by a professional at each campus resource.

1. **Dean of Students' Office**

   _____

   _____

   _____

2. **Academic Dean's Office**

   _____

   _____

   _____

3. **Counseling Office**

   _____

   _____

   _____

4. **Academic Support Center**

   _____

   _____

   _____

5. **Library**

   _____

   _____

   _____

6. **Computer Center**

   _____

   _____

   _____

7. **Career Center**

   _____

   _____

   _____

INTRODUCTION TO THE LTL JOURNAL

Learning is not only learning new information, or even applying what you've learned to new circumstances. It's also the ability to see the world around you in a new way.

When you acquire new skills, and respond in a new way, your goals and values change. New skills are new means; they may imply new goals. Suddenly something becomes possible that wasn't possible before. New goals force you to find new means to fulfill them. For example, if you begin a nursing curriculum, and perform extremely well in chemistry, your new skills may re-direct your goals: You may decide to prepare yourself for medical school. Your new skills are new means that can change your goals; in turn, they force you to find the means to accomplish your new goals.

We're in the midst of an information revolution, a rapidly changing world, where the central skill is to adapt to new circumstances, to learn *how* to learn. But much of formal education is still fighting for the ideals of the industrial revolution, of the factory, where it was important to master a routine. Thus, in today's high schools, students can often earn good grades through rote learning alone. Students are still asked to memorize the steps of a process, not to understand them.

With LTL, you'll build on your existing critical thinking skills, and acquire new skills. You'll become an *active* learner: You'll be someone with the ability to perceive problems and find the means to solve them. You'll acquire the key skill needed in today's technological society – the ability to adapt to changes in society and in the workplace. In this process, you'll develop your own view of reality, clarify your existing values, and find new directions. You'll question what you learn, break down new information into parts, re-examine it, see new possibilities, make new connections, and eventually stake out your claim.

As you work through this process, we'd like you to keep a journal. Start with where you are now – *what are your goals, your strengths, the areas which need improvement?* In each chapter of this book, as you acquire new skills, we'll ask you to reflect on the changes you see in your goals, and your view of yourself as a learner. Your new means may change your perception of what you can do, what you value, and what you hope to achieve.

This will be a journal of your own thoughts and feelings. Use what you're learning in this course as the basis for your thoughts. *What did you learn in this chapter that helped you this week – in and out of school? What messages are you giving yourself about your efforts, and your chances of reaching your goals?*

Don't worry about grammar and sentence structure. This journal is for you – to read and reflect on where you are now and where you want to be. Write as much or as little as you want.

Drop us a postcard. Or send us e-mail. Let us hear from you if you'd like to share some of your adventures in learning with others coming after you.

REACHING FOR THE TOP 1
A PRE-COURSE SELF-ASSESSMENT

Find out where you are now. Answer the questions on this inventory. Each group of questions reflects a chapter in this textbook. When you complete the inventory, score yourself and fill in the *Reaching For The Top* bar graph.

Be honest with yourself. You'll have a chance to see how far you've come by taking this inventory again and comparing your before and after *Reaching For The Top* charts. Rate yourself from 1–5 on each category below, with 1 = lowest and 5 = highest.

How We Learn
1. I know when and where I study best, and use this information to plan my study time.
2. I know if I'm a "big picture" or a "detail focus" learner, and have found ways to make up for what I'm missing.
3. I know if I'm a left- or right-brain learner, and use this information to study most effectively.
4. I know how messy or neat my optimal work environment is, and have set up my work environment to match my needs.
5. I know what the key barriers to my learning are, and have found ways to overcome them.

Generating Questions From Lecture Notes
1. I write my notes to the left of a 3-inch margin.
2. I record as much as possible, inserting * when I'm confused.
3. I generate questions from my lecture notes, making sure that I'm writing enough higher-level questions.
4. I write "What if...?" and Creative Questions about information I'd like to know about that was *not* mentioned in lectures.
5. I test myself on my lecture-note questions for 5 minutes every night.

Reading to Answer Questions
1. I write pre-reading questions and read to answer my questions.
2. I use my reading for self-testing.
3. I concentrate on math problem-solving questions when reading math-based material.
4. I use effective speed reading techniques.
5. I look for the distinctive "voice" when reading literature and poetry.

Time/Task Management
1. I have a good estimate of how long it will take me to do my school work and other work.
2. I break up complex tasks into manageable parts.
3. I take short, creative breaks.
4. I monitor my progress in completing major projects.
5. I map out a large task, and work backwards, ensuring that I have enough time to complete the task.

Preparing for Exams
1. I generate exam-type questions to prepare for exams.
2. I use visual organizers to prepare for exams.
3. I test myself when preparing for exams.
4. I have an effective strategy for taking objective tests.
5. I have an effective strategy for taking essay exams.

Writing, Research, & The Internet
1. I write well-constructed paragraphs.
2. I have an effective strategy for writing term papers.
3. I back up my written ideas with evidence.
4. I know how to do research using the Internet.
5. I know how to do research using an electronic card catalogue.

Being All That You Can Be
1. I am good at taking initiative.
2. I can see the positive side of things.
3. I have high self-esteem.
4. I have effective ways of helping myself overcome self-doubts.
5. I act in accordance with my values.

Relationships
1. I am good at making and keeping friends.
2. I feel confident in a romantic relationship.
3. My relationships are free of racism.
4. My relationships are free of sexism.
5. I act in an ethical way in my relationships with others.

Being Healthy
1. I use effective methods to reduce stress.
2. I eat in a healthy way.
3. I get enough exercise.
4. I have a responsible approach to sexual activity.
5. I am free from addictions.

For Adult Students: Going Back to School
1. I know where to find campus resources for adult students.
2. I balance school and work well.
3. I have an effective way to balance my responsibilities to school and my responsibilities to my spouse.
4. I have an effective way to balance my responsibilities to school and my responsibilities to my children.
5. I have an effective way to balance my responsibilities to school and my responsibilities to my employer.

Practical Matters
1. I know how to live on a budget.
2. I have an effective way to finance college.
3. When choosing my courses and extra-curricular activities, I take into account transferable skills.
4. I have a plan to establish a contact network.
5. I have clear career goals.

Where are you now?

Add up your total score. Your score on each category has a possible range of 5 (if you rated yourself 1 on each item) and 25 (if you rated yourself 5 on each item). Fill in the bar graph on page 15.

The next page shows a bar graph completed by one student, who rated herself as follows:

How We Learn: 12 points
Lecture Notes: 5 points
Reading: 10 points
Time/Task Management: 15 points
Relationships: 8 points

Writing, Research, & The Internet: 15 points
Being All That You Can Be: 12 points
Preparing for Exams: 10 points
Going Back to School: 12 points
Practical Matters: 8 points

Sample Pre-Course Self-Assessment

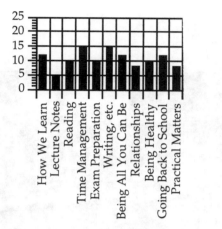

Pre-Course Assessment

Chart the results of your own self-assessment here:

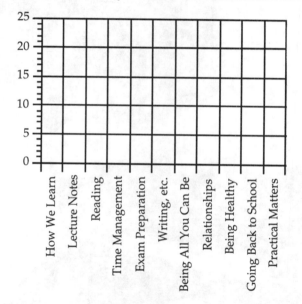

WHY ARE *YOU* IN COLLEGE?

In this chapter we've introduced some central issues you'll encounter as a college student: the benefits of going to college; achieving academic success with LTL; negotiating an unstructured curriculum; and meeting goals, both personal and academic.

Now that you're here, examine *why* you're here. The official reason for going to college is to learn. And it remains an important reason. But it's not the main motive for many people. *Writing in your LTL Journal, list the reasons why you decided to go to college.* Be honest with yourself. It's always good to be clear with yourself about what you're doing – even if you might later change your views.

At the end of this course, look back at this list. A semester of college will give you enough information to see what you've written in a new way. Are there changes in your reasons for going to college? If so, what are they?

Chapter 2:
HOW WE LEARN

We'll explore some issues related to learning in this chapter. You'll gain an overall perspective on learning which will help you identify aspects of how *you* learn – and who you are in the community of learners you've just joined.

You'll start by examining some barriers to learning, including both the fear of failure and the fear of success, learning disabilities, the pressures of time, relying on rote memorization, and the impact of peer pressure. You'll read about the dangers of too many extra-curricular activities, and of using a learning style that doesn't work for you. You'll begin to think about special problems encountered by adults returning to school. And you'll look at how you can overcome the limitations posed by these barriers, and work towards success.

In the next section of this chapter, we'll introduce you to Learning to Learn® (LTL), which forms the basis of this book. You'll learn how research on successful learners led to the development of *Learning to Learn® – which has been recommended for national dissemination by the U.S. Department of Education as the most effective student success program for college students.*

The subject of learning styles is discussed in the next section of this chapter. You'll look at the full range of learning styles: Are you a left- or right-brain learner? Do you focus on details, or are you a "big picture" learner? Do you need a structured, or an open-ended approach to learning? When and under what conditions do you learn best? In this section, you'll get a chance to evaluate your learning styles along these various dimensions.

Finally, you'll learn about the structure of learning, and how the key LTL skills are organized in that structure.

BARRIERS TO LEARNING

Before we talk about how learning occurs, let's explore some of the barriers to learning. If you recognize any barriers that prevent your best learning, we can help you devise strategies to work around them, so they no longer stand in your way. We won't suggest climbing the mountain straight up, facing it head-on; but finding a path *around* the mountain.

Fear of Failure

You may have experienced failure in the past and let it define you. If so, when faced with a new challenge, you put on armor – expecting failure from the start. You tell yourself, "No matter how hard I try, it won't work. Besides, if I really try, and fail, it will mean I can't succeed. Why try?" So you put up barriers – missing classes and appointments; staying up too late; "arranging" to fail before you try.

Getting around this barrier In this course you will learn a special set of new skills in the LTL system – skills that comprise the *most successful* learning system for college students. Read some of the **Student Voices** passages. Do these students remind you of yourself? *Try just one skill* – generating questions from lecture notes. See if it works for you right away – on your next test. When you see the results, try another new skill. You may have to get used to success.

Fear of Success

This may seem a strange kind of fear. Why would anyone be afraid of succeeding? But a growing body of research shows that many people *are* afraid of succeeding. Often this is because of conflicting expectations in society. For example, women have traditionally been care-givers. Until recently, women in our society have been expected to fill only the role of housewives – supporting the successes of their husbands. These expectations are rapidly changing. Fifty years ago, women comprised only 1% of a class entering medical school. Today nearly 50% of students entering medical school are women. But for *individual* women, the differing expectations may be very real and painful. The strength of long-held pictures people get of themselves in our society can produce internal conflicts, so that it seems easier to fail than succeed.

Fear of success can also occur when there are enormous stakes in success and failure. For example, if you are the first person in your family to go to college, you may feel a huge responsibility – one that can be a burden. You may also feel that, by succeeding, you will be entering a new world – and that your connections to the world you know will fade.

Getting around this barrier The stresses related to fear of success are all about developing a new self. It's scary to step out into a new world, and to begin to let go of an old image, building new dreams and a new sense of possibility. The first step is to acknowledge that fear: Anything new, even a wonderful change, is stressful. As you continue, you might give yourself new self "messages." "Translating" negative self-doubt statements into positive ones can help you get past this barrier. In Chapter 8, "Being All You Can Be," we'll give you models for how to translate negative messages of self-doubt – how to change negative feedback into positive feedback.

Learning Disabilities

For the last 30 years, a good deal of attention has been given to the problem of learning disabilities. There are both positive and negative effects of this attention. Increased school funding for students with learning disabilities has enabled more students to succeed. But there are also negative impacts – self-labeling which can lead to a special kind of failure: *"I don't take notes because I'm an auditory learner;" "I can't write because I have a writing disability;" "I can't pay attention in class because I have Attention Deficit Disorder,"* etc.

Getting around this barrier LTL skills help college students at all levels. "A" students continue to do well in school – but spend less time studying. Students who have never done well academically have sudden and continuing success. But the LTL system has a special impact on students who have been diagnosed as learning disabled: It opens up the "prison" doors and dissolves some of the most stubborn academic disabilities. (For example, you will no longer have to tape lectures and listen to them over and over. The LTL question-generating note-taking process will free you from that chore.)

Pressures of Time

Many people have multiple responsibilities these days. But there are still only 24 hours in a day. One (not very effective) way of coping with the pressures of time is procrastination – to put off until tomorrow what you could do today.

What kinds of tasks are most often put off until another day? The big, complicated ones that loom ahead in the distance, and seem to grow larger with each passing day – like writing a term paper, or doing your taxes.

People also find it hard to schedule time for ongoing tasks, like finding 2–3 hours each week to read a chapter in a biology textbook. Why is it so hard to schedule this time? Because life breaks in and plans break down, interrupting the most "perfect" schedule.

Getting around this barrier With LTL, you'll learn a new approach to dealing with time, not to try to devise and stick by a rigid schedule – but to focus on *task* management. You'll begin to break up large tasks into manageable parts that fit into life as it actually is – with its unexpected emergencies and interruptions.

My story

I was a classic learning disabled child. When I entered school, I had a lot of curiosity, a larger-than-average vocabulary, and great expectations for learning.

But I couldn't learn to read. I could "get" some distinctive words, like "elephant", but the letters in all the small words seemed mixed up. I was a "mirror reader." For example, I could not tell the difference between "d" and "b" and could not scan words from left to right. I kept changing the direction of where and how I looked at words on a page, sometimes from left to right, sometimes from right to left.

I struggled like this for several years, feeling confused and frustrated at why I could not do what seemed to come so easily to other children. I was placed in special classes, and received lots of help, but nothing seemed to work. When I was nearly 10, entering the 5th grade, everything changed for me. I had a wonderful teacher, Mrs. Mildred Kelly, who seemed to know what to do – and it worked. Within a few months, I became a reader. A real reader – who read everything, and found a door open to a new world.

Did I "recover" from my disability? In most ways, yes. I have graduate degrees from Harvard and the University of Michigan, and am respected in my field. But I still have trouble telling left from right; get lost easily; and have a terrible sense of direction. Using new learning skills, I found a way around the most important barriers to my success. And getting lost? Well, I find my way around town by looking for private landmarks, instead of depending on my own internal compass.

In graduate school and in 15 years as a college learning center director, I looked for a systematic way to teach what I learned from Mrs. Kelly to my students. Working with Joshua Slomianko, I found that way: Learning to Learn® has been recommended by the U.S. Department of Education as the most effective learning system for college students. My mother said, "You were a kid who had a hard time learning. And now you're teaching people how easy it is to learn."

– Dr. Marcia Heiman, co-author,
  Learning to Learn®
  Thinking Skills For The 21st Century

Relying on Rote Memorization

Most students see school learning as different from other kinds of learning. Why? Because school is one of the few places where you have to *memorize* to get ahead – because school is a closed environment. "Cramming" for exams is a time-honored custom: You memorize tonight what you forget tomorrow – *after* the exam.

The problem is that rote memorization is difficult, boring – and not very effective. Even using a memory system which teaches you "tricks of the trade" may not work – even for short-term memory (the kind of memory needed to recall information the morning after a night's study). For example, suppose you're studying for a history exam. As a memory device, you make up a nonsense word, where each letter stands for one of the 10 terms of a treaty. You'll probably remember the word. But under the pressure of an exam, you might get confused or forget what the letters stand for!

But even if rote-memory "tricks" work for you, their use is limited and cumbersome beyond tests asking for definitions of terms. In college, you'll be expected to do more than "Define X." You'll be asked *higher level* questions. If you rely on rote memorization, you'll have the added problem of trying to "translate" from the memorized pattern to the pattern of the questions asked by the field.

Getting around this barrier With LTL, you'll learn to use *questioning* and *visual learning* methods in an active way. Your new skills will help you think of what you're learning in terms of the *questions* raised by the fields you're studying – the kind of thinking you're expected to use on exams. LTL skills rely on *natural learning skills* used in open environments – skills that help you recognize faces and places, cook a meal, drive a car, or play basketball.

Peer Pressure

In high school you may have been reacting to another barrier to learning. Social pressures are serious in high school, when teenagers are just beginning to establish their own identities. On one hand, teenagers want to establish the boundaries of the self. They want to be unique. But the power to assert their uniqueness can only be achieved by joining others in similar situations with similar interests.

For many teens, establishing an identity involves doing exactly what authorities – parents and teachers – do not want them to do. Part of teen rebellion is asserting yourself and fitting in. If your group rebels against instructions – and instructors – there may be pressure to put down academic achievement as something only for "nerds."

Now that you're in college, you might find that your priorities have changed. But you face two obstacles. First, your self-image is at war with the image of what a "good" student is. (Is it cool to get good grades?) Second, you're out of practice – and you don't have the right skills. You've never learned how to study, and college is a lot more academically demanding than high school.

Getting around this barrier Part of your problem will take care of itself in a new context. Now that you're in a new environment, things will start to sort themselves out. Research on human behavior change shows that a change in social context creates conditions where new habits can be formed. Make sure that your new friends are serious about college and what it can help them achieve. New friends who are motivated to do well can create *positive* peer pressure for you to succeed.

Applying the LTL methods to your content courses will make up for your lack of experience in learning how to learn. You'll predict exam questions, develop good learning habits, and do well in school.

Extra-Curricular Activities

You may be in college for extra-curricular reasons – you're planning to be a basketball superstar; you want to "party" away from home; you liked the non-academic side of high school – belonging to clubs, school organizations, sports teams. You see college as a new kind of amusement park. This can become a barrier if it means that you ignore your academic work.

Getting around this barrier It's true that there's a strong social side to the college experience. And academic success may seem a low priority to students on sports scholarships. But don't miss the chance to shape the rest of your life by focusing on the non-academic side of college life. A low GPA may mean that you're suspended from the team; or you might lose a valuable scholarship. And what's more important, you're forfeiting the rest of your life: You'll miss gaining new skills and finding new goals.

If extra-curricular activities are important to you, and you want to *add* them to your college work, try the LTL Task Management strategies (Chapter 5). They'll help you do more in less time.

Using a Learning Style That Doesn't Work For You

If you're not learning in a way that comes natural to you, you may face obstacles to learning. You'll find out about learning styles later in this chapter – and you'll get a chance to find out what your optimal learning style is. For the moment, think back on any learning situation – in school or out – where there was a very poor learning "fit." It may be that your acquired learning habits are at variance with your own best, natural learning style.

Getting around this barrier Using the self-assessment on page 40 ("What is Your Learning Style?"), find out your own pattern of learning styles – and make changes that fit your learning needs. For example, if you're a visual learner, you may want to take courses where your visual skills are at a premium. If you're a detail-focus learner, a pre-law curriculum might fit your needs. If you're a night person, try to avoid early morning classes.

Problems of Adults Returning to School

As an adult returning to school, you face many obstacles to learning. You've been out of school for a long time, so your learning skills are rusty. You have many responsibilities – perhaps a family and a job – and doing *everything* is a constant juggling act. And you might face a certain amount of resistance from your family and co-workers, who know and appreciate you as you have been, and who are uncomfortable with surprises.

Getting around this barrier Chapter 11, "Going Back to School," is devoted to helping you solve the special problems you face as an adult returning to school. For the moment, you should know that, despite the barriers, adults returning to school have a very high rate of success in college. With your added maturity, clearer purpose and goals, you have many advantages over younger students.

USING YOUR BEST THINKING SKILLS

The Active Mode

Think about how you think when you're doing something you're good at – anything from playing pick-up basketball to playing chess. You try out a strategy – and see if it works. You look for clues – and find ways to use them. That is, you experiment, take feedback, and internally ask yourself questions about what's working.

This kind of *active thinking* is harder when the information is new to you – for example, when you enter a biology laboratory for the first time. At first, it *all* seems new to you. You've never been in a lab. You don't know where to start. You're afraid of making a mistake. You can't fall back on tried-and-true strategies, and you're not sure how to tell if you're going in the right direction.

If all this seems too much for you, and you "turn off" your mind, you're not thinking critically. But if you begin to call on your own experiences, things will settle into place. For example, imagine you calm down and recognize that the lab is a kind of "kitchen" – and you like to cook. You begin to look at your lab manual as a kind of cookbook. You arrange what you need – just as you do when you're working from a recipe. Since you've found a way to connect something new to skills you already have, you can begin thinking critically again – asking yourself questions about what you're doing, looking for clues that you're on the right path, checking what you've done, making small corrections, then asking yourself more questions about where you are and what you need to do.

You're using *active thinking skills.*

THINKING TOOLS OF SUCCESSFUL LEARNERS

Many of the barriers you face as a new college student can be overcome by learning to use your existing assets – your own best thinking and problem-solving strategies. You'll learn to do that in this course – applying learning methods based on *natural* thinking skills. These strategies will help you become an *active learner* and a successful student. They'll also help you solve personal problems and meet personal goals.

What Learning to Learn® can do for you

This book contains the Learning to Learn® system (LTL). *The U.S. Department of Education has identified LTL as the most effective learning system for college students.*

What does that mean? It means that LTL students
- ◆ predict up to 80% of their exam questions;
- ◆ have higher GPAs in all subject areas;
- ◆ "work smarter, not harder". LTL students don't rely on memorization – so they *learn more in less time;*
- ◆ are 20–40% more likely to graduate from college than are students not using LTL.

LTL is based on Four Thinking Tools used by most successful learners. These are:
- ◆ *Asking questions* – asking yourself questions about new information
- ◆ *Breaking tasks into small, manageable parts* – to help you get things done
- ◆ *Focusing on goals* – setting and achieving small and large goals
- ◆ *Getting feedback on learning progress* – finding out what you know – and what you need to know.

The Four LTL Thinking Tools

These Four Thinking Tools are not just academic skills. They are skills you use every day – usually without being aware of them. For example, crossing a street in traffic involves using all four of these thinking tools. Crossing a street:
- ◆ You ask yourself *questions:* "How far away are the cars and how quickly are they traveling? Will I make it safely across the street if I cross now or should I walk to the corner and cross at the light?"

- ◆ By asking yourself questions, you're *breaking a complex task into smaller parts* and finding the most important aspects of the situation.

- ◆ Your behavior is *goal-directed:* You want to get across the street.

- ◆ You have to pay attention to *feedback* – or you might get hit by a car.

If you *consciously* use these four thinking tools – especially in areas where you were on "automatic pilot" – you'll be surprised at what happens.

Natural Thinking Skills

We've said that thinking tools of successful learners are the same as the skills you use in everyday life.

Since you use the Four LTL Thinking Tools on a daily basis, they are *natural* to you. Thinking is one aspect of *doing*. With Learning to Learn®, you'll learn how to make active thinking more *present* in your academic life. You might forget some of the steps in this book – in fact, we encourage you to be flexible, inventive, make changes – and build new learning strategies with these four thinking tools. The gains resulting from this process will be lasting – because *we're not teaching you anything new*. We're helping you *externalize* your own natural thinking – so that you become aware of and have access to your own best thinking skills.

In Your Words:
The Four LTL Thinking Tools

You may already be using some of these strategies in many areas of your life. The following exercise asks you to look at how you currently use this way of thinking. When you see that you are *now* using these Thinking Tools to accomplish things you do well, it will be easier to see how to use them to learn something new.

Think of an activity you do well – a hobby, like fixing cars, gardening, playing pick-up basketball, painting, cooking – whatever is in your life.

Name your activity. Then list some of the things you do when you perform this activity. (Remember, this exercise will help you see how you *now* apply these strategies to an activity you're good at. No one will judge you on your answers.)

_____

_____

_____

_____

_____

_____

_____

_____

_____

Asking Questions

How do you use this Thinking Tool when you perform your chosen activity? Write your answer in the space below.

_____

_____

_____

Hints: *How do you find the information you need to do your chosen activity? What questions do you ask yourself before beginning your activity?*

Breaking Complex Tasks into Manageable Parts

How do you use this Thinking Tool when you perform your chosen activity? Take three minutes to write your answer in the space below.

_____

_____

_____

Hints: *Do you break your overall goal into sub–goals? What are the parts of this activity? Where are your stopping places? If two people were helping you, what would you tell them to do? When you perform this activity, what do you do first? What do you do next?*

Focusing on Goals

How do you use this Thinking Tool when you perform your chosen activity? Take three minutes to answer below.

_____

_____

_____

Hints: *What do you do to keep your mind from wandering? How often do you think about reaching the intermediate goals of your chosen activity? Do you remind yourself of the overall goal of your activity? What are the rewards of this activity?*

Getting Feedback on Progress

How do you use this Thinking Tool when you perform your chosen activity? Take a few minutes to answer below.

_____

_____

_____

_____

Hints: *Are you getting closer to accomplishing your overall goal for this activity? How can you tell if things are going well? How do you know if you're doing a good job? Can you tell when you're going in the wrong direction?*

Empower Yourself
Solving Problems
With The Four LTL Thinking Tools

You already use the Four LTL Thinking Tools when you perform activities you're good at – but probably without being aware of them. They're a natural part of the way you think. With LTL, you'll become more aware of your *naturally occurring thinking skills*. The Four LTL Thinking Tools are the basis of LTL. Throughout this course, we'll add skills which show a variety of ways of using these thinking tools.

When you encounter a problem at school, at work, or in your personal life, think it through, using the Four LTL Thinking Tools.

1. ***Ask yourself questions.*** What is the problem? Have I ever seen this problem before? Is it similar to a problem I know how to solve?

2. ***Divide the problem into parts.*** What are the parts of the problem? Do I know how to solve part of the problem? Do I need more information to solve other parts? Can I find a solution by putting the parts in a different order?

3. ***Work towards specific goals.*** Do I have a clear picture of the outcome I'm looking for? Can I work backwards from that goal – dividing the problem into parts and asking myself questions along the way – to find a solution?

4. ***Get feedback on your progress.*** Is there a way I can check to see if I'm going in the right direction? Do I know where I am in the process? Am I achieving my objectives along the way to my overall goal?

All of these strategies are interrelated. Once you've gone through these steps, begin again by asking yourself new questions, finding new parts of the problem and its solution, and using new information. The new information may call for a revision of your checklist. You have a sense that you're moving forward. You're progressing to new levels of activity. In fact, you're re-creating yourself. You're evolving, developing new ways of coping. For example, when you get feedback on your progress, you might decide to revise some of your smaller goals. You might change your direction, and commit more resources; set aside more time; change *how* you do things as well as *what* you do.

If you haven't found the solution, re-cycling will help you find it. If you *have* found a solution to your problem, move forward: How can you apply this solution to other problems?

In this way, you'll not only solve the problem at hand. You'll also *predict problems and find solutions for the future*. More importantly, you'll develop new skills, find new strengths, and generate the necessary confidence to tackle new challenges. In short, you'll take the initiative, and be daring without being foolish.

Solving Problems With The Four LTL Thinking Tools

Working with a partner in your class, identify a problem you both often face, and apply the Four LTL Thinking Tools towards solving that problem.

Do your work here:

_____

_____

_____

_____

_____

_____

_____

_____

_____

_____

_____

_____

✔ THINK ABOUT THIS

In the past you've used the Four LTL Thinking Tools without being aware of them. The next time you're working on a project, and get "stuck", try these Thinking Tools. Notice their effect. Use them to think through and solve your problems. You'll become more aware, more conscious, and better able to successfully accomplish what you set out to do.

Student Voices

Eddie Cole

Learning to Learn? I think it's great. I just wanted to play ball and become a pro. I was on probation before LTL. I was kind of down and out. I didn't even want to take LTL. But once I got into it, it really changed things for me. Now I can get A's and B's, even in hard subjects. With all my questions, I know what's going to be on my tests and I don't even have to study too long.

I learned that there's more to life than basketball. I'm a computer science major now, and I'm doing pretty well. When I finish this degree at the community college, I'm going into business management at a four-year college.

What would I tell other students about LTL? It will change their lives.

LEARNING STYLES

What Are "Learning Styles?"

Different students learn in somewhat different ways. Some students are more analytical, others more holistic in their approach to new information; some learn better when working independently, others require direction. Time of day may be a factor: "Night" learners burn the midnight oil; "morning" learners feel most awake and aware early in the day. We'll explore these and other learning style issues in this section – and you'll get a chance to determine your own learning style – what comes naturally to you. You might be a more visual than auditory learner; or one who benefits from a certain environment, more or less crowded, more or less noisy, than the norm.

DIFFERENT KINDS OF LEARNING STYLES

◆ Are you mainly a verbal (left-brain) or a visual (right-brain) learner?

◆ Do you naturally focus on details? Or do you have a dynamic, changing focus, looking for the "big picture?"

◆ Are you comfortable in a highly structured learning setting? Or do you need a more open environment?

◆ Do you learn best in the morning or at night? Before or after food? Can you do certain kinds of learning better at some times than others?

You might think that certain combinations naturally go together. For example, do you think that all artists – visual, creative learners – are also "big picture" learners? Do you believe that all scientists are verbal, logical thinkers – instead of non-verbal, visual learners?

If you think those things, think again.

The painter Georges Seurat had a strong *visual imagination*. But he constructed his paintings as several thousand points of color, each reflecting slight changes in the light on the figures and landscapes he painted. So he was *very focused on details*. But he was *not a high-structure learner*. Most of his paintings were done outdoors, where he could control little or nothing of the changing view.

And the scientist Albert Einstein may have had a primarily *visual imagination:* His most important discoveries began with complex, highly visual thought experiments – like daydreams very well imagined in the mind's eye.

We'll explore some of these areas on the following pages.

LEFT- AND RIGHT-BRAIN LEARNING STYLES

Why do people have different learning styles? The structure and function of the brain can explain some of these differences. The brain is made up of two sides – the left cortex and the right cortex. These two sides are connected through a complex network of nerve fibers. The two sides of the brain control different kinds of mental activities.

In most people, the **left** cortex controls **logic, reasoning, words, and numbers**; the **right** cortex controls such mental activities as **imagination, pattern recognition, color, and daydreaming**.

Many people are clearly left- or right-brain dominant. For example, George Washington and the Greek philosopher Aristotle were left-brain dominant: Their thinking was logical, rule-governed, internally consistent, and verbally based. In contrast, it appears that the painter Marc Chagall and the dancer Isadora Duncan were primarily right-brain dominant.

You may be a person with a strong visual imagination. If so, you may have found school to be frustrating in the past. You may have felt that you didn't fit into the structure of what was required in school. That's because you have a *different learning style*. You may be *right-brain dominant*.

But you still have to operate in the logical, left-brain world.

Or you may be highly verbal, but unable to "get" fields like physics, where strong visual learning skills are important.

The good news is that you can learn to effectively use *both sides of your brain*. Research shows that it is possible to strengthen the non-dominant side of the brain – and that doing so enhances the functioning of both left and right cortexes.

Using Both Sides of Your Brain

In this course you'll learn how to be more aware of and use your natural thinking skills. You'll learn to integrate and strengthen both sides of your brain through the LTL exercises.

LTL and Left-Brain Learning

You'll learn to generate questions from lecture notes and readings. The questioning process is a kind of mental exercise that strengthens the left side of your brain. **Generating questions** from written material (Chapter 3) will help you (1) think clearly through complex issues and (2) externalize your thinking, so you can examine what you think about both new and old information.

For example, here are some lecture notes and a Mirror Question that directly reflects the information in the notes:

How does teamwork help employees become more productive?	*Teamwork increases productivity by (1) pooling information and problem solving; (2) helping employees learn from each others' experiences; (3) decreasing down time.*

Here's a Mirror Question generated from key words in two textbook headings:

What is the Hazard. Communic. Standard, & what does it require of chem. manuf. employers?	**Improving Workplace Safety: The Hazardous Communication Standard**

The Hazardous Communication Standard (HCS) is designed to protect workers from the safety hazards involved in working with chemicals. The HCS law now affects every manufacturing company using chemicals.

HCS Requirements of Chemical Manufacturers

According to HCS, chemical manufacturers are required to meet special standards. They must let their workers know about hazards by using (1) special labels and (2) Material Safety Data Sheets.

All safety hazard labels must have 6 parts: They state the name of the chemical; the name, address, and emergency phone number of the company that made or imported the chemical; the physical hazards involved (Can it catch fire? Is it radioactive?); important storage or handling instructions; health hazards (What illnesses can it cause?); and basic protective clothing, equipment, and methods for working with this chemical.

LTL and Right-Brain Learning

When you construct Question Charts and Key Word Diagrams (Chapter 6), you'll be combining verbal and visual skills.

Question Charts

Question Charts will help you compare and contrast complex information – arranged by **questions** – in visual form:

How have new policies prevented workplace accidents?

New Policies:	*Employee decision-making*	*Improved communication*	*Less demanding shifts*
What are some benefits of the new policies?	Employees take action in a crisis	Information flows easily between employees at all levels	Employees are alert to dangers
What are examples of accidents avoided by this policy?	Navy deck worker can halt operation if something is wrong when air strike is launched	Air controller–pilot communication resulted in 10-fold decrease in accidents since 1960s	Diablo Canyon nuclear power plant has excellent safety record
What is an example of an accident that might have been prevented by this new policy?	1986 Challenger disaster (NASA management did not listen to warnings of engineers)	Air Florida DC crash in 1982 – junior officer did not give needed information to airplane pilot	Exxon Valdez oil spill

Key Word Diagrams

Key Word Diagrams (Chapter 6) will let you draw *any* kind of diagram to connect ideas abbreviated into key words. Like Question Charts, Key Word Diagrams will help you combine **verbal and visual thinking skills**.

Here are two examples of Key Word Diagrams that answer questions:

"Should the government help large companies that may fail?"

Pro	*Con*
–safeguards workers' jobs	–may encourage poor business practices
–high costs of unemployment	–goes against idea of free market
–increases gross national product	
–costly federal "rescue"	

"How can small businesses use creative testing of new products to compete with large corporations?"

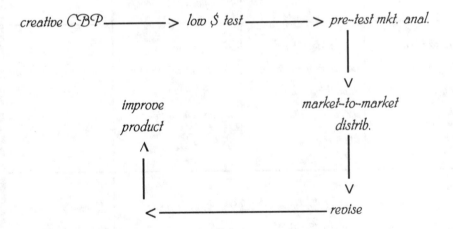

Mind Maps

Mind Maps (Chapter 6) can help you "see" your thinking. Starting from a central picture that represents the topic of the Mind Map, you'll draw lines and small pictograms radiating out of that key idea.

Here's a Mind Map that summarizes the effects of Eli Whitney's work:

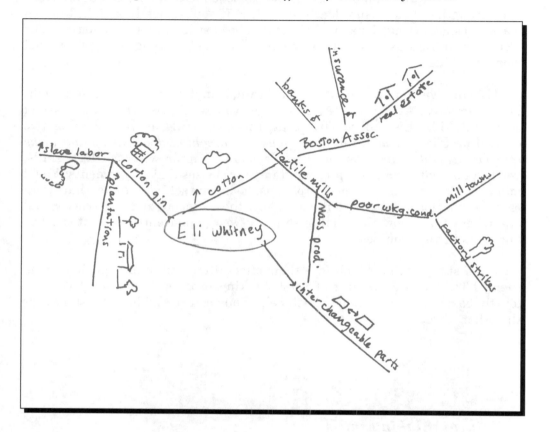

Picturing Ideas

Picturing Ideas (Chapter 6) lets you draw a simple picture to recall technical ideas. For example:

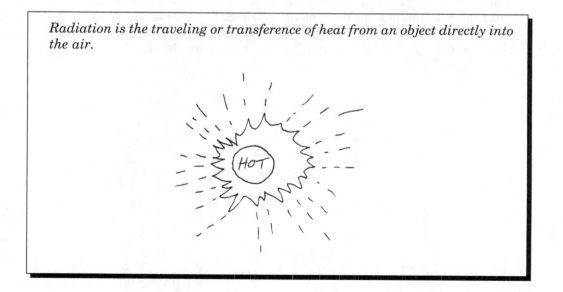

Radiation is the traveling or transference of heat from an object directly into the air.

Integrating left- and right-brain thinking

All of these visual organizers will help you integrate verbal (left-brain) and visual (right-brain) thinking.

If you're mostly a left-brained learner, question-generating will be easy for you. Drawing a diagram of the possible consequences of changes in an event will strengthen your visual learning skills. If you're mostly a right-brained learner, constructing visual organizers will be easy for you. Constructing your visual organizers as answers to questions will help strengthen your verbal learning skills.

LTL will give you practice with "left brain," analytical thinking and "right brain," creative expression. After awhile, you won't view LTL as a set of separate skills. Instead, you'll see all the LTL skills as variations of two central practices: *generating questions* and *breaking down ideas and tasks into manageable parts*. As you become more familiar with the LTL skills, you'll "play" with the ideas presented in your classes and assignments: You'll make *variations* on assigned problems, ask yourself *questions* that were raised – but not necessarily answered – by the material, and construct visual organizers that show the relationships between apparently unrelated ideas and facts in your courses.

Unlike study skills, which lose their effect after you stop explicitly using them, LTL will become part of your thinking process. You'll see LTL as a fourth basic skill, reasoning, which helps you acquire and have mastery over the other three.

✔ **THINK ABOUT THIS**

Natural thinking skills

Think of how well you drive a car – you're taking in and responding to visual signals at a very fast rate. It's like a speeded-up question/answer activity, where you're quickly looking for and responding to feedback around you. All of this is a kind of *internal question-asking*. In the LTL questioning exercises, you'll learn to slow down a bit and make that internal question/answer more obvious to you. By putting those thoughts into words, you'll *externalize* your thinking – bringing your thoughts into the light of day, where you can examine them more closely.

DETAIL-FOCUS/BIG PICTURE
LEARNING STYLES

Detail-Focus learners are good at analysis, seeing the parts of an item or event. In the workplace, they tend to be good administrators. Detail-Focus learners get things done, and done the right way; but they may have trouble with "the vision thing." They may see the trees so clearly that they don't notice the whole forest.

In contrast, Big Picture learners understand the importance of working towards a large, perhaps unreachable, goal. Big Picture learners tend to be visionaries, people who want to make changes, who see things in an unconventional way. The problem is that Big Picture learners may not be practical enough to see the details needed to make their dreams come true.

So whether you're naturally a Detail-Focus or Big Picture learner, you're more likely to reach your goals if you develop some skills from the "other side." The LTL skills can help you become a more "balanced" learner.

If You're a Detail-Focus Learner...

Questions that begin with "How...?" "Why...?" and "What if...?" (Chapter 3) will help you think broadly about a topic. In finding the answers to these questions, you'll go beyond the precise detail of "What is...?" Questions, which usually reflect only simple facts. *("What is the temperature outside?" "What is a 'photoautotroph'?")*

Your questions can lead to a chain of related questions. They can also produce a kind of creative tension, since their answers may take some time to find – and in some cases, the answers may not be available. If you're a Detail-Focus learner, you naturally think of "How...?" "Why...?" and "What if...?" Questions when you're focused on step-by-step work. But you may ignore these kinds of questions when you're looking at the project as a whole. Also, as a Detail-Focus learner, the open-ended quality of asking these "How...?" "Why...?" questions may bother you. Or you might ask *too many* "What if...?" Questions. You might be too cautious, and let "What if...?" Questions keep you from acting on a problem.

Solutions are often found during the period of creative tension evoked by "How...?" "Why...?" and "What if...?" Questions; not everything must be answered *now*. As an **exercise**, you may want to write more "How...?" and "Why...?" Questions about a problem you're trying to solve. Leave the questions unanswered, and come back to them in a day or two.

In Your Words:
Asking Detail-Focus Questions

Think of an important goal you want to accomplish this year (academic, personal, social, or work-related). Write some questions starting with "What is...?" "When...?" "Where...?" and "Who...?" about what you need to do to reach this goal.

_____

_____

_____

_____

_____

_____

If You're a Big Picture Learner...

If you're a Big Picture learner, you'll welcome the open-ended quality of *"How...?" "Why...?" and "What if...?"* Questions. In fact, asking these kinds of questions is a *natural thinking skill* you use when you're thinking about projects you enjoy, on or off the job. So it will be easy for you to be aware of "playing" with these questions as problem-solving tools. But you may overlook the details within the big picture. As an **exercise**, you may need to focus on asking questions that reflect simple facts, like *"What is...?" "When...?" "Where...?" and "Who...?"*

In Your Words:
Asking Big Picture Questions

Think of an important goal you want to accomplish this year (academic, personal, social, or work-related). Write some questions starting with "How...?" "Why...?" and "What if...?" about what you need to do to reach this goal.

_____

_____

_____

_____

_____

_____

_____

_____

HIGH AND LOW STRUCTURE LEARNING STYLES

Another category of learning styles is High and Low Structure. High-Structure learners are very organized, and enjoy learning in organized settings. Low-Structure learners are just the opposite.

If You're a High-Structure Learner...

If you're a High-Structure learner, it's important to find ways to give structure to your learning when you work on your own – so you don't lose your way and waste a lot of time. You also need a quiet work setting, where there are few distractions.

Setting specific goals for yourself with a Task Management Checklist (Chapter 5) will help you build structure into unstructured time.

Asking yourself questions will help focus your learning. Asking questions will help you study in a self-directed way. Getting into the habit of asking yourself "How...?" "Why...?" and "What if...?" Questions will give you more structure as you work and learn.

If you're a High-Structure learner, you may find that Mirror Questions come easily to you, but you need to work on asking "What if...?" Questions whose answers are open-ended.

If You're a Low-Structure Learner...

You may be the kind of person who hates to work in a structured environment. Only you can find your papers – but you know where they are. You like to lean back, put your feet up on the desk, and think about solving a problem. You enjoy working and learning on your own, in a low-pressure setting. You can deal with noisy environments; you may even find that you can learn when there's noise – like TV in the next room – that would distract someone else. You can concentrate in a visual or aural mess – focus in and be unaware of chaos around you.

But there's a down side. You may be so unaware of what's going on around you that you daydream.

If you're a Low-Structure learner, questioning skills will keep you from wool-gathering. Asking yourself "How...?" "Why...?" and "What if...?" Questions will help give you direction.

You also need to give yourself concrete **feedback** on your progress to keep moving in a productive direction. How can you do this, and still not be boxed in by rigid goals?

Productive Environments
For High- and Low-Structure Learners

Working with another student, picture optimal working environments for a High-Structure learner and a Low-Structure learner. In what ways would these environments be different? How would they be similar? Are there any differences in how each should apply the Four LTL Thinking Tools? (For example, students with a high need for structure would naturally use more goal-setting and looking for feedback; people with low structure may ask themselves more questions about an activity.)

Write key words describing optimal learning conditions for both types of learners:

High-Structure Learner	Low-Structure Learner

WHEN DO YOU LEARN BEST?

Is there a time of day when you learn best? Are you a morning person? Night person? Do you learn best after food? Or does eating make you sleepy?

Do you read best in the morning, just after a cup of coffee? Or is your mind going too fast to slow down and comprehend new information then? If so, is your "fast mind" period the best time for your writing?

Does being hungry make you generate a lot of ideas – so that you write well then? Or does hunger interfere with your clear thinking?

Is there a time of day when you can best read fiction (lighter reading) or biology (heavier reading)? Or is it best for you to alternate this reading – light/heavy/light?

Take some data. What happened just before you really studied well for a math test? Did solid homework in a biology class? Understood poetry? Wrote clearly and well? Look at:

◆ *the time of day;*

◆ *what happened just before your "breakthrough;"*

◆ *the surrounding aural/visual distractions;*

◆ *when you last ate; and*

◆ *other special conditions surrounding your learning.*

That is, you're more than just a "morning person" or a "night person." If you take data on when you do your best work – your best work in different areas – you'll have a better picture of when *you* learn best.

How does the concept of The Four Thinking Tools fit the theory that people have different learning styles?

Everyone uses these four skills in thinking and problem solving. With the LTL skills, you'll learn to *integrate* all four thinking tools: You will build on the learning styles you now use well – and strengthen the areas you need work on. For example, if you are now primarily a right-brain, visual learner, you'll learn to build on that skill, and strengthen your left-brain, verbal learning.

WHAT IS *YOUR* LEARNING STYLE?

Circle the items you'd mark "Yes."

Left-/Right-Brained Learning
1. When someone gives you directions, can you "see" where you're going in your mind's eye? If you write down the directions, do you draw a little picture or diagram for yourself – perhaps with arrows?
2. Do you look for a logical "system" to complete a project?
3. Do you often understand a situation before you can put what you've seen into words?
4. Do you often need a reason *why* before you do something?

Detail-Focus/Big Picture Learning
1. Is your checkbook usually balanced?
2. Would you feel comfortable if you turned around in a circle, and saw huge mountains as far as you could see in all directions?
3. Do you plan vacations carefully?
4. Do you have big dreams – but don't know how to make them real?

High-Structure/Low Structure Learning
1. Is your desk usually neat?
2. Was your mother always after you to clean up your room at home?
3. Do you usually study in the same place?
4. Do you break rules because you forget what they are?

Key

Left-/Right Brained Learning
You're probably left-brain dominant if you circled 2 and 4.
You're probably right-brain dominant if you circled 1 and 3.
If you circled other combinations, you don't have a clear dominance pattern.

Detail-Focus/Big Picture Learning
You're a Detail-Focus learner if you circled 1 and 3.
You're a Big Picture learner if you circled 2 and 4.
If you circled other combinations, you don't have a clear detail-focus/big picture pattern.

High-Structure/Low Structure Learning
You're a High-Structure learner if you circled 1 and 3.
You're a Low-Structure learner if you circled 2 and 4.
If you circled other combinations, you don't have a clear high-/low-structure pattern.

When Do You Learn Best?
To answer this question, you'll have to take data on when and under what conditions you perform different kinds of learning tasks best. (See "When Do You Learn Best," page 39.)

Don't Let Labels Limit You

We are all unique, with different strengths and preferences stemming from both experience and innate tendencies. Although differences of talent and preference exist, it's important to remember that we are more similar than we are different – and that we're already performing much more complex tasks in everyday life than will be required in the formal settings of school and the workplace: Researchers in artificial intelligence found that daily living tasks are much more complex than academic tasks. They've taught computers to perform formal academic tasks. But the daily living tasks we take for granted are much too hard for computers.

What does this mean? It means: *Don't let the label of a particular learning style or learning disability limit you.* For example, if you've been told that you're an auditory learner, don't let that stop you from taking notes. (If you rely on your auditory strength alone, you won't have a record of what was said; and your visual learning skills, which need to be stronger, will get weaker.)

Think of this analogy: Most cars can travel at 160 mph, when the speed limit is 70. They have more capacity than they need. In a similar way, human beings use only a fraction of their intellectual capabilities in formal settings.

Anybody who functions normally in daily life performs much more complex activities than academic work requires. If you can handle the complexity of everyday life, there is no reason you should fail in the simpler, more structured environment of formal learning in college.

So if you have an unusual learning style or a skill deficit, take heart. You're only using a small part of your natural thinking skills. We can help you bridge the gap. Success is only a strategy away.

In Your Words:

Don't Let Labels Limit You

In what ways do you feel you are now limited by your unusual learning style or learning disability?

_____

_____

_____

_____

_____

_____

Look back at this statement at the end of the semester. See what changes you were able to make by using LTL.

THE STRUCTURE OF LEARNING

All learning – in and out of school – has three stages: Input, where information is gathered; Organization, where new information is given structure, and the learner sees its relationship to past knowledge; and Output, where the learner comes up with a product or a process.

In school, note-taking and reading fall into the Input Stage; in the Organization Stage students fit new information into a pattern of previously known information; taking exams and writing papers are in the Output Stage. The key LTL skills fit into this structure of learning in the following way:

1. **Input.** Writing questions (from lecture notes and books).

2. **Organization.** Arranging what you've learned into Question Charts and breaking up your homework assignments into a series of smaller tasks.

3. **Output.** Testing yourself, using questions you've written and information you've organized; writing to answer questions, or constructing Question Charts, Key Word Diagrams, and Mock Exams.

The following diagram shows how the major LTL skills are related:

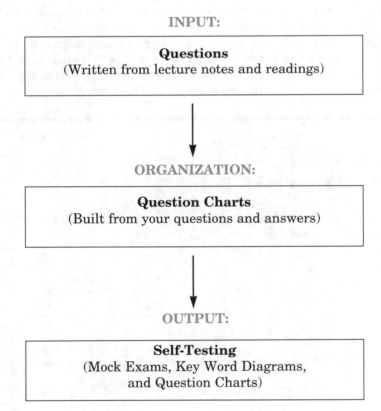

INPUT:

Questions
(Written from lecture notes and readings)

ORGANIZATION:

Question Charts
(Built from your questions and answers)

OUTPUT:

Self-Testing
(Mock Exams, Key Word Diagrams,
and Question Charts)

Both Sides of Your Brain Games

1. Taking a Mental Picture

In this game, you'll practice taking a mental picture. Here are the steps:

1. Look closely at something.
2. Close your eyes.
3. Try to recall what you saw. "See" what you saw in your mind's eye.
4. Repeat this process 3 times.

You can try this individually, practicing when you're on a bus or waiting in line at the Post Office. Or you can try this activity as a game in class.

If you're playing this game in class, you will need:
◆ *2 teams of students;*
◆ *2 sets of "busy" pictures – pictures that have a lot going on in them;*
◆ *a stop watch with a hand that counts seconds; and*
◆ *2 chalkboards or 2 flip charts.*

In each round, one member of each team gets 5 seconds to view the picture; closed eyes; 3 seconds; closed eyes; 2 seconds; closed eyes.

Each team member then tells his/her team as many details as possible – as well as the "big picture" story of the picture (i.e., it's a 4th of July celebration). A designated team member writes whatever is recalled on the chalkboard or flip chart. Each detail counts 1 point; the "big picture" description counts 5 points.

The team whose members get the most points wins the game.

2. Picturing Ideas

Each team is given a set of 3″ x 5″ cards. Each card contains a brief written policy listed in your college's student handbook or catalogue. The set of cards for Team A is identical to the set given to Team B.

1. Form 2 teams.
2. A member of each team gets the Card #1 of the team's set of cards.
3. The student with the card looks at it, then draws a simple picture of it – like the simple picture "describing" *radiation* on page 33. (One or two key words can be added to your picture if needed.) The student with the card does *not* show the written card to anyone else on the team.
4. Team members gather around the "artist." The object of the game is for team member(s) to call out the meaning of the term. Whichever team first calls out the correct meaning of the picture wins the round.
5. Another member of each team gets Card #2, and becomes the designated "artist" for that round.
6. Play 5–6 rounds of the game.

Chapter 3:
GENERATING
QUESTIONS FROM
LECTURE NOTES

Are you often bored by your instructors' lectures? Do you watch the clock in class? Talk to your friends? Fall asleep?

Why are you bored? Because sitting in a lecture is a passive situation. But you *can* turn this into an active learning process by using questioning techniques – by having a kind of internal dialogue with the speaker.

The ideal teaching situation uses the Socratic method, where the teacher and student are engaged in a question/answer dialogue. Of course, this ideal situation doesn't exist in a lecture class with one teacher and 30 or 300 students. But you can approach this ideal by creating an *internal dialogue* where you *ask yourself questions* and look to confirm or deny your guesses while you listen.

By generating questions from lecture notes, you'll be able to turn a passive situation into a kind of video game of the mind – where instead of sitting passively, you're reacting quickly, seeing if you can guess the next step, "get" what's coming next.

The skills you'll learn in this chapter will help you *predict exam questions*. You'll learn to distinguish between relevant and irrelevant information and think analytically. And you'll learn to externalize your thinking – to be aware of your thoughts and think "outside the box" of conventional rote learning. This ongoing internal dialogue will help you solve problems in and out of school.

Questioning
– the Key to Learning

In Chapter 2 we talked about four natural learning skills used by all successful learners – which are used by *everyone* in the informal learning situations of everyday life. The most important natural learning skill is *questioning* – something you do when you cross a street, shop in a grocery store, or listen to another person.

Questioning is a central part of the way people respond to the world around them. It shows that they are curious, helps them take initiative, adapt to the environment, and adjust their responses to changing conditions.

Often people are not aware that they're using this questioning process. Many things go by so quickly that you can hardly "hear yourself think." For example, when you drive a car and quickly avert an accident, a very quick internal set of questions-and-responses occurs.

In this chapter, you'll learn to externalize and become more aware of your thinking by asking yourself questions. You'll begin to understand both your instructors' objectives and the questions that are central to the fields you're studying. Using LTL questioning skills will help you:

◆ *predict exam questions* from your lecture notes;

◆ *quickly review information;*

◆ *listen with better understanding;* and

◆ *become an active learner* – looking for the answers to your own questions as you listen to a lecture.

> ### *Thinking About Learning:*
> ## Why are questions central to LTL?
>
> Through the questioning process, you're learning to use the scientific method in the broadest sense. You form an hypothesis about what you're going to hear – and your guess is confirmed or denied by what is actually said.
>
> Questions also provide a *frame of reference* which can help you organize the facts you're learning. It's hard to retain isolated facts. Information organized into a pattern is more easily recalled and applied. By learning what questions the field asks, you'll begin to understand the structure of the fields you're studying, and you'll have a framework in which to put new information.
>
> In school, you're usually trying to focus on facts. You try to memorize seemingly unrelated bits of information. By asking questions of what you learn, instead of focusing on isolated facts, you'll get a sense of the field. You'll begin to direct your attention to *structure* – the structure expressed by the questions the field asks. When you generate questions from your course material, pieces of information will fall into their proper place (i.e., as they are organized in the structure of the field) and will be retained in patterns – easier to recall and to apply in a meaningful way.

STUDENT SAMPLE

Here's a page of lecture notes taken by a student before she began LTL instruction.

Before Learning to Learn®

Political Pref.	church all 1	2	3	Vichy — (1940 — 44) church year 4	Rural 5	No Relig 6
Left	.11%	30%	40%	55%	24%	87%
Other	89	70	60	45	26	13

- possible to classify pol. systems in other ways - gave ex. - helpful - scheme pointed to certain aspects of pol. syst.

         Lecture 1-15-70
                Thursday

FRENCH Political System

hard to draw parallels between diff developing pol. systems

political conflicts can merge out of the past as well as contemporary times. (Past Development / Past Relevance / other sources of conflict) ✱

1. French past   subdivide chart / Quad 1 — Pol. dev. stable / pol. dev. un stable
    changes can occur along horizontal lines   or
    within quandats - change of Rules.
    3rd, 4th & 5th rep - diff sets of rules - but all accept competition
    Vichy - didn't accept competition (def)
✱Political development attainment of satisfactory
         Rules & institutions

weakness diff between dev. countries in past & dev. countries today
       FRANCE   LATIN AMERICA
1. in past - devel countries had usually reached economic development first
   today - reach pol. stability first
2. France - nation state : 19th Century national loyalties stronger
3. France - beauracracy - things could be carried out.
4. parties Russian, Chinese etc. weren't around in past
    Notion of party, - New

There's a lot of information here, but it's hard to see what it's about.

STUDENT SAMPLE

Now glance at the notes below, which the same student took while using LTL skills. These are the notes of a successful student.

After Learning to Learn®

Where does competition begin? — [legal and factual competition within Comm party for leadership Invented by Lenin

For what purpose was the party organized? — Party organized before revolution to make real revolution (MARCH 1917 - Collapse, Nov. Revolut. Then converted into control after Revolution (In spite of small #'s were successful. No opposition but legitmate (Mex. leg. but none)

Ideology - "party directs and orients": "increasing objective historical law etc" (FROM NEWSPAPER)

What is the connection between party and Revol? — Party is ideological part because system emerged out of Revolution
Men who made Bolshevik Revol were inspired by an ideology (MARXISM)

What are the basic parts of Marx's philosophy? — Marxism
1. private property divided men into classes
2. in Capitalist dom. people own property
3. if abolish private property - abolish class structuring - abolish. of state

What additions did Lenin make? — Lenin's Additions
1. after Bolshevik's take over - Repression will be in the interest of the people
2. to reorganize the society (iron discipline leading role of the party.
Function of Ideology (to justify rule)

In the "after" notes, the student generated questions from her notes.

How did this student get from *before* to *after*? We'll show you in the next few pages.

TAKING LECTURE NOTES

Steps for Taking Notes

1. *Draw a line for a 3-inch wide left-hand margin.*[1]
   A wide margin will give you a place to write your questions later.

2. *Take notes on the right-hand side of the page.*
   Take your notes on the wide side of the page, to the right of your 3-inch margin line.

3. *Take notes as a "recorder."*
   Take as many notes as you comfortably can. Don't worry about getting every word, and don't try to understand the notes as you write.

4. *Use blank lines (____) to mark missed information.*
   Blank lines are cues for writing in missing information later.

5. *Use asterisks (*) to mark points of confusion.*
   Asterisks will help you remember to ask for information to clear up your confusion later.

6. *Leave the left-hand page blank.*
   You can use this page later to insert your own variations of the information presented, "What if...?" and Creative Questions, Question Charts, and Key Word Diagrams.

7. *Abbreviate words.*
   Abbreviations help you write more in less time.

Hints:

◆ Don't stop writing in an effort to understand the lecture. Your understanding will come later, when you begin to write questions from your lecture notes.

◆ Don't worry if your notes look messy or some words are misspelled – the notes are only for you.

---

[1] If your college is located near a law school, buy law-ruled notebooks or notebook filling paper for lecture notes. This kind of notebook paper has a 3-inch margin on the left side of the page.

USING ABBREVIATIONS

Some instructors may talk too quickly for you to write down what they're saying. Using abbreviations for terms that are often repeated can help you solve this problem.

Here are some commonly used abbreviations:
writing = wrtg (leave out vowels: reduce "–ing" to "–g") and = + with = w/

One method of abbreviating calls for dropping off the ends of long words:
abbreviation / abbreviated = abbrev [2]
organization / organized = organ

Most fields have terms that are used over and over again. For example, if you looked through a page of notes from an accounting course, you might find that the following words are often repeated:
depreciation   corporation   compensation   revenue

You might abbreviate these words as follows:
depreciation = deprec   compensation = comp
corporation = corp   revenue = rev

This process is more than simply a way of abbreviating lecture notes. Finding repeated terms to abbreviate will draw you to the key terms of the field. When you notice key terms repeated in a given field, you're effortlessly *identifying some of the important ideas in that field.*

These key-term abbreviations can also help your learning. When you look over your notes, your eyes will be automatically drawn to the abbreviated terms. You'll see the key words at a glance – reinforcing your learning of these concepts.

Steps for Using Abbreviations
1. Review your notes, looking for words that are often used.
2. Circle these words and make up your own abbreviations of them.

Assignment
1. Look through your notes from classes you're taking.
2. Find repeated words which you can abbreviate.
3. Begin a "dictionary" of these words in your notebook.
4. Add to this list when you come across more terms that are often used in your courses.

Bring your abbreviation lists to class.

---

[2] The actual ending – whether you mean a noun or verb form – will be clear from the context.

LEAVING NOTEBOOK PAGES BLANK

Don't take notes on every page of your notebook. Write your notes and questions on right-hand notebook pages and leave the left-hand page blank.

You can make your own *variations* of the problems presented in technical courses. For example, in a math course you'd make up your own variation of a problem worked out in class – using the formula given, but inserting new values.

For technical courses, like math or computer science, use the left-hand page for:
◆ abbreviations and technical terms glossary; and
◆ your own variations of problems presented in class.

For non-technical courses, like sociology or psychology, use the left-hand page for:
◆ *your abbreviation glossary;*
◆ *questions that interest you, but were not raised in class;*
◆ *Question Charts and Key Word Diagrams.*

STUDENT SAMPLE

In the sample below, the student did not take lecture notes on the left-hand page. She left this page blank during the lecture and later made her own variations of the problems presented in class.

Making Variations in Math-Based Courses

If problems in an electronics class deal with finding the energy stored in an inductance, *make up your own problems* of this kind on the left-hand page.

Making up variations is a key to learning in technical fields like computer science. For example, if you're taking a computer science course in Clipper, you'll learn how to create a multiple data file. Make up variations on the examples presented in your computer science class.

Taking Notes with Formulas or Graphs

When you're taking technical notes that include formulas and graphs, you may feel like putting down your pencil and trying to understand the material that's being discussed. But it's really not the right time to stop writing. That is, if you don't record the information, you won't have a chance to read and think about it later. If the information isn't in your notes, you won't be able to make up variations, test your understanding, or predict exam questions.

Keep taking notes – even when the information isn't clear to you. You don't have enough time to learn new information the first time you hear it. You need time to "play" with the new ideas, especially in technical areas, where the ideas are new to you. If you keep taking notes, you'll have a chance to question and understand the information later.

Remember, you can always insert an * when you get confused during a lecture. But if you stop taking notes, you'll never know when you got confused.

Student Voices

Billy Roach

I was a B-average student in high school, but when I got to college, I flunked three out of five of my first-semester courses. Then I took the Learning to Learn course. With the LTL methods, and how my school-work improved, my attitude changed drastically.

Now I have a 3.5 and I love school. I love to learn. I love it. And grades don't matter to me the way I used to think they would. Now I love knowledge. I love to learn about everything, to read about everything.

Questions About Taking Notes With LTL

I never use my notes for studying.
Why should I bother to take notes in class?

With LTL, you'll learn how to *predict exam questions* from your lecture notes. These questions will be the key to how you learn – and they'll help you see what's important.

Should I copy over my notes?

No. Your notes will improve in appearance, organization, and clarity when you generate questions from them. If you write questions from your notes after class, before long you'll find that you listen in a more organized way in class. And your notes will "automatically" improve.

Should I try to listen and not write when I don't understand something?

No. Keep writing so that you miss as little as possible. If you have lots of information in your notes, you'll be able to "work" with them later, generating questions and seeing what you still don't understand.

What if I can't write as fast as my instructors talk?

That's why you should insert blank lines when you miss information, and use abbreviations as often as you can. As you practice these note-taking methods, you'll miss less and less. For now, ask a friend or your instructor about the information you missed.

I don't seem to understand much in class if I just keep taking notes.
What should I do?

Your listening skills will improve when you become aware of the kinds of questions your instructors are raising. You'll start anticipating, listening for implied questions as your instructor changes topics.

What if I can't read my notes after class?

Whenever your notes are unclear to you, try reading them aloud. If you look at your notes after class, reading them aloud will help trigger your memory, so you can fill in what you missed.

Should I take notes in seminar classes? What about discussions
among students in class?

It's true that you learn something in every class you attend. Some of what you learn will be on exams. But the main pay-off will be that what is said in seminars can provide an occasion for your own response – a stepping stone for expressing your own ideas, perhaps in a paper you plan to write. Take abbreviated notes in seminar classes – notes that will help you recall the key points under discussion – so you can "play" with the information later.

GENERATING QUESTIONS FROM LECTURE NOTES

Playing Jeopardy

Have you ever played the game "Jeopardy?" In this game, players are given answers – and the winner comes up with the matching question. Using LTL, you'll get a lot of practice with "Jeopardy." You'll look at the information presented in class as a series of answers to questions. By asking these questions, you'll understand a lot about what's important in the field and to your instructor: You'll learn to ask yourself the questions raised by the fields you are studying. Nobody knows all the answers in any field. What the professional knows is to ask the relevant questions – and where to find the information. You'll acquire these skills – and approximate the behavior of professionals in the fields you're studying.

Asking Mirror Questions

When you generate questions from lecture notes, you're playing the Jeopardy game – writing questions that were answered by the information in the notes. We call these Mirror Questions – since they *reflect* the facts and ideas in lectures. Mirror Questions will help you practice the *prediction game* – changing a passive environment into an active one. They'll help you stay awake in class – and *predict exam questions*.

Steps for Writing Mirror Questions

As soon as possible *after* the lecture,

1. *Write questions that are answered by the information in your notes.*

2. *Write your Mirror Questions in the 3-inch, left-hand margin of your notes.*

3. *Write complete questions.*

4. *Write 4–5 questions for every page of notes.*

In Your Words:
Seeing the Patterns of Questions

Write questions from your lecture notes in one of your academic courses for a week. Then look back at your questions and see if you can find a *pattern* of questions. What are some of the *key questions* asked in that course?

_____

_____

_____

_____

_____

Questions About Writing Mirror Questions
From Lecture Notes

How many questions should I write for an average page of notes?

Most handwritten note pages have 4–5 major new ideas, or short "sections" – so you'll usually need 4–5 questions for a page of notes.

How can writing Mirror Questions from notes help me take tests?

You're predicting exam questions. To improve your memory of information for exams, cover the "answer" side of your notes and test yourself on the questions you've written. Later on, we'll show you how to predict both essay and objective test questions. (See Chapter 6.)

Should I write my questions in complete sentences?

It's a good idea to start by writing questions in complete sentence form – this will help you think with questions. After a while, you can use abbreviated questions – but always use some form of question (e.g., "Why...?"). Your memory of information will improve when you get into the habit of asking yourself questions about the material you're learning.

What if I can't think of questions for all of my notes?

If you can't find a question for part of your notes, you probably didn't understand part of the notes; or you weren't able to write enough down. Write a question mark (?) in the margin of your notes opposite this section. Ask a friend or your instructor about this information later.

I don't want to change the way I take notes. Why should I use this technique?

This technique will help you predict exam questions. It's also the basis of the LTL system – all the other LTL skills build on it. ***Try this experiment:*** Use this method for two courses – and don't use it for two other courses with a similar level of difficulty. Or make your own variations on this method. Make your decision based on the results: What are your final grades like in these courses? How much did you have to study for them?

Should I generate questions from notes taken in a seminar class?

Sure. Generating questions will help you think about what was said – and how it's connected to the rest of what you're learning in that class.

In Your Words:
The Mirror Question Exercise

Working with another student, write Mirror Questions based on your notes from a page of lecture notes from a content course.

SUMMARY QUESTIONS

What is a Summary Question?

A Summary Question sums up the theme, or main idea, of the notes.

Steps for Writing Summary Questions

1. Write a question that
   – summarizes your Mirror Questions for the lecture, or
   – asks about the theme for that lecture.

2. Write your Summary Question at the top of the first page of the day's lecture notes.

Hint:

◆ If you get stuck – and can't come up with a Summary Question – connect Mirror Questions by using "and," and form one large sentence. Then polish it into a Summary Question.

A Question About Summary Questions

What if I can't think of a Summary Question?

Ask yourself: What is the connection between my Mirror Questions? What is the topic of the lecture? Can I write this topic in a question form?

In Your Words:
Writing a Summary Question

Working with another student, write a Summary Question based on the notes you just used for writing Mirror Questions.

Use the space below for your work.

_____

_____

_____

_____

_____

_____

Assignment

When you finish writing your lecture note questions each day, write a Summary Question for the lecture as a whole.

WRITING HIGHER-LEVEL QUESTIONS

To predict exam questions, it's important to ask *good* questions – the kind of questions your instructors – and other professionals – ask about the material you are studying.

For example, if most of your questions start with "What is..." you'll miss the more complex, interesting connections.

In the student samples below, three freshmen started writing simple, "What is?" Questions. They nearly failed their first hourly exam.

When they began writing higher-level questions, they saw more significant relationships in the information – and earned high grades in the course.

STUDENT SAMPLES

Writing Higher-Level Questions

The following questions were generated from lecture notes by three students who were just beginning to apply LTL skills to their work in an oceanography course:

Student A:	*What is a mid ocean ridge?*
	What is the speed of continental drift?
Student B:	*What is a delta?*
	What is turbidity current?
Student C:	*Name and describe the four types of dams.*
	What is isostatic balance?

These students were asking "What is?" Questions – questions too simple for oceanography. By writing higher-level questions from notes and books, their questions – and grades – got much better:

Student A:	*Contrast water hitting hard rock with waves rolling up on a beach of sand.*
Student B:	*How does the theory of "plates" relate to the age of the sea floor?*
Student C:	*How do we use knowledge of the earth's magnetic field reversal to explain sea floor drift?*

ASKING GOOD QUESTIONS

**I'm just a student. Won't I ask unimportant questions?
How can I ask myself the kinds of questions that my
instructor thinks are important?**

It's true that asking good questions is a *process:* It doesn't just happen automatically. You have to make a conscious effort. But using the steps below, you won't have a problem.

Here are some things you can do to improve the quality of your questions – so that you really *will* predict exam questions.

Steps for Writing Good Questions

1. Ask "What is...?" Questions for new terms. (e.g., "What is a *'normative statement'*?")

2. Ask questions beginning with *Why/How/Compare* for most other information. Write questions that cover more than simple facts.

3. *Write 4–5 questions* for a page of lecture notes.

4. Write a *Summary Question* that tells you about the topic of the day's lecture.

5. Write *complete questions* – not just key words. Writing real questions will help your thinking process. You'll begin to think like your instructors – and *you'll predict more exam questions.*

6. *Write 50-point questions* – as in the exercise below. These questions will help you see the "big picture," combine important ideas you're learning about – and predict essay-exam questions.

In Your Words:
Writing 50-Point Questions

Imagine that you're an instructor for one of the academic courses you're taking now. You're making up a 50-point essay question. Look through your lecture notes for that course, and write the question in the space below.

_____

_____

_____

_____

_____

_____

ASKING SUBJECT-RELEVANT QUESTIONS

As you begin the process of generating questions, it's important to keep in mind another aspect of asking good questions: Your questions should be relevant to the fields you are studying.

In Your Words:
Asking Subject-Relevant Questions

In the chart below, match question types with fields. What kinds of questions do you think each of these fields most often asks? Working with another student, discuss and fill out the chart below. (Add a field of your choice in the "etc." column.)

	Electronics	*Accounting*	*Psychology*	*Etc.*
What is the relation between... and ...?				
Define...				
How does X work?				
What was the effect of...?				
What is the structure of...?				
What is the function of...?				
Compare and contrast...				

USING MIRROR QUESTIONS
TO PREPARE FOR EXAMS

Writing questions can really help you study for exams if you practice **self-testing**.

Spend 5–10 minutes a night testing yourself on your lecture note questions.

You might be great at predicting exam questions. But real learning – the kind you can use in a creative way when you need to – happens over time. Testing yourself for a few minutes every day can make a big difference on an exam.

When testing yourself:

◆ Cover your answer notes, and see how much you can remember.

◆ Test yourself in an *active* way: Say the answers aloud to yourself, or write down a few key words or phrases from your answers.

Assignment

Write questions from your notes for two of your academic courses and bring these notes to your freshman seminar class next time.

GOING BEYOND THE INFORMATION GIVEN:
"What if...?" and Creative Questions

What are "What if...?" and Creative Questions?
"What if...?" and Creative Questions help you think imaginatively about whatever you are learning. *They are not Mirror Questions that directly reflect the information given.* Instead, they go beyond the information given.

Where do I write my "What if...?" and Creative Questions?
Write these questions on the left-hand page of your notebook – the page we asked you to leave empty for charts, examples – and for "What if...?" and Creative Questions.

"WHAT IF...?" QUESTIONS
"What if...?" Questions are most important to anyone learning math-based material. If you don't make variations of the problems given in class, you won't be prepared for new problems presented on exams.

When you ask "What if...?" Questions, you're asking the kind of question experts in the field ask themselves.

Drawing a simple diagram will help you see the consequences implied by "What if...?" Questions. The example below shows two series of events affecting a farmer's harvest. One set of events relates to the farmer's actions. The other relates to weather conditions.

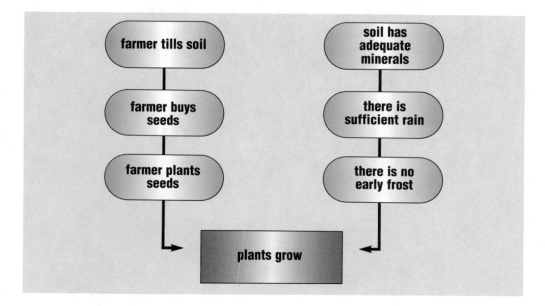

What if any of the factors change? There could be a very different result.

Steps for Writing "What if...?" Questions
1. Imagine a change in facts or ideas presented.
2. Write a "What if...?" Question about that change.
3. If helpful, draw a simple diagram that shows the facts or ideas that might change.

In Your Words:
Writing "What if...?" Questions

Working with another student, write "What if...?" Questions from your notes for one course. Draw a simple diagram that shows the steps or events that might change.

Do your work here:

CREATIVE QUESTIONS

Creative Questions ask about facts and ideas that were not presented. They are questions you ask when you become curious about a topic.

Steps for Writing Creative Questions

1. After writing your Mirror Questions, ask yourself questions that were not answered by the material.

2. Write your questions on the empty, left-hand page of your notebook.

In Your Words:
Writing Creative Questions

Writing with another student, write a few Creative Questions from your notes for one academic course. Write your questions in the space below.

_____

_____

_____

_____

_____

_____

_____

EVALUATIVE QUESTIONS
– A Special Kind of Creative Question

We've said that Creative Questions go beyond the information given. Asking *evaluative questions* is important in college – and throughout life. These questions reflect your *judgment* of the information presented. For example, not everything you read is true. Like everyone else, authors have a bias. Here are some things to look for in asking evaluative questions:

◆ Does the lecturer present credible evidence to support his/her arguments?

◆ Does important information seem to be missing? (For example, until recently, history textbooks have been almost exclusively devoted to the accomplishments of white men – as if women and people of color did not make important contributions.)

◆ When reading, notice if the author uses language that shows a bias. (For example, look at the descriptive adjectives used. Does the author use positive descriptions of one group, and not of another?)

◆ Do you agree with the priorities suggested by the way the information was presented? Can you think of a different order of priorities? Is it better? If so, why?

Can you see ways to use evaluative questions elsewhere in your life – beyond your classes?

Questions About "What if...?"
and Creative Questions

Where should I write my "What if... ?" and Creative Questions?

The empty left-hand page of your notebook is a good place for these questions.

I'm supposed to learn new information. How can I be expected to go beyond it and ask "What if...?" Questions?

"What if...?" Questions ask you to make variations in the information you're given. In writing these questions, write down the "facts" as you're learning them, and change one part.

How often should I ask myself "What if...?" Questions?

There are no "rules" for this. If you're learning about facts and ideas in a field where change is prevalent, like computer science, you'll need to make more variations than in fields that are more static.

What if my Evaluative Questions show that I disagree with my instructor?

The exchange of ideas is what higher education is all about. If writing Evaluative Questions leads to an area where you don't agree with your instructor, bring up your ideas in class or during your instructor's office hours. College teachers love to exchange ideas which might result in important, interesting discussions. But be prepared to give reasons for your disagreement. This kind of interchange will open up a whole new area of experience and opportunity for you.

Asking Good Questions Beyond College

We've talked about the role of Mirror Questions in helping you predict exam questions. But Mirror Questions can be used in many other ways – in and out of school. Asking Mirror Questions can help you correctly interpret new information you receive, either orally or in writing. For example, imagine that you have a new job, and your boss has just given you a complicated set of instructions. If you misinterpret the instructions, you'll have a hard time solving the problem at hand. Asking Mirror Questions will help you focus on the information given and check your understanding of it.

Creative and "What if..." Questions can help you head off problems by anticipating them. Creative Questions will help you see problems in a new way; and "What if..." Questions will help you think of solutions for changed circumstances.

In Your Words:
Asking Good Questions Beyond College

We've talked about asking better questions from notes, and you've learned about the importance of asking good questions – questions asking "How?", "Why?", "Compare...", "What if...?", and Creative Questions. But of course, *asking good questions is also a key problem-solving skill.* Working with another student, identify a personal, school, or job-related problem you face.

◆ Brainstorm "How?" and "Why?" questions to clarify the parts of the problem;
◆ Ask yourself "What if...?" Questions to anticipate new scenarios; and
◆ Ask yourself Creative Questions to arrive at problem solutions.

Begin this process by using the space below:

_____

_____

_____

_____

_____

_____

_____

Assignment

The next time you receive complex directions – from an instructor, a friend, or from your boss – stop a moment and jot down the question(s) the directions imply. Ask Mirror, Creative, and "What if...?" Questions. Do you have a clearer idea of the directions? Do you need more information?

CLASSROOM ISSUES

Most college classes have either a *lecture* or a *seminar* format. Some combine both formats.

LECTURE CLASSES

In lecture classes, you are expected to show up on time for classes and take notes. Here are some things you should be aware of:

◆ Show respect for your instructors. Don't antagonize your instructors by showing up late for class or by talking during class.

◆ Don't eat during class.

◆ Raise your hand to ask questions if you don't understand a point being made.

Many instructors value students' classroom participation – and even grade students on their participation in class.

Do you feel uneasy about raising your hand in class? Do you think you might not say what you mean to say? Or that you might phrase your question poorly? *Try writing your question down before you ask it*. Your "What if...?" and Creative Questions will help you think of interesting questions to ask in class.

SEMINAR CLASSES

Classes which have a seminar format are designed to be supportive and caring environments, where students can feel free to express new ideas.

If you view a seminar class as an open environment, you will help foster maximal learning – and make the experience of the seminar interesting for yourself and others. What does that mean? It means that you'll be cooperative and participatory instead of competitive; it means that you'll offer constructive, positive feedback when commenting on others' ideas. An open environment is a growth environment. You can allow yourself ten mistakes for every good idea, and no mistake is fatal to your self-image. You'll help create a stimulating environment where students view each other as resources.

On the other hand, if you view your classmates as competitors, and always try to win attention for yourself at other students' expense, you'll help foster a closed, negative environment – where people help each other fail.

*How would you use the **Four LTL Thinking Tools** to solve problems you have in this area? If this is an area where you'd like to make some changes, turn to the Four LTL Thinking Tools exercise at the end of this chapter.*

GETTING TO KNOW YOUR PROFESSORS

One of the main differences between high school and college is how students are expected to relate to instructors.

In high school, the best teachers are also counselors. They help you through the rough times. They know about your personal circumstances. They've probably met your parents. If you have difficulty with a particular assignment, they'll try to help you with it.

College is more like the real world. Your relationships with your instructors will be more formal. For example, unless your instructor is a graduate student, it's customary to address college instructors as "**Professor**" Smith or (if the instructor has a Ph.D.) as "**Dr.**" Smith.

While available for help, college teachers will be less accessible than your high school teachers were. For example, college teachers are usually able to meet with students only during scheduled office hours. Classes are often very large – particularly in the first two years of college – and classroom participation may be very limited. In fact, some of your professors may not recognize you outside the classroom.

You may establish a warm relationship with one or more of your college teachers, but this is not the norm. College teachers have many responsibilities other than teaching. They must write publications in their area of expertise; participate in departmental and other professional meetings; and serve on a wide variety of college committees.

Because your college teachers have busy schedules, it's useful to be specific and goal-directed when you see them. For example, if you're confused about solving a proof in a math class, *don't* ask, "How do you do this kind of problem." The explanation will be too long; and you won't remember it anyway. Instead, work through the kind of problem you're having difficulty with before meeting your instructor. When you meet with your instructor, say:

"I can do this problem until this part. Here's where I get stuck."

While relationships between college teachers and students are highly structured, college teachers can have a lasting impact on your life. (In my case, three college professors made a big difference in my life. I'm still in touch with one of them – thirty years later. The other two have long since forgotten me. They were important to me *by example* – not because they knew me personally.)

Self-Evaluation Checklist for Generating Questions From Lecture Notes

Throughout this book we'll provide self-evaluation checklists to help you monitor how well you're using this skill in your content classes.

1. Is there material for which you have not written questions?   Yes/No
2. Have you written a summary question for each lecture or meeting?   Yes/No
3. Do most of your questions ask "How?" or "Why?" – not "What is...?"   Yes/No
4. Do you leave the left page of your notebook paper blank, and later add questions that interest you, but that were not answered in class?   Yes/No
5 Do you draw a blank line (____) where information was missed, and later try to fill in the missing material?   Yes/No
6. What level of question do you ask? Do your questions appear to be "automatic," or do they thoughtfully mirror the material?   Yes/No
7. Have you developed a system of abbreviations for commonly-used terms in each course?   Yes/No
   Do you have a glossary of these abbreviations and the words they represent?   Yes/No

For technical courses (e.g., math, electronics, computer science)

1. Do you write questions for all your notes – including problems and formulas?   Yes/No
2. Do you leave the left page blank and later use it for writing problem variations?   Yes/No
3. Do you write problem-solving questions ("How does it work?") for math-based problems in your lecture notes?   Yes/No
4. Do you place an asterisk (*) in your notes when you become confused during a lecture?   Yes/No

For all courses

1. Do you test yourself for 5–10 minutes after you've written questions from a lecture?   Yes/No
2. Have you shown your lecture note questions to your content-course instructors so they can tell you if you're on the right track?   Yes/No

If you do these things on a regular basis, you'll be on your way to being a very successful student.

THE PREDICTION GAME

Your instructor will ask your class to form teams of 3–4 students. Each team will compete for "prizes" determined by the class. The members of each team will try to predict exam questions. The team that predicts the highest number of *actual mid-term exam questions* wins.

What's the best way to predict exam questions?

◆ Generate questions from your lecture notes and textbooks.[1]
◆ Ask questions starting with *Why... How...* and *What if...*
◆ Make up "mock" exams – as if you were your course instructor.
◆ Practice breaking down past exam questions into component sub-questions.
◆ Combine Mirror Questions from lecture notes and books into 50-point questions, and compare these questions to essay exam questions from previous years.

Assignment

Generate questions from your lecture notes, and bring these course notebooks to your freshman seminar class.

Discussion and Review

How do this chapter's LTL skills illustrate the Four LTL Thinking Tools?

The LTL Journal

Continue your journal of your thoughts and feelings. How can asking questions help you see your life more clearly?

---

[1] You'll learn how to generate questions from textbooks in Chapter 4.

Chapter 4:
READING
TO ANSWER
QUESTIONS

Have you ever found yourself reading and re-reading a passage, and not getting much out it? Do you just want to get to the end of a chapter – whether or not you understand or remember any of it?

When you're assigned a reading, you have no idea if it will be interesting or relevant. As in lectures – where you have no control over format – you have no control over the content of your assigned readings. With LTL you can arrange for an *active* learning environment where the *process* will take you beyond disguised rote learning – and enable you to develop your own point of view and come up with original thoughts in discussions, papers, and exams – just like generating questions from lecture notes helped you become an active listener.

This will accomplish two things: It will make the *process* more enjoyable, and the *pay-off* much greater than anticipated.

In this chapter, you'll continue the prediction game. You'll learn how to read to answer questions in a variety of assigned readings – including textbooks, readings without headings, and supplemental readings. We'll show you how to make speed reading work, by combining it with reading to answer questions. Finally, you'll learn about subject-specific applications of LTL reading methods – in literature and poetry; computer science; math-based texts; and in texts which include graphs, tables, and diagrams.

READING TEXTBOOKS

Steps for Reading Textbooks

1. Glance over the headings, subheadings, and illustrations in the chapter.

2. Write questions from headings, subheadings, pictures, and charts.

3. Read for answers, underlining key words and phrases.

4. Revise your questions if needed.

Hints:

◆ There is no "best" question. Just write a question that gives *you* a direction for reading.

◆ The headings, subheadings, and illustrations are the cues that will trigger your memory. They're also the best starting point for writing questions – to test your memory.

◆ Write several questions from the headings. Or write a question that combines ideas from several headings – whichever is most useful to you to start the process.

In Your Words:
Writing Questions From Headings

1. You've been assigned a chapter called "The Healthy Heart" for a nutrition class. Here are the chapter's major headings and subheadings:

> ### *Diet for a Healthy Heart*
> > *The role of vitamins*
> > *Trace Minerals*
> > *Caution – fats, sugar, salt*
>
> ### *Exercise*
> > *A daily exercise program*
> > *Dangers of over-exercise*
>
> ### *Important Dos & Don'ts*
> > *Smoking – how it can damage your heart*
> > *The relaxation response – how it can help your heart*

Write an essay-type question that will cover the chapter's main points.

Hint:

◆ If you have a problem writing this question, use "and" to connect the topics.

_____

_____

_____

_____

2. Turning to one of your textbooks, write questions from the chapter's title and major headings and subheadings.

Hint:

◆ Write questions in the margins of your textbook, so that you can easily refer back and forth between questions and answers when you're reviewing for an exam.

_____

_____

_____

_____

STUDENT SAMPLE

Notice the **Combined-Heading Question** in the margin – the student used key words from *all four headings and subheadings* in this question.

NOTE:
Your aim is understanding – and finding cues to trigger what you've learned for later recall. You'll read to find and **underline** *key word answers* – so you can easily access your questions and answers for later use. You *won't* highlight whole passages – turning pages into yellow, blue, or whatever the color of your highlighter is. (You'll never find a use for a whole passage – and even if you do, you won't be able to repeat it.)

AFFECTIVE DISORDERS

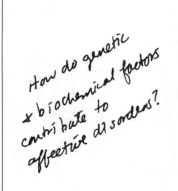

How do genetic & biochemical factors contribute to affective disorders?

ORGANIC FACTORS

What produces the mood extremes that are characteristic of affective disorders? According to one view, some of these conditions—especially the bipolar variety—are *endogenous,* that is, produced by some internal, organic pathology.

GENETIC COMPONENTS

The belief that such an organic pathology exists is based on several considerations. As in schizophrenia, there is the rather specific therapeutic effect of certain drugs (described below). And again, as in schizophrenia, there is good reason to suppose that at least some forms of the disorder have an important hereditary component. This is almost certainly true for the bipolar condition. The average concordance for identical twins of whom one suffers from bipolar affective disorder is 67 percent, while the comparable figure for fraternal twins is 16 percent (based on Slater and Cowie, 1971). The evidence suggests that the genetic factor is much weaker or perhaps altogether absent in unipolar cases.

BIOCHEMICAL HYPOTHESES

The genetic evidence is a strong argument for the view that there is some biological factor that underlies bipolar affective disorders. This view is further bolstered by the fact that in bipolars, the switch from one mood to the other is generally quite divorced from external circumstances. The most plausible interpretation is that there is some internal, biological switch.

One hypothesis is that the disorder is based on a biochemical defect that involves the supply of various neurotransmitters, specifically, the *catecholamines,* at certain critical sites in the brain. When there is an oversupply, there is mania; when there is a shortage, there is depression (Schildkraut, 1965). Some evidence comes from the study of certain therapeutic drugs. Drugs which deplete various catecholamines lead to mood depressions in normal persons. Conversely, drugs which increase the available amount of these transmitters act as *antidepressants.* An example is *imipramine,* a drug widely used in the treatment of depression. Imipramine leads to an increase in the available supply of certain catecholamines.

In Your Words:
Reading Textbooks

Apply the steps for Reading Textbooks to the passage on the next page.

Steps for Reading Textbooks (Review)

1. Glance over the headings, subheadings, and illustrations in the chapter.

2. Write questions from headings, subheadings, pictures, and charts.

3. Read for answers, underlining key words and phrases.

4. Revise your questions if needed.

Hints:

◆ Remember that there is no one "best" question.

◆ Use words from 2–3 headings, subheadings, or illustrations for each *Combined-Heading Question*.

◆ If you need more information, read the first sentence under each main heading.

Student Voices

Marionette Peavy

Learning to Learn has helped me in many ways, in school and out of school. I'm not only using the techniques in school, but also I'm using them outside to take care of personal business. Using LTL, I understand myself much better and my organization is great.

As far as my future, well, I always had the feeling that I wanted to be a lawyer, but I never liked reading. I hated reading. And to become a lawyer you have to read. So I'd always say, "Okay, I want to be a lawyer, but I can't stand reading, so I'll be something else." But once I got into Roxbury Community College, and took the Learning to Learn program, I feel that I can be a lawyer, a doctor. I can be anything I want. I can read with understanding now. I can understand exactly what's going on, and say, "Okay, I can take care of this. I understand this."

Write your questions here:

Developing Capable People

Glenn's theory

Stephen Glenn identified three perceptions and four skills needed for developing capable people. By perception, he means a belief a person has about himself – one that will affect the person's performance. For example if I perceive (believe) that you're interested in what I have to say, I'll be encouraged by that. As a result, I'll do a better job. But if I suspect that you're not interested in my ideas, I won't have confidence and may do a poor job. People's perception affects their performance. Glenn defines skills as abilities, strengths, and talents that can be improved.

The three perceptions of capable people

1. <u>Personal capability</u>: Personal capability is the belief that I can achieve my goals. If I believe that I'm capable, I'll try to solve problems, take risks. I'll have a positive attitude about my prospects for success.

2. <u>Personal significance</u>: Personal significance is the belief that I'm needed; that I'm not replaceable; that I'm a unique person; that I count; that if I'm not here, I'll be missed; that I'm worthy of respect; that my opinions are worthwhile.

3. <u>Personal control over events</u>: Control over events is the belief that I'm the maker of my destiny, that I can affect my future, that I'm not just subject to fate. If I don't think I have personal control, I'll blame my mistakes on others, on fate, on my upbringing, etc.

The four skills of capable people

1. <u>Intrapersonal skills</u>: Intrapersonal skills help people control their emotions, and to discipline themselves. For example, if I'm a morning person, I'll schedule my most important jobs for the morning. If certain social situations are not good for me, I'll avoid them.

2. <u>Interpersonal skills</u>: Interpersonal skills help people work with others, to get along with others, to cooperate, communicate, negotiate, share, and listen. The more I can improve these skills, the more willing others will be to accept my ideas.

3. <u>Systemic skills</u>: The systemic skills are understanding cause and effect, being responsible, adaptable and flexible. If I have strong systemic skills, I'll understand that my actions have consequences, and that if I act a certain way I'll obtain certain results. I'll see that I can adapt to different situations in order to control them.

4. <u>Judgmental skills</u>: Judgmental skills help people choose to do the right thing at the right time. Good judgmental skills will help me act in an unselfish way that benefits those around me.

Written by Dr. Michael L. Brooke.

What if I ask a question that was not answered by what I'm reading?

This is not a wasted effort: What's important is that you were actively reading for information. If you then revise your question, it will serve as a memory cue when you test yourself for pre-exam review.

Why should I combine a heading and subheadings in making up a Combined-Heading Question?

Writing **Combined-Heading Questions** is better than writing a question for each heading. With fewer questions, there's less busywork, a new level of understanding – and a bigger pay-off.

◆ Combined-Heading Questions will help you see the *connections* between the ideas in headings and subheadings. The connections suggest what will be in the next heading or subheading. So you'll see the author's ongoing argument – how the trees add up to a forest.

◆ Combined-Heading Questions help you understand the author's ideas as you read. You'll be able to read larger "chunks" of information with understanding – which will make your reading not only rewarding – but also more likely to continue.

What if there isn't enough information in the headings to write a question?

Try reading the first sentence under each heading for clues to writing Combined-Heading Questions.

Reading Without Headings

What if I'm reading material without headings?

This method is similar to what happens when there's not enough information in the headings. It's a structured approach to finding key words – generating your own "headings."

Make up a question combining a couple of key words from the first sentences of 3–4 paragraphs. *For example:*

Flying Cars: A Dream That Never Got Off the Ground

The auto-airplane never took flight with the buying public. Although several models were in daily use during the 1950s and one amazing model got close to full production, the problems of nationwide distribution could not be overcome. Federal agencies curled up in horror at the thought of hundreds of thousands of amateur pilots meeting daily over major cities. The design of a good airplane, which stresses light weight and high power, clashed with the ideal qualities of an automobile: sturdy, cheap, and roomy.

The flying car, which may now seem only a wild fling in our romance with the automobile, peaked during a postwar love for anything with wheels, especially four wheels. It was a time of garish models shaped to grab front-page photographs: two Ford offerings of the mid-'50s were the bubble-topped Lincoln Futura and the torpedo-like Ford FX-Atmos, a car with fins big enough to shame a shark. General Motors replied with the titanium-bodied, gas-turbined Firebird II. But progress sidestepped them all and left them as prey for collectors and museums.

A flying car seemed so useful that it was dreamed of before there were even cars or aircraft – a gliding carriage was built in 1808. Many schemes followed, and the first car to really fly arrived not long after Orville Wright touched down on the sands of Kitty Hawk. In 1917 the Curtiss Autoplane, an aluminum-framed car with three wings, appeared at the Pan-American Aeronautical Exposition in New York City. It wasn't for the Model T crowd: a pilot-chauffeur sat in front and two passengers basked in their own velvet-curtained and leather-lined compartment. It did fly, though not briskly. American inventor Glenn Curtiss dropped the idea with the nation's entry into the European war.

The second-cut, circled key words chosen by the learner were:
never took flight; public; flying car; postwar; useful

Three possible questions from these key words are:
1. *Why did the flying car, which seemed so useful during the postwar era, never take flight with the public?*
2. *Why did the public reject the flying car, even though its usefulness was obvious during the postwar era?*
3. *If the flying car was useful, why did the public reject it, and why did that happen during the postwar era?*

Steps for Reading Without Headings

1. Read only the first sentence of each paragraph.
2. Underline 3–4 key words in each first sentence.
3. Circle the key words that seem most important.
4. Write your question.
5. Read to answer your question.

In Your Words:
Reading Without Headings

Write your question here:

Apply these steps to the reading below:

Since ancient times, the family, not the individual, has been the central unit in the Chinese peasant village. Each family was run like a small autocracy, with the principal power residing in the father. The father controlled all family income and property and arranged the marriage of his children.

Even in old age, the father retained the authority, since wisdom of the elderly was highly respected. While the culture produced very strong bonds of affection between parents and children, by law, parents had absolute authority over their offspring; the father was entitled to sell his children into slavery or execute them for disobedience.

As age had authority over youth in ancient China, so men dominated women. Girls' marriages were arranged. A young Chinese wife had few rights in her new home. She was dominated both by her husband and by her husband's mother. She also had few personal rights. Her husband might take a second wife or discard her entirely if she produced no male heir. In addition, the Chinese peasant woman had no economic freedom. She rarely owned property and could not earn income from

housework – the only work available to her. While she may have had a fine natural intellect, she was kept totally illiterate. In addition, until the 20th century, Chinese women were forced to endure the crippling custom of foot-binding. This meant that, from the age of five, Chinese girls were forced to bind their feet tightly so as to prevent normal growth of the feet. The "lily feet" produced through this custom broke the arches of the feet of growing young women, whose adult feet were no longer than a child's.

The rights, duties, and patterns of authority and subordination were carefully ordered for all members of the extended Chinese peasant family. Husbands ruled over wives; sons were viewed as superior to daughters; and mothers were subordinate to their sons. Everyone had an exact place and set of expectations. The wives of the oldest son knew their roles and responsibilities, as did the children of the youngest son.

SUPPLEMENTAL READINGS

What if I'm asked to read several small paperbacks in addition to my textbook?

1. Reading for a General Overview:
Reading books with several related concepts
(Examples: Paperbacks assigned for marketing or psychology courses.)

Most assigned readings without headings are of this type:
The author has a few important points to make, and a lot of the book is made up of examples illustrating these key points. If you are assigned this kind of reading, use variations of the following method:

Steps for Reading Books with Several Related Ideas
   a. Read the first paragraph of a chapter, a paragraph in the middle of the chapter (chosen at random), and the last paragraph of the chapter.
   b. Underline key words in each of the paragraphs. Write an essay-type question that includes key words from all three paragraphs. Read to answer that question.
   c. You're reviewing the book as it relates to your goal – its place in the course you're taking.

2. Reading for Details:
Reading complex material

   a. Look for an overview of the chapter.
   b. Mark off 3–4 paragraphs with a pencil.
   c. Use the steps for Reading Without Headings for each "chunk" of 3–4 paragraphs that looks important. (See page 79.) This method will allow you to look for details when you find information that looks important.
   d. *Don't* underline whole lines or highlight passages – that just makes it harder to find the answers to your questions later on, when you review for tests.

Assignment
   For each of your non-math-based courses,[1] take the list of assigned readings and label them **1** (general overview) or **2** (details) for the level of question-asking you think you'll need for each kind of reading assignment.

---

[1] You'll learn how to read math-based textbooks on pages 89–92.

SPEED READING

READING 100 PAGES AN HOUR
OR, HOW DO I READ 10 BOOKS FOR A COURSE?

Is speed reading hard to learn?
No. Anyone can learn to read faster by practicing. Reading at normal reading speed (less than 600 words per minute), you've trained your eyes to read word by word, line by line. Speed reading simply means training your eyes to operate at their full potential. Instead of reading every word separately, your eyes will be able to take in groups of words at a time. As with any new skill, the key to successful speed reading is practice. To train your eyes to scan written words more quickly, you'll have to develop new reading habits.

Steps for Reading 100 Pages an Hour
Your goal is to read 100 pages an hour, or 25 pages every fifteen minutes.

1. Select the section you want to read, and mark off 100 pages with a paper clip.

2. Generate a pre-reading question from the first, a middle, and the last paragraph in the section.

3. Make sure there is a clock in the room so you can time yourself.

4. Sit at a desk, in a straight-back chair.

5. Pace yourself by moving the pen across each line more quickly than usual, and try to keep your eyes moving with it.

6. Remember, you want to get to the paper clip before 15 minutes are up.

7. Check yourself: As you were reading, did you have fragments of visual images that related to the content you were reading?

Hint:

◆ Don't worry about your comprehension. This is primarily an exercise in visual scanning and hand-eye coordination. Your initial goal is to train your eyes to read faster – not to remember every detail, but to have a general idea of what you're reading.

Questions About Speed Reading

How can I understand the information if I read so quickly?
When you read less than 600 words per minute, you have the sensation of "hearing" the words as you read. Through long habit, you interpret that as understanding. So you're reading slightly faster than you might read aloud. But you *know* that you can process information more quickly than you can "hear" words in your head. For example, if you're driving a car, you can react and adjust to new information faster than you could describe what you're doing. At low reading speeds, the information is processed through your auditory cortex. When you're reading faster than 600 words per minute, you process the information directly through the visual cortex.

Why doesn't speed reading work for most people?

Since the information is going directly to your visual cortex, you need to have a way to monitor that you're not just daydreaming during the exercise. Make frequent stops and check for images while you're engaged in this activity. Without this feedback, your speed reading activity might be worse than slow reading.

Also, after a week or so of practice, "frame" your speed reading by generating *pre-reading questions* before you read. That is, combine this technique with *Reading to Answer Questions*. Without pre-reading questions in mind, you'll get scant benefits from this skill.

How long will it take for me to attain high reading comprehension?

If you practice this method for 20 minutes a day, your speed and comprehension will improve dramatically – even at high reading rates – in about 6 weeks.

How do I know that the technique is working?

The best way to know you're reading fast enough is to be aware of how you feel while you're reading. When you first try speed reading, if your heart is beating more quickly, and you're feeling anxious and rushed, you're going fast enough. You may also find that your eyes feel tired. Once your eyes get used to the new speed, these signs of anxiety will disappear.

Will I remember any of what I've read?

At first, you may not remember as much as you would like. This is to be expected – you've been trained to read every word. Since your eyes are skimming the pages, you'll probably miss some details of the book you're reading. As you practice in this skill, your eyes will adjust to the new speed and your comprehension will increase. Trained speed readers read very fast with extremely high comprehension.

How can I force myself to read faster?

Many students find that the pressure of the clock is enough to force them to read faster. If the clock doesn't work for you, try reading 25 pages 15 minutes before an appointment you *must* be on time for. Make sure that you're reading in the proper atmosphere; adjust the lights before you start. Sitting at a desk in a straight-backed chair will help you focus on the exercise.

Some students find that they can read faster if they establish a reward that they get only after they reach a 25-page goal. Such a reward may be a visit to a friend's room, a phone call, or a snack.

How do I read ten books for a course?

When you're assigned a lot of paperbacks for a course, you're not expected to know details in them. Each assigned book should give you an answer to *one or two of the major questions raised by your course.* For example, you might ask yourself, *"What was court life like at the time of Louis XVI?" "Which personal events influenced Queen Victoria's life?"* Look through your notes before you read one of these books and find the relevant question(s) the book should answer. With these question(s) in mind, speed read your book.

Which courses should I use speed reading for?

Try assigned readings in the humanities and social sciences, With technical, math-based courses, slow down and work through the material as you read. (See pages 86 – 94.)

READING LITERATURE AND POETRY

There are two levels of reading literature and poetry in college classes:
1. Reading for personal meaning, and
2. Reading for recall and literary understanding.

Both are important.

To begin with, use a variation of *Reading Without Headings* as a pre-reading activity for reading novels, plays, or poems.

◆ ***If you're assigned a novel,*** read the first, a middle, and the last paragraph of each chapter, except for the last chapter. (To appreciate the suspense in the novel, read this chapter as written, beginning to end.) Ask yourself questions about the plot and the relationships between the characters. Then read to see if your questions were on target.

◆ ***If you're reading a play,*** try to guess what will happen in each scene. Then read the scene to see if you guessed correctly.

◆ ***When reading poetry,*** read the first, middle, and the last line of the poem. Try to visualize the poem, and imagine what it means. Then read it to fill in the spaces in your picture.

After pre-reading, read the piece through from beginning to end.

Reading for Personal Meaning

What's important to you? You might view reading assigned fiction and poetry as a drag – an exercise in getting the "right" answer.

But you can bring something new to your reading of fiction and poetry – your own unique experience and the sensory imagery that forms how you see and hear the world. For example, a student who plays classical piano brought a unique, personal view to her reading of James Joyce's short story, "The Dead." She "heard" the music in Joyce's language, and wrote a very personal critique of the story for her English class.

If you recall and repeat a known answer, you'll do pretty well in literature classes. You'll get "B" grades. But if you come up with a new response, you're likely to get "A." You'll also get more out of these classes – and personally, you'll have a greater feeling of self-worth. When you bring your own unique experience to reading, you discover something new. That's a totally different pleasure.

Reading for Recall and Literary Understanding

Question Charts (see Chapter 6) will help you organize and remember information in literature and poetry classes. For example, here's the outer "shell" of a Question Chart you might build to compare and contrast three poems. Your questions would come from questions you generated from your lecture notes – that is, the kinds of questions raised by your instructor in class.

	Robert Frost's "Mending Wall"	Carl Sandberg's "Chicago"	Emily Dickinson's "I'm a Nobody"
How are metaphor and simile used?			
How is sensory imagery used?			
How is alliteration used?			
What is the central message of the poem?			
What does the poem mean to you?			
Other questions?			

Or, you might compare the major characters in the novel, *The Lord of the Flies*, in a Question Chart that asks questions like:

◆ *What aspect of human personality does each character represent?*

◆ *How did their actions reflect their personalities?*

◆ *What events occurred as a result of each character's actions?*

◆ *How did each character view "The Beast?"*

Identifying the "Voice" in Literature

On exams, students in literature and poetry classes are often asked to identify an author or literary character, given a short passage or speech. Why is this kind of exercise considered so essential? It shows that you recognize a "voice" in literature – that you can see what makes the voice of this author or character distinctive.

Do you have to memorize literary passages in order to succeed at this exercise? Not at all. When learning anything new, people see large distinctions before they see small ones. Applying this principle to identifying a literary voice will help you do well in literature and poetry classes – and it will help you enjoy and recognize the unique qualities of these voices.

Steps for Identifying "Voices" in Literature

Start by identifying authors, then literary pieces; then characters within a given piece. For example, suppose you're taking a course on modern American playwrights:

1. Read 2–3 consecutive speeches from a play by one playwright. Then read 2–3 speeches from another playwright. Ask yourself questions about what makes them sound different from each other. Anything you notice is fine – just turn back and forth between the two playwrights until you have a "feeling" for the sound of the playwright's voice.

2. Do the same exercise between two plays written by a given playwright.

3. Within a given play, read three speeches, randomly chosen, from different characters in a scene. What do you hear? Visualize? Go back and forth until you get a sense of the "voice" of each character. You'll understand what you're reading more clearly – and you'll be able to identify which character is talking in a speech that appears on an exam.

Assignment

If you're taking a literature or poetry course, apply these strategies to your assigned readings.

READING COMPUTER SCIENCE

LTL skills in computer science will help you read computer science in an *active* way. For example, imagine that you're taking a beginning course in computer science. If you're reading a chapter on control structures in BASIC, you'd follow these steps:

Steps for Reading Computer Science

1. *Glance through a chapter's introduction, summary, headings, and sub-headings.*
   Example:
   The major headings for Chapter X are:

   Branching Control Structures
        The IF statement
        The DO CASE statement
   Looping Control Structures
        The DO WHILE loop
        The FOR...NEXT loop
   Using Control Structures

2. *Guess at the chapter's main topic.* Write your guess in your own words.
   For example, you might say:
   "It looks like the chapter discusses statements for branching that are like highway signs showing which way the next step of the program goes."

3. *"Translate" the chapter's main topic into an example from daily life.*
   For example:
   *" 'IF' is a control statement. What does 'if' mean in daily life? Well, when I drive my car, I'll stop the car **if** I come to a red light. **If** there's no red light, I'll continue driving. So <u>that's</u> what the author means by an IF control statement: Make a change IF something happens — IF a piece of information is given. IF not, continue in the way things have been going."*

4. *Work through each section of the chapter,* writing examples of new terms, then reading to see whether your examples were correct. If not, make the necessary changes.

5. *Read the problem sections of each chapter.* At first, the problem sections of a computer science textbook may look hard to read. You'll be tempted to skip over them. Don't skip them! They contain the chapter's most important information.

6. *Keep a list of the terms you defined by example.* They are the tools of your trade.

Remember, steer your course, don't drift – and you'll get there faster.

Tips for Actively Reading Computer Science

Here are some ways to make your reading of computer science more active:

1. *Say each problem out loud to yourself* – or to a friend. If you don't know how to start this activity, ask your computer science instructor to show you how he or she "talks" through a problem.

2. *Put an "*" in whenever you get "stuck"* — whenever you can't talk through the problem, or the logic of a step is unclear to you.

3. *Make a checklist of your most common errors.* Show your * marks to your computer science instructor. He or she may spot a pattern that shows an error you're making. Make a list of these errors. Keep your list with you as you solve problems. Edit for these errors when you get "stuck" again on other problems.

4. *Write variations of the problems in each section of the chapter.* This is important because the discipline of computer science is directed towards applying computer science concepts to new situations.

5. *Work through flow charts.*
   — Read the flow chart out loud. Talk through the process the flow chart describes.
   — Make up an example and mentally "run" it through the flow chart.
   — Cover part of the flow chart with a 3″ x 5″ file card and try to predict the rest of the chart. Draw your prediction on the card. Give yourself feedback by uncovering parts of the chart and comparing what you've drawn with the actual chart.
   — Using the text's example and one of your own, experiment with changing parts of the flow chart. Ask yourself what effects these changes would have on the process.

Questions About Reading Computer Science

Why would I want to talk problems out loud?

When you "translate" symbolic language into your own words, you'll be surprised how much easier it is to understand. You may want to work with a friend in the course, talking the problems out loud together.

I'm not taking computer science. Is there anything I can use from this section?

Sure. If you're learning to use different computer programs, but you're not studying computer science, try organizing information about different computer programs into a **Question Chart**. (See Chapter 6.)

For example, if you're learning to use Microsoft Word, Excel, and Wordperfect, compare the three programs and ask questions about their operations, when to use them, and how to find and use the menus for these operations. Then use your Question Charts to get what you want out of these programs.

In Your Words:
Reading Computer Science

Practice turning the example chapter's main topic into an example from daily life. The chapter's headings and subheadings are:

Branching Control Structures
   The IF statement
   The DO CASE statement
Looping Control Structures
   The DO WHILE loop
   The FOR... NEXT loop
Using Control Structures

Below are some other "control statements." Make guesses about what they may mean and write examples of them from real life situations. Ask yourself, *"In daily life, when I'm asked to 'Do' something, what does that mean? What's an example of that?"*

◆ DO
Your daily life example:

_____

_____

_____

◆ OTHERWISE
Your daily life example:

_____

_____

_____

◆ ENDCASE
Your daily life example:

_____

_____

_____

Don't be afraid to make mistakes at this stage. That kind of fear might stop you from using your common sense. At this stage, it doesn't matter if your guesses are wrong. The point is to become an active reader. If you make a guess about the meaning of a new term, you'll read to find out whether your guess was correct. You can make changes if you need to.

Assignment
If you have a computer science course, apply these strategies to your assigned reading and exercises.

READING TO SOLVE MATH-BASED PROBLEMS

Most students read problem-solving textbooks – in math, the physical sciences, statistics, etc. – as if they were reading a novel. They read a chapter from beginning to end as if it were a story. But the purpose of math-based textbooks is to teach problem-solving methods. The important information is in sample problems and diagrams, not in the written word.

All of this means three things. When taking a math-based, problem-solving course:

1. *Focus on learning problem-solving methods.*

2. *Pay attention to sample problems in the chapter.* Written text should be treated only as a means of understanding the problems.

3. *Actively work through the sample problems* – since they contain the key information in the chapter. There should be as much writing – solving problems – as reading in working with a math-based textbook.

Steps for Reading to Solve Problems

This method will help you become a more active, problem-solving reader:

1. *Look through the chapter to get a general overview of its contents.* Glance through a chapter's introduction, summary, headings, and subheadings. During your survey, write questions in the book's margins for headings and subheadings.

2. *Read through the problems at the end of the chapter.* Bracket the problems that seem to ask for the same problem-solving process or formula. (We'll talk more about this later.)

3. *Find the sample problem* in the chapter that matches the first group of problems at the end of the chapter.

4. *Divide the chapter into reading units.* For example, read from the beginning of the chapter until the first sample problem.

5. *Read to solve problems.* Try to work through the sample problem in the chapter.

6. *Check your understanding.* Solve one of the matching problems at the end of the chapter.

7. *Take a break with an open question* – one you'll answer when you come back.

8. *Find the sample problem* in the chapter that matches the second group of problems at the end of the chapter.

9. *Continue until you complete the chapter and its problems.*

Analyzing End-of-Chapter Problems

Here's a method that will help you find clues to group together similar end-of-chapter problems. Even if the book groups similar problems together, you'll need to make your own groupings among the problems presented. This method will help you tell the difference between identical problems (with different values for practice) and those which call for a new formula.

The problems below are elementary, but they illustrate the practice – which applies to the most sophisticated problems.

We've analyzed and grouped together the following problems.

1. A golfer sank a putt 5 seconds after the ball left the club face. If the ball traveled with an average speed of 3.5 feet per second, how long was the putt?

Given	Find
time = 5 secs. speed = 3.5 feet per sec.	distance

2. A truck traveled 640 miles on a run from Atlanta to New York City. The entire trip took 14 hours, but the driver made two 30-minute stops for meals. What was the truck's average speed?

Given	Find
time = 14 hrs. – 60 mins. speed (two 30-min. stops) = 13 hrs. distance = 640 miles	average

3. A car travels for three hours at an average speed of 55 miles per hour. If the driver's mind wanders for a couple of seconds, how far will the car have traveled during that time?

Given	Find
time = 2 secs. average speed = 55 m.p.h. Unnecessary information: 3 hrs.	distance

These problems all have the same kinds of given and unknown ("find") information: time, speed, distance. It's reasonable to guess that *they're variations of the same problem,* calling for the same kind of solution.

Analyzing these problems shows that they have the same givens and the same unknowns. So *they're really the same problem, requiring the same method of solution.*

Using Given/Find for problems at the end of a chapter, you'll learn to focus on the math-based parts of the chapter. And you'll begin thinking about the questions that the problems raise – even *before* you start reading the chapter. Your reading will be *problem-centered* – which is what's needed for a math-based course.

The following pages contain Given/Find exercises.

In Your Words:
Analyzing Problems With Given/Find

Working with another student, bracket together the problems that are similar to each other, and fill in the Given/Find columns.

Exercise 1: Physics

1. What centripetal force is required to keep a 4 kg mass moving in a circle with a radius of 4 m at constant speed?

Given	Find

2. A body which weighs 73 lbs moves in a circle of radius 3 ft at a speed of 10 ft / sec. What centripetal force is acting on it?

Given	Find

3. A force of 5 nt applied to one end of a rope keeps an object tied to the other end, moving at a speed of 4 ft/sec in a horizontal circle of radius 6 m. What is the radius of the object?

Given	Find

4. What is the gravitational force between two objects, one having a mass of 10 kg and the other having a mass of 3 kg, when they are 3 m apart?

Given	Find

Exercise 2: Electronics

1,000 ohms = 1 K; K stands for "thousand ohms"

1. A resistance of 10,000 ohms has 55 volts across it. Find the current flow.

Given	Find

2. A current of 5.5 milliamps passes through a resistor of 70 K. What is the voltage across this resistor?

Given	Find

3. A resistance of 62 K is connected across 130 volts. What is the current flow in the resistor?

Given	Find

4. Two resistors are connected in series, rated at 1.5 K, 10% and 2.2 K, 20%. Find the limits of the resistance variations in the combination.

Given	Find

5. Two resistors connected in parallel have ratings of 3.9K, 20% and 22K, 20%. Find the limits of the resistance variations in the combination.

Given	Find

Assignment
   If you have a math-based course, apply this skill when reading your textbook.

READING GRAPHS, TABLES, AND DIAGRAMS

Most students skip over graphs, tables, diagrams, etc. This is a serious mistake: On a biology exam, you may be asked to trace the flow of blood through the heart; on an electronics exam, you'll be asked to answer questions about diagrams. These kinds of test items appear on exams in all technical fields.

Here's a method that can help you through these courses.

Steps for Reading Graphs, Tables, and Diagrams

1. Work through illustrations in your text or lecture notes.

2. When possible, make variations of the graph, etc. in the margins of your textbook or lecture notes. Change the values and see if you can create an accurate version of the graph or diagram with your imaginary data.

3. Translate the illustration into words. Write your translation in the margin of your text or notes.

4. If it's hard to read the illustration, make your own simple drawing, and say the process aloud to yourself – as if you were explaining it to someone else – as you trace over your drawing.

CALVIN AND HOBBES © 1992 Bill Watterson. Dist. by UNIVERSAL PRESS SYNDICATE. Reprinted with permission. All rights reserved.

In Your Words:
Reading Diagrams – A Prediction Game

For active learning, talk through the process pictured in a diagram before reading the explanation in your textbook. In the example below, you'd trace the flow of blood through the heart using the diagram – then check your understanding by reading the explanation. (This is important because you'll be given only the diagram on an exam, and you'll have to learn to use it – not the words – as a learning tool.)

Working with another student, talk aloud the diagram below. One of you should "read" the diagram out loud, without looking at the written explanation. The other should read the explanation, and give feedback on how close the "reading" of the diagram is to the written explanation.

THE HUMAN HEART – Blood returns from the systemic circulation through the superior cavae. It then enters the right atrium and is pumped into the right ventricle, which propels it through the pulmonary arteries to the lungs. In the lungs, the blood is oxygenated. Blood from the lungs enters the left atrium through the pulmonary veins. It is pumped to the left ventricle and then through the aorta to the body tissues.

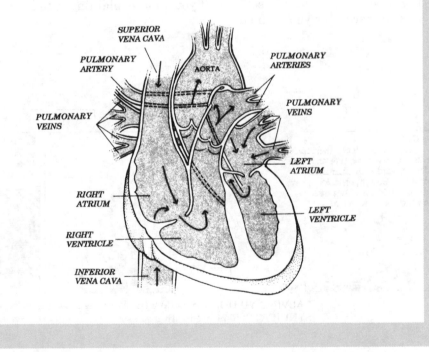

Assignment
If you're taking courses that use graphs, tables, and diagrams, apply this skill, and bring your work to class.

Self-Evaluation Checklists

Reading Textbooks

1. Did you scan the chapter by reading the headings, subheadings, and other clues to create our overview question?   Yes/No
2. Did your first question relate to the chapter title?   Yes/No
3. Do your Combined-Heading Questions use ideas from all the headings and subheadings in each section?   Yes/No
4. Did you guess at the answers to your overview and combined-heading questions?   Yes/No
5. Did you read to answer your questions?   Yes/No
6. Did you revise and add questions as needed?   Yes/No

Reading Without Headings

1. Did you read the first paragraph, a middle paragraph, and the last paragraph of the article or report?   Yes/No
2. Did you write 1–2 questions from information in these paragraphs?   Yes/No
3. Did you read to answer your questions?   Yes/No
4. Did you revise your questions as needed?   Yes/No

Supplemental Readings

When Reading for a General Overview,

1. Did you read the first paragraph of a chapter, a paragraph in the middle of the chapter, and the last paragraph of the chapter?   Yes/No
2. Did you underline key words in each of the paragraphs?   Yes/No
3. Did you write an essay-type question with key words from all three paragraphs?   Yes/No
4. Did you read to answer that question?   Yes/No
5. Did you review the book in relation to the course you're taking?   Yes/No

Reading for Detail

When Reading for Detail,

1. Did you read the first sentence of 3–4 paragraphs?   Yes/No
2. Did you underline, then circle, a few key words in each first sentence?   Yes/No
3. Did you write a question using key words from each first sentence?   Yes/No
4 Did you guess the answer to your question?   Yes/No
5. Did you read to answer your question, and underline key words of the answer?   Yes/No
6. Did you revise and add questions as needed?   Yes/No

Speed Reading

1   Did you sit at a desk, in a straight-back chair?   Yes/No
2. Did you use a paper clip for every 25 pages, and time yourself?   Yes/No
3. Did you generate a pre-reading question from the first, a middle, and the last paragraph in the section?   Yes/No
4. Did you pace yourself by moving the pen across each line, keeping your eyes moving with it?   Yes/No
5. Did you get to the paper clip within 15 minutes?   Yes/No
6. Did you "see" fragments of visual images that related to the content you were reading?   Yes/No

Reading Literature and Poetry

1. Did you use a variation of *Reading Without Headings* as a pre-reading activity?   Yes/No
2. Did you use Questions Charts to read for recall and literary understanding?   Yes/No
3. Did you compare speeches and authors, looking for the distinctive "voice?"   Yes/No

Reading Computer Science

1. Did you glance through a chapter's introduction, summary, headings, and sub-headings?   Yes/No
2. Did you write your guess about the chapter's main topic in your own words?   Yes/No
3. Did you "translate" the chapter's main topic into an example from daily life?   Yes/No
4. Did you write examples of new terms, then read to see if your examples were correct?   Yes/No
5. Did you read the problem sections of each chapter?   Yes/No
6. Did you keep a list of the terms you defined by example?   Yes/No

Reading to Solve Math-Based Problems

1. Did you get a general overview of the chapter's contents?   Yes/No
2. Did you read through and group end-of-chapter problems?   Yes/No
3. Did you match problems in the text to those at the end of the chapter?   Yes/No
4. Did you divide the chapter into problem-solving units?   Yes/No
5. Did you read to solve problems, working through sample problems?   Yes/No
6. Did you take breaks between these units?   Yes/No

Reading Graphs, Tables, and Diagrams

1. Did you work through illustrations in your text or notes?   Yes/No
2. Did you make variations of graphs, etc.?   Yes/No
3. Did you translate illustrations into words?   Yes/No
4. Did you make your own simple drawing of the illustration, saying the process aloud to yourself?   Yes/No

THE COST/BENEFIT GAME:
WRITING QUESTIONS IN TEXTBOOKS

So you think you'll sell your books for $10.00 more if you don't write questions in them.

You're probably right. If you're taking 5 courses, that's $50.00 a semester.

Form 2 teams, and ask yourselves the following questions:

◆ How much are you spending for each course?

◆ What's your tuition for a semester in college? A year in college?

◆ What difference would getting a C or an A or B mean you applied to law school?

◆ Do you have other questions?

The team that comes up with the most detailed, "real-life" answers in the shortest period of time wins the game.

Discussion and Review

How do this chapter's LTL skills illustrate the Four LTL Thinking Tools?

The LTL Journal

Continue your journal of your thoughts and feelings. How can the skills in this chapter help you solve life skills problems?

Chapter 5:
TIME/TASK MANAGEMENT

Like most students, you probably procrastinate, putting off large assignments, like reading a 30-page chapter in biology or starting work on a term paper. You do this because you have a hard time concentrating, you're overwhelmed, and you think you won't get much real work done unless you set aside more time – time that you don't have. The problem gets worse, your assignments pile up, you've got so much to do – and you don't know where to start.

Sound familiar? Would it help to bite the bullet and finally set up a schedule of what to do when? Maybe. But have you ever tried to set up a schedule and really follow it? With will power, you might keep to the schedule for a week or two. But over the long haul, most people can't keep up. They can't pre-plan the amount of time they actually need. Things in real life interrupt – and disrupt – the "perfect" schedule.

This is *not* a standard chapter on time management. The best-planned schedule is made useless by unpredictable events. Instead of helping you schedule your *time,* we'll help you focus on the *tasks* you have to get done. We'll show you how to use a Task Management Checklist that will let you break up complex tasks into manageable parts – and fit them into your life as you are now living it.

What's Wrong With Most Time Management Systems?

The short answer is that they're based on the wrong assumptions – and work against, not with, unexpected developments.

Most time management systems ask you to make up a schedule and stick to it.

There are two problems with this approach:
◆ It assumes you're organized enough to know how much time you need to do your work;
◆ If you were able to stick to a pre-designed schedule, you wouldn't need this program in the first place.

Most people are pretty disorganized. They're not very good at estimating time – especially how much time they need for difficult tasks; they tend to procrastinate; and they don't set goals for themselves. You're probably not too different. But don't get discouraged. Help is on the way.

What's Different About The LTL Time/Task Management System?

You'll learn how to:
◆ focus on getting tasks done;
◆ take data on your use of time;
◆ build on the way you now use time;
◆ break up large assignments into small, 10–15 minute tasks;
◆ take creative breaks;
◆ make up weekly checklists of these small tasks; and
◆ fit your assigned tasks into your life.

When you finish checking off the tasks on your checklist each week, you'll be caught up with your academic work.

How Do You Use Your Time?

To begin with, let's see where you are now.

For each statement, circle the number that best reflects your feelings.

		Never	Occasionally	Frequently	Always
1.	I have enough time to complete my work.	1	2	3	4
2.	I feel on top of my assignments.	1	2	3	4
3.	I think I get enough sleep.	1	2	3	4
4.	I stay up late, doing important tasks.	1	2	3	4
5.	I feel guilty that I don't have enough time for the people I care about.	1	2	3	4
6.	I'm able to set aside a period of personal time each day.	1	2	3	4
7.	I find time for some kind of social activity each week.	1	2	3	4
8.	I don't have any time for myself.	1	2	3	4
9.	I'm always doing something for other people in my family.	1	2	3	4
10.	When I have to write a paper for school, I put off writing until a few days before it's due.	1	2	3	4
11.	I cancel social activities because I feel I don't have time for them.	1	2	3	4
12.	I get my work done on time.	1	2	3	4
13.	I find myself making excuses about why my work isn't done.	1	2	3	4
14.	I feel good about how I use time.	1	2	3	4
15.	I feel that something is hanging over my head, and that I don't have enough time to do my work.	1	2	3	4
16.	I feel tired.	1	2	3	4
17.	I don't know what to do first.	1	2	3	4
18.	I organize my time well.	1	2	3	4
19.	My family and friends help me get things done.	1	2	3	4
20.	I'm good at setting and reaching my goals.	1	2	3	4

Step #1

Taking Data: How Do You Spend Time Now?

On the next two pages you'll find an empty schedule. Use it to follow yourself around for a week and see how you actually spend time. Notice small and large breaks you take, like playing a hand of cards or drinking soda.

◆ When do these breaks occur?
◆ What are you doing before you take these breaks?
◆ How long do you spend with the task *before* taking a break?
◆ How long are your work breaks?
◆ Do you easily get back to work after a break?

When you begin using the LTL Task Management Checklists, you'll be able to use your "time wasters" as rewards for working through your checklist.

Don't try to change your habits, just take some data on them. Use key words and abbreviations (e.g., br = breakfast), so you can fit in as much information as possible.

Before you begin taking data on yourself, estimate the amount of time you spend studying each day or the amount of time you spend on each subject in a week's time.

Your estimated use of time

Your courses

Weekly estimated time spent studying for this course

_____   _____

_____   _____

_____   _____

_____   _____

_____   _____

Data Collection Chart

	Mon.	Tues.	Wed.	Thurs.	Fri.	Sat.	Sun.
AM 8-9							
9-10							
10-11							
11-12							
PM 12-1							
1-2							
2-3							
3-4							

Data Collection Chart

	Mon.	Tues.	Wed.	Thurs.	Fri.	Sat.	Sun.
4-5							
5-6							
6-7							
7-8							
8-9							
9-10							
10-11							
11-12							

Step #2

Interpreting the Data

Now that your week of data-collecting is over, let's look at what you've learned.

◆ Were any days or periods of time more productive than others?

◆ Can you tell why by looking at your schedule? (For example, you may find that you did more productive work when you were *working through* your physics problems in your textbook than when you were just passively *reading* your physics textbook. *Doing* a physics problem is an active task; *reading* a physics textbook can put you to sleep (unless you're reading to answer your own questions).

◆ Does any of this information give you clues about rearranging some of what you do to make your life easier (and more productive)? (For example, would it make sense to read a chemistry chapter in three short sessions instead of one long one, since you tend to fall asleep during long study sessions? Did you study best late at night? In the morning? Before or after meals?)

◆ Did the amount of time you actually spent studying match your estimated study time? What percentage of the time you reserved for study time was actually spent studying or writing?

Step #3

Setting Priorities With a Task Management "To Do" List

Do you often feel overwhelmed? Do you set up schedules and try to live with them?

Don't think about *time* management. You're not going to be judged on how much time you spend on your work – but on the products you come up with, how much you learn and apply.

Think about *task* management – the tasks you need to get done.

Find out what's important to you – what comes first. Begin by writing a "To Do" list – all the things you really need to get done in the near future. That's your Master "To Do" list of tasks, including the sub-tasks that are small steps – part of a larger project.

Using a "To Do" list is easy. Make a list of what you need to get done tomorrow. Then use the list tomorrow throughout the day. Check off each item as you do it. (You'll be surprised at how good it feels to check off the items on your list.) Put tasks you don't complete on the next day's list. A lot of the larger tasks can be divided into smaller parts – so you can have manageable tasks on your list each day. (That's how to deal with projects that seem too big to start – break them down into *manageable parts*.)

You're using the **Four LTL Thinking Tools** – asking yourself *questions* about what you need to do; setting *goals;* breaking large tasks into *small parts*; and getting *feedback* on your progress as you check off each task.

Step #4

"To Do" Lists

You've begun to write questions from lecture notes. In this process, you're learning to look at facts and ideas as a series of answers to implied questions. You're better able to see the *parts* of what you're learning.

We just talked about using Task Management "To Do" Checklists. Here are some steps for using these checklists:

Using Task Management Checklists

◆ Make a list of your major tasks.
◆ Break up the tasks into smaller sub-tasks.
◆ Write a Task Management Checklist of the tasks and sub-tasks.
◆ Take rewarding breaks. (See Step # 7.)
◆ Check off each sub-task as you complete it.
◆ Review your checklist at the end of each day – and at the end of each week.

How do you break up a major task into sub-tasks? The Task Management "To Do" Checklist below shows how a major task, organizing a committee meeting, is really a series of smaller tasks.

Organizing committee meeting

– reserve room

– call committee members

– write memo about meeting

– send out memo

– check presentation equipment & supplies

– order coffee & donuts

Step #5

Task Management Checklists and LTL Skills

As you become more familiar with LTL, you'll find that you can break up most of your studying time into 10–20 minute LTL tasks. You'll be able to break down a large task – such as reading and studying a chapter in biology – into a series of small tasks. With LTL methods, you can complete your homework assignments by turning them into a series of LTL tasks.

Examples:

◆ generate questions from lecture notes: *5 minutes*

◆ cover the "answer" side of the notes and "test yourself": *10 minutes*

◆ make up a Question Chart for one of your courses: *20 minutes*

◆ find the answers in your textbook: *20 minutes*
   (You'll read much faster and remember more with this kind of directed approach.)

◆ put key words from your reading into your Question Chart: *10 minutes*

Step #6

Using a Task Management Checklist for Academic Tasks

You'll have more time for yourself when you divide complex academic tasks into smaller parts. Your daily Task Management Checklists will be composed of small tasks that can be completed in 10–20 minute segments. The Task Management Checklist below includes LTL tasks for lecture notes and reading assignments. The student checked off completed tasks and wrote down how long they took to complete.

Computer graphics class

✓ *Write questions from lecture notes: 5 minutes*

✓ *Cover "answer" side of notes & test myself: 10 minutes*

- *Ch 4 – skim & write Q's*

- *Take break*

- *Read to ans. Q's (1st half of ch.)*

- *Take break*

- *Read to ans. Q's (2nd half of ch.)*

- *Do questions 1–4*

Step #7

Using Time-Breaks as Rewards

People often stretch out breaks to avoid the punishment and frustration of work when their efforts don't accomplish much. We all hate waste. With LTL, you're likely to take less "endless" breaks, because the LTL skills keep you going – you're always playing the prediction game of finding answers to your own questions.

But it *is* important to take work breaks. Are there things you like to do that take only a few minutes? You'll know you like to do them because you've been spending time on them instead of working – in unplanned work breaks. For example, 'phoning a friend, playing a song on the guitar, or whittling a piece of wood might be "time-wasters" that would fit in well here.

In the same way you made an effort to improve the quality of your work time, improve your fun time during breaks. Make a checklist of 10-minute activities you like to do. Choose the activity. Decide which fits best now. Take your fun time as seriously as your work time. Improve it. Don't get into a rut.

Use your 10-minute time breaks like this:

- ◆ Do a task with a defined goal in mind (writing questions for one history chapter or five chemistry problems).

- ◆ When you reach a goal, decide on your next task.

- ◆ Take a break (with some definite time in mind: 10 minutes is good).

- ◆ Work towards the next goal you've set for yourself, etc.

In Your Words:
Taking Creative Breaks

Ask yourself:
- ◆ What are some brief, rewarding activities I can do on my breaks?
- ◆ When do I usually take breaks now?
- ◆ What am I doing before these breaks?
- ◆ How long do I usually spend with a task before taking a break?
- ◆ How long are my breaks?

Steps for Taking Creative Breaks

1. Plan breaks to reward yourself for completing sub-tasks.
2. Write your breaks on your Task Management Checklist.
3. Build your Task Management Checklist around your current use of time.

Step #8

Using Question Charts
in Task Management Checklists

The following Task Management Checklist contains several LTL skills – writing questions from lecture notes, reading to answer questions, and building Question Charts for a course in marketing. (See Chapter 6). The student checked off completed tasks and wrote down how long they took to complete.

Marketing

✔ *Write questions from lecture notes: 5 minutes*

✔ *Cover "answer" side of notes & test myself: 10 minutes*

– *Skim chapter 4 & write Q's*

– *Take break*

– *Read to ans. Q's (1st half of ch.)*

– *Take break*

– *Read to ans. Q's (2nd half of ch.)*

Step #9

Preparing for Exams
With Task Management Checklists

Task Management Checklists can help you prepare for exams, as shown in this Task Management Checklist. (See Chapter 6 for Key Word Diagrams.)

Art History

✔ *Write lecture note Q's: 3 minutes*

✔ *Write questions from lecture notes: 5 minutes*

✔ *Cover "answer" side of notes & test myself: 10 minutes*

– *Write major essay questions*

– *Write Key Word Diagrams*

– *Test self on Question Chart*

Assignment

Apply Task Management skills to complete your homework assignments. Each week, make up Task Management Checklists to cover your week's work. Bring your checklists to LTL class. Take data on your work when you're doing a small task for the first time. How long does it take you to complete each sub-task? This data will tell you whether a given sub-task fits easily into your ongoing daily activities. If not, you'll need to set aside a small amount of time for it. Check off each sub-task as you complete it.

Review your checklist at the end of each day: How much have you completed? Which task (or sub-task) do you want to work on next?

Student Voices

Sandra Frasier

Learning to Learn has helped round off my life. It helps me not only in school – not only by helping me with my courses – but to do other things. To get things done on time, to think about my future. It makes you think about what you want to do with your life. Those are serious questions.

My life goals are better as a result of LTL. I'm able to direct myself and – because I have direction now – I know how to get there, step by step.

What would I say to another freshman coming into this course? I would strongly recommend this course to anyone – first year or senior year, graduate or undergrad. It would help a great deal in anyone's life. It's positive.

Using Task Management Checklists For Daily Life

Task Management Checklists can be helpful for more than managing your time. By breaking up complex tasks into manageable parts, you can turn big problems into a series of small tasks, and you can see what your priorities are – what comes first, what next, etc.

◆ Working with another student, think of something non-academic that you plan to do, but that will take some planning. It could be saving money for a car or vacation, or solving a series of problems with your roommate. Use questions to break the problem into parts, and give yourself assignments in a Task Management Checklist. Don't start by worrying about the order of the tasks. After you've brainstormed the tasks, you can arrange them in a logical order.

◆ Using data from your Data Collection Chart, identify periods of inefficiency. Can you spot a bottleneck – a place where things often go wrong? Working with another student, brainstorm alternatives: Would it help to break up large tasks into smaller ones? Rearrange the tasks? Use others as resources? Restate your goals? Do your short-term objectives and tasks relate well to your larger goals?

Looking Towards the Future

When you learn to use LTL Key Word Diagrams (see Chapter 6), you'll see that you can create a powerful problem-solving tool by combining them with Task Management Checklists. For example, you might create a Key Word Diagram for mapping the parts of the task, and insert informal deadlines. This will help clarify your goals.

Using Task Management Checklists For Daily Life

Using the space below, create a Task Management Checklist which will help you solve a problem in your personal or academic life.

THE TASK MANAGEMENT GAME

Divide the class into 2 teams. Team 1 makes up an example of a "crisis" study problem. (e.g., *Tom has 3 papers due in 3 weeks; he also has to prepare for exams in history and biology, and he's on the basketball team.*)

Team 2 must construct a Task Management Checklist, breaking up the tasks into LTL parts, within 5 minutes. Missed steps count against the team that's "up."

Using Natural Thinking Skills

Asking questions, breaking up complex tasks into parts, focusing on goals, and looking for feedback – all these are natural thinking skills. These skills are used in all successful learning – in and out of the classroom. But most students don't bring these learning skills into the classroom. If you're new to a field of study, you probably don't see what you're learning as a set of *answers to central questions*. You may see a specific assignment – like reading a chapter in biology – as *one* hard job, instead of what it really is – a series of *small, manageable tasks*. You don't get immediate *feedback* on your progress from teachers, and you may not know how to assess your own learning progress. You may confuse means with ends, and your *goals* may not be related to your instructors' objectives. (For example, you may just aim at reaching the end of the chapter – not at finding the answers to questions asked by the field you're studying.)

In school, you're asked to memorize facts and answer other people's (your teachers') questions. You've been asked to see "book learning" as something that's not related to daily-life learning. So you may not use your natural thinking skills in school.

In this course you're learning to apply your natural learning skills to your school work. You're using concrete, practical "translations" of the Four LTL Thinking Tools.

Discussion and Review

How do this chapter's LTL skills illustrate the Four LTL Thinking Tools?

The LTL Journal

Continue your journal of your thoughts and feelings. How can Task Management Checklists help you organize your life more clearly?

Chapter 6:
PREPARING FOR EXAMS

**By Using Both Sides
of Your Brain**

If you learn new information, you may still have a problem recalling and using it on exams. In this chapter, you'll see how to fit what you've learned into the shape required by your professors' questions.

INTEGRATING LEFT- AND RIGHT-BRAIN LEARNING

In Chapter 2, you were introduced to Left- and Right-Brain Learning. We talked about the left side of your brain – the verbal side that asks **questions**, and the right side of your brain – the **visual** side that learns best by "picturing" ideas.

Do you have any trouble recalling what you've learned – especially on exams? In this chapter, you'll learn to use visual organizers to help you remember information under the pressure of exams. Question Charts and Key Word Diagrams will "trigger" your memory when you're taking exams.

Question Charts, Key Word Diagrams, and Picturing Ideas are all **visual organizers** – they use both the **left and right sides of your brain**. You'll learn to prepare for exams with visual organizers – so you can "see" with your mind's eye when you take an exam. By combining words and pictures, you're using – and integrating – both sides of your brain.

QUESTION CHARTS

Do you dislike school learning because you need to memorize so much information? Do you have a problem organizing and recalling large amounts of new information? Do you often miss connections between information that's new to you and what you already know? With **Question Charts**, you'll learn to organize information in ways that will help you understand and remember it better. And you'll find that you spend much less time memorizing, and more time thinking about, what you learn.

STUDENT SAMPLE

> ### A Completed Question Chart
> Here is a completed Question Chart. Notice that:
> ◆ All questions apply to all the items in the chart.
> ◆ None of the questions can be answered with "yes" or "no."
> ◆ Some of the answers were found in the student's lecture notes ("L"), others from the textbook ("T").

Compare the Major Political Parties of Japan

	Liberal Democrat	Socialist	Communist	Komeito
How did the party become organized?	Progressive & liberal T64	Social masses T64	Illegal before 1945 L55	Buddhism & Japanese nationalism L65
Which groups provided the most support for the party?	Business leaders Rural people White collar workers L62	Labor unions students L63	Local rural electorate & students T302	Soka Gakkai L65
What was the party's domestic policy?	Cooperation w/business Establishmnt of defense forces L62	Anti-business L63	Develop awareness of indust. workers & peasants T302	Small group organization L66
What was the party's foreign policy?	Militaristic L62	Neutral Anti-estab. L63	Indep. from foreign infl. T302	Anti-militar. Neutral L66
What was the party's main problem?	Corruption of campaign funds L62	Couldn't solve internal probl. or inspire youth loyalty L63	Incompat. w/Japan nat'l char. T230	*Not in book or lecture notes–* *LOOK UP!!*

In Your Words:
About Question Charts

Working with a partner, what do you notice about this Question Chart?

_____

_____

_____

Do you think it's important to compare the items by using questions? Or would just labels without questions be okay? Why?

_____

_____

_____

Looking at the first question, you'll notice that the professor didn't talk about how the Liberal Democratic or the Socialist parties become organized. What would happen to a student who didn't write a Question Chart – and who found this question on an exam? *"Discuss the origins of the four major political parties in Japan."*

_____

_____

_____

Who should write a Question Chart – students or professors?

_____

_____

_____

How do you think Question Charts might help at exam time?

_____

_____

Is it hard to construct a Question Chart?

No. Here's the "shell" of a Question Chart that you might build if you were taking a course on world religions. The items to be compared – in this case, different religions – are across the top of the chart. Questions that can be asked about all the items to be compared run down the left side of the chart.

Notice that the "header" of the Question Chart is a **Summary Question** that the chart answers.

What are some key distinctions between these world religions?

	Hinduism	Buddhism	Islam	Taoism	Judaism	Chrisitianity
What / who is the "higher power" in this religion?						
Which "wants of man" does this religion address?						
Who was the founder / leader of this religion?						
What rituals or practices are part of this religion?						
What are the major written documents in this religion?						
Where and how do the followers of this religion worship?						
How does this religion address death?						
Etc. questions						

BUILDING QUESTION CHARTS

Steps for Building Question Charts

1. Before you build a Question Chart, write a *Summary Question* that tells the purpose or topic of the chart.

2. Place items to be compared across the top, questions down the left side.

3. Use comparison items from the same category.

4. Write questions that apply to all comparison items.

5. Avoid questions answered by Yes/No.

6. Ask complete questions.

Hints:

◆ Check the items across the top. Are they in the same category (e.g., types of fruit, types of companies, etc.), so that you can compare and contrast them?

◆ Are your questions broad enough to be asked of each item you're comparing?

◆ Use "empty" cells as cues to do research. What do you need to know to fill in this cell?

Student Voices

Gyun Kim, Accounting Major

Learning to Learn organized me, helped me concentrate, and made me want to do my course work. Asking questions helped me see the whole global picture, and Question Charting helped me connect it all together. That's really important for accounting courses, because in accounting everything is related, and if I didn't have LTL, I'd be trying to learn everything case by case.

You can't do that and do well in accounting. You have to have a picture of how it all connects. With LTL, I'd go into an exam and just "see" the Question Chart in my head, so I'd know which journal entries I had to use for different cases.

In Your Words:
Building Question Charts

Working with another student, draw the shell of a Question Chart on any topic that interests both of you. (It doesn't have to be an academic topic.)

Remember to write a Summary Question before building your Question Chart.

Do your work here:

Questions About Building Question Charts

Where do the questions in a Question Chart come from?

You wrote these questions in the margins of your notes and reading material. You can generate more questions through brainstorming – asking yourself, "What questions do I need to compare the items in this Question Chart?"

Why should I write a Summary Question before building a Question Chart?

Because the chart as a whole should be an answer to a question. Writing a Summary Question first will give direction to your thinking as you build the Question Chart. Notice that you are retracing in reverse the steps you learned earlier in LTL. For example, when working with lecture notes, you wrote Mirror Questions first – *then* you wrote a Summary Question. You were uniting disjointed information into a whole. Now you're building a structure – starting with a plan and filling it in with content.

How can Question Charts help me study for tests?

Question Charts are excellent tools to use when preparing for both essay and objective tests. Question Charts often help students predict questions on essay tests. *If you are expecting multiple-choice questions, write a number of Question Charts.* We'll show you an example of this use on the next page of this chapter.

Building Question Charts can also show you what you *don't* know – and what you need to look for. An *empty cell* in a Question Chart is a cue to look up new information.

When do I build Question Charts?
Are both small and large charts good?

Make up Question Charts when you might find it useful to compare two or more items within a category. Question Charts can be small – asking 2–4 questions about 2–3 items in the same category – or large and expanding. (For example, you might add more topics to be compared across the top of the chart; or new questions as you learn more about these topics.)

If you can't fit all of the important facts and ideas into the cells of a Question Chart, insert page numbers referring to facts and ideas in your notes and textbooks. (See the Question Chart on Japanese political parties on page 116.)

When you're making up a complex Question Chart, you might *color code* it for different kinds of facts or ideas.

Why is a yes/no or one-word answer not enough to put in a cell of a Question Chart?

You need enough key word answers to remind you of the complete answer. Your real question is not just, "Should I buy this car?" or even "Is this car reliable?" but "How reliable is this car when the weather is poor?" In that case your answer might be: *"reliable: snow – front wheel drive – good traction; heavy rain – engine doesn't stall out; cold – car starts."*

What if there's an empty cell in a Question Chart?

An empty cell shows that you don't know – or haven't yet found – the answer. An empty cell can point you towards finding new, useful information.

PREDICTING OBJECTIVE TEST QUESTIONS WITH QUESTION CHARTS

It's hard to study for objective tests. There are so many details, and you don't know how to predict what's important.

But Question Charts can help you. Let's see how.

Here's an example that shows the relationship between Question Charts and multiple-choice test questions.

In Geography 101, you've spent a month studying rural life in several Asian countries. Starting with a Summary Question, you've built a Question Chart covering material studied during this time. Here are some of the items (countries), and the questions that were raised in class about them:

Summary Question: ***Compare the rural economies and social organization in four Asian nations. How are they similar? Different?***

Question Chart:

	Japan	*China*	*Vietnam*	*Laos*
What are some important cash crops for export?				
What is the social class system like?				
What kinds of farming methods are used?				
How large are the farms, and who works and owns them?				

PREPARING FOR OBJECTIVE TESTS WITH QUESTION CHARTS

If you filled in the cells on this Question Chart and tested yourself on it, you'd be prepared for your next objective test. Your Question Chart could predict *all* the multiple-choice questions on the exam:

1   The caste system divides society into rigid social classes in:
    A. Japan   B. Vietnam   C. China   D. Laos

2. Tea and cotton are important cash crops for export in:
    A. Vietnam   B. Japan   C. China   D. Both A & B

3. The government has asked farmers to work together in cooperative groups called communes in:
    A. Vietnam   B. Japan   C. China   D. Laos

4. Many farmers do not own any land, but instead farm the land of large landowners in:
    A. Japan   B. Laos   C. China   D. Vietnam

5. The government has attempted to produce a "classless" society in:
    A. Japan   B. Vietnam   C. China   D. Both B & C

6. Silk is an important farm product in:
    A. China   B. Japan   C. Laos   D. Both A & B

7. The country with the most modern, efficient farming methods in Asia is:
    A. Laos   B. China   C. Japan   D. Vietnam

8. Ancient methods of farming are still used throughout much of:
    A. Japan   B. China   C. Laos   D. Both A & C

9. Small farmers working their own land are commonly found in:
    A. China   B. Laos   C. Japan   D. Both A & C

10. Rice is a key export of:
    A. China   B. Laos   C. Japan   D. None of these

In Your Words:
Question Charts and Exam Questions

If the Question Chart on page 122 were complete, where would you find the answers to these 10 questions? *Write the number of each question in the appropriate empty cell of the Question Chart.*

✔ THINK ABOUT THIS

This example shows that the details needed for **multiple-choice** questions can be predicted through the use of Question Charts. Question Charts can also help you predict the questions on **True/False** tests. A lot of detailed information falls into patterns – and empty cells in a Question Chart can point you towards information you need to find.

In Your Words:
Building Question Charts From Objective Tests

I. *Here are questions covering the "early man" section of an anthropology exam:*

1. *Which of the following is believed to have made bifacial tools?*
   a. Ramapithecus
   b. Australopithecus africanus
   c. Australopithecus
   d. Homo erectus

2. *Upon what evidence is the conclusion based that Australopithecus robustus was an herbivore?*
   a. canine teeth
   b. sagittal crest
   c. patterns of molar wear
   d. both a and c

3. *The first evidence of man-made shelters occurs at which of the following stages of man's evolution?*
   a. Ramapithecus
   b. Australopithecus boisei
   c. Homo erectus
   d. Australopithecus africanus

4. *Which of the following of man's ancestors lived during the Pliocene era?*
   a. Australopithecus africanus
   b. Homo erectus
   c. Ramapithecus
   d. Australopithecus robustus

5. *Evidence from dentition and archaeological sites indicates that Australopithecus africanus was:*
   a. a carnivore
   b. an herbivore
   c. an omnivore
   d. of these

Working with another student, construct the shell of the Question Chart that would have helped you predict all of the above questions.

Build your Question Chart here:

II. You're taking a biology course, and you've just taken an objective exam. *Here are the test questions on the role of glands in the human body:*

1. *Insulin is secreted by the:*
   a. adrenal glands
   b. pancreas
   c. pituitary glands
   d. none of the above

2. *When you're angry, your body produces hormones from the:*
   a. pituitary glands
   b. pancreas
   c. thyroid glands
   d. adrenal glands

3. *The thyroid glands are located in the:*
   a. stomach
   b. head
   c. neck
   d. pelvic area

4. *A giant can result from overproduction of the hormone from the:*
   a. adrenal glands
   b. pancreas
   c. pituitary glands
   d. thyroid glands

Working with another student, construct the shell of the Question Chart that would have helped you predict all of the above questions.

Build your Question Chart here:

Steps for Predicting Objective Test Questions

1. If you expect objective tests, build Question Charts covering material that can be compared and contrasted (e.g., different theories in psychology; different parts of the brain; different accounting methods).

2. Check the content of your charts against the questions your instructor asked on past tests. This will assure that the Question Charts you're creating will predict the kinds of questions your instructor asks.

3. Test yourself by covering up the cells of your Question Chart.

STUDYING FOR OBJECTIVE TESTS: DEFINING TERMS

If you've been writing questions from lecture notes, you know which new terms will be tested on a future exam: Look for your *"What is...?"* Questions.

How do you study for this kind of exam? It's hard to memorize lots of new terms. Here's an exercise that can help you solve this problem:

1. ***Set aside a separate section of your notebook for your new terms.*** (In courses where there are lots of new terms, you may want to keep the left-hand pages of your notebook empty, and write new terms and definitions there.)

2. ***Define each term by example.*** For example, in a psychology course you may learn the term "regression" meaning *"to act in childlike ways, usually in response to an emotional crisis."*

   Don't try to memorize the formal definition of the term. Instead, look for an ***example*** of it. In your textbook, the definition-by-example might mention a child, lost at a carnival, crying like a baby. A key word for this example would be *"carnival."* Since that has meaning for you, list the example key word in your glossary:

   regression / crying child lost at carnival

3. ***Make up a sentence using the new term.***

4. ***Say your "definition" – your own example – out loud*** when you study these terms. If you work on your list for *five minutes* every night, *you won't have to worry about exams.*

If you have an exam coming up soon, and you haven't been preparing like this, test yourself aloud in 5-minute practice sessions, with short breaks in between. Review from the beginning of the list each time, so that you really know all the terms. For each 5-minute segment, add a couple of new terms. For example, if you have 30 new terms, study 6 terms for 5 minutes, then take a little break. When you come back to the list, review the first 6 terms – and add 2–3 new terms.

✔ **THINK ABOUT THIS**

Make up lots of Question Charts if you're taking courses with objective test questions. Some charts will be short, covering a topic reviewed in class for a few days. Others will be more complex, covering larger parts of the course.

TAKING OBJECTIVE TESTS

Here's a checklist for taking objective tests:

◆ Glance through the whole test first. Estimate the amount of time you'll have for each answer (e.g., 2 minutes for 30 questions).

◆ Underline the key words in the stem of each questions (e.g., "The main <u>cause</u> of <u>air</u> <u>pollution</u> is…").

◆ On each item, first eliminate answers you know are wrong. For example, items containing words like "all," "always," or "never" are often wrong.

◆ Watch for choices like "all of the above" or "a and b only." There may be more than one correct answer listed among the choices.

◆ Do all items you are sure of first. Put an asterisk (*) next to those you're not sure of. Put a check (√) next to those you don't know at all.

◆ Do the asterisked items second, then the checked items. ***Don't change your answers.*** Your first answers are most likely to be correct. Use information from the answers you're most sure of as clues to answer questions you're less sure of.

◆ On math tests, *check your work by estimating answers.* For example, if you're multiplying two 2-digit numbers, your answer needs at least four digits.

◆ Check over your test after you've finished it. When you're given a separate machine-scored test sheet, make sure the numbers you mark match those in the test booklet.

ESSAY EXAMS AND KEY WORD DIAGRAMS

> ◆ *Ann studied hard for an essay exam, and came into the classroom well-prepared. She has three essay questions, given equal weight, and one hour in which to complete the exam. When she starts to answer the third question, she notices that she has only 15 minutes until the end of the exam. Her mind goes blank.*
>
> ◆ *Mike writes a lot on his essay exam for marketing, but he doesn't write his points clearly. When his instructor returns the exam, Mike sees that he lost 20 points on this question. He tells himself, "I just didn't have enough time to write everything I know about that question."*

If these situations are familiar to you, Key Word Diagrams will help.

Key Word Diagrams will help you perform well on essay exams – so that your essay answers match what you really know.

Using Key Word Diagrams

You predict that the following test question will be on your economics midterm:

"Should the government provide guarantees and loans to failing companies?"

You'd make up a **Key Word Diagram** answer to this question, using your notes and readings to help you find the right key words.

This question calls for the most common Key Word Diagram, the **Pro/ Con T**. You'd write pro and con key words in a diagram like this:

Pro	*Con*
safeguards workers' jobs	*encourages business inefficiency*
high costs of unemployment	*against laws of free market & productivity*

THE HIDDEN PRO/CON T IN "DISCUSS"

Sometimes the pro/con aspect of a question is hidden in the way the question is written. For example:

"Students learn more in high school today than they did fifty years ago. Discuss."

If this question were on a real exam, you'd be expected to state both sides of the question – not just give your opinion. A pro/con answer is most appropriate here. You might write a Key Word Diagram like this:

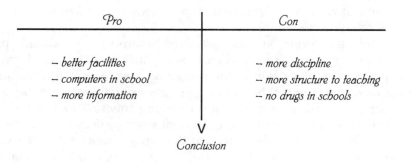

	Pro		*Con*
	– *better facilities*		– *more discipline*
	– *computers in school*		– *more structure to teaching*
	– *more information*		– *no drugs in schools*

V
Conclusion

Compare/Contrast Key Word Diagrams

For example, you might use a **Compare/Contrast** Key Word Diagram to answer the question. *What are the most common sources of errors on the job?*

People	*Machines*	*Material*
lack of attention	*age of machines*	*raw mat'l too thin*
over-tired	*computer errors*	*raw mat'l too rough*
poor training		

Chain of Events Key Word Diagram

The Key Word Diagram below answers the question, *How does gasoline deliver power to an automobile?*

gas ⟶ *carburetor* ⟶ *air/gas mixture* ⟶ *cylinders* ⟶ *spark plug spark* ⟶

explosion ⟶ *piston turns crank shaft*

Cause/Effect Diagram

If you're asked to discuss cause/effect relationships, you might use a **Cause/Effect Diagram**.

The following Cause/Effect Diagram – with arrows indicating cause and effect – might be useful for the question, "What are some of the causes of product variations in manufacturing?"

temperature changes ⟶ *metal expands*

low humidity ⟶ *static electricity* ⟶ *damaged circuit boards*

dirt, vibration, air flow ⟶ *damaged electronic parts*

Reducing Exam Anxiety With Key Word Diagrams

The following illustration shows how LTL prevents exam anxiety. At home, you'll generate Mirror Questions from your lecture notes and books – and combine them into a Summary Question. You'll draw a Key Word Diagram – an abbreviated essay-exam answer.

At an actual essay exam, you feel prepared because you've already practiced taking the exam at home. You read each essay question, then jot down its Key Word Diagram. Your Key Word Diagrams make up a *pool of information to answer the essay questions.* When you begin answering your first essay question, you use your key words as a checklist – checking them off as you write. If you think of an idea for Question 2 when you're answering Question 1, you can add to your Key Word Diagram for Question 2, then go back and finish your first essay. *You have a place to put ideas as they come to you,* a visual format to recall what you learned, and a way to check that you haven't forgotten anything.

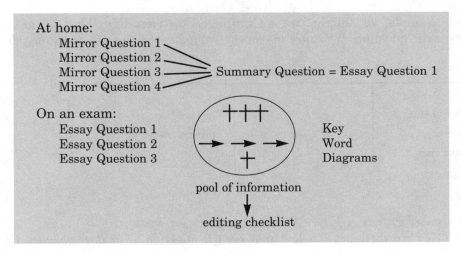

More Complex Key Word Diagrams

The kind of diagram you draw is also important, since *visuals* will help you recall information, and because the structure of your diagram will help you organize your answer.

At times you may need more complex diagrams. For example there may be two or more independent factors leading to a given result. In a nutrition course, you might learn that a person's height is determined by both environmental factors (such as good nutrition) and genetic factors. You might express this idea in a Key Word Diagram:

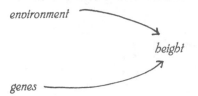

STUDENT SAMPLE
Complex Key Word Diagrams

Key Word Diagrams can take any form. Anything will work if it (a) shows how the key words are related and (b) helps "trigger" your memory of the ideas in the diagram.

For example, here's a complex Key Word Diagram that answers the question, *"What are some causes of ground water contamination?"*

Causes of Ground Water Contamination

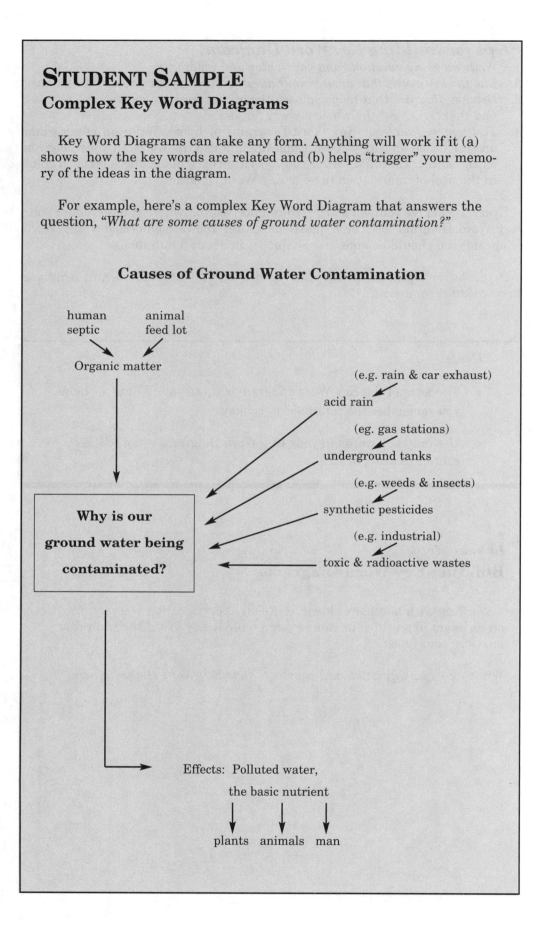

Steps for Building Key Word Diagrams

1. *Write an essay question* from your notes and readings.
2. *List the key words that answer your question,* using your notes and readings.
3. *Draw a diagram* that helps you see the connections among your key words, and that "triggers" the whole answer for you.
4. *Test yourself* on your Key Word Diagrams at home. Write an essay exam answer based on a Key Word Diagram, and use the words in your diagram as an "editing checklist." After you've written each point, check off each point in the pool of information in your Key Word Diagram.

Every week, give yourself a brief, 10-minute "exam," where you reproduce your Key Word Diagram for 2 or 3 questions. (After you've memorized a Key Word Diagram, you should be able to reproduce it in about 3 minutes.)

If you haven't practiced with Key Word Diagrams all semester, *at least use them to study for exams.*

Hints:

◆ The form of the Key Word Diagram is up to you. Whatever helps you remember the information is okay.

◆ Use only key words in your Key Word Diagrams – not whole sentences and phrases.

In Your Words:
Building Key Word Diagrams

Working with another student, write an essay question you might expect on an exam in one of your courses, and build a Key Word Diagram that answers your question.

Write your essay question and construct your Key Word Diagram here:

THE MIND MAP
– A Special Kind of Key Word Diagram

A Mind Map represents ideas in both Key Word and symbolic or pictorial form. Created by the British author and brain researcher Tony Buzan, a Mind Map can help you "see" your thinking. Starting from a central picture that represents the topic of the Mind Map, you'd draw lines radiating from the picture. Each line would contain one expression and/or symbol. You'd use colors to emphasize key points.

The Mind Map below summarizes key ideas about Central America.

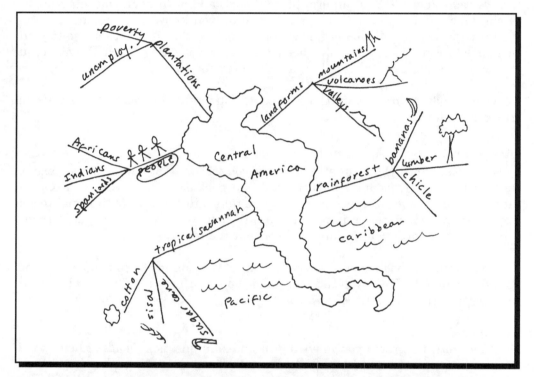

Like other Key Word Diagrams, a Mind Map can be used to study for exams. In abbreviated form, it can also be quickly reproduced at an exam, as an aid to help you organize and recall key points of your answer to an essay question.

> ✔ **THINK ABOUT THIS**
>
> A Mind Map can provide an interesting visual "translation" of a complex information. But it's very complicated. Unlike a simple Key Word Diagram, a Mind Map is not easily used during exams. Under the pressure of an exam, you won't have the time to reproduce a Mind Map or use it to guide your essay exam answers.
>
> So take the time to condense a Mind Map into a simple Key Word Diagram for use during an essay exam.

Assignment

Draw a Mind Map that answers one of your "50-point" predicted exam questions from a course you are taking now.

A Question About Key Word Diagrams

How can a Key Word Diagram help me while I'm taking an essay exam?

When you take an essay exam, your *first response* should be to reproduce your Key Word Diagrams. If the questions are somewhat different from those you expected, still begin with Key Word Diagrams. You can make needed changes once you've got your diagrams down on paper. The Key Word Diagrams you practiced at home will help "trigger" new information – which you can add as needed.

If you begin by writing your Key Word Diagrams, you won't forget parts of the answer as you write. You can use the key words and phrases in your diagram as a checklist to help you put all the information you know into your essay. And your diagram will help you organize your essay, so that it makes sense to your instructor. Finally, since you've been practicing your Key Word Diagrams at home, you won't have to cram the night before the exam.

Write the diagrams in your exam booklet. You might get *credit* for them if you run out of time.

Assignment

Use a Key Word Diagram at home as if you were taking an open-book exam, and write an essay from it. Don't refer to your book or notes as you write. Guess and make up things, as if you were about to take a test and were "bulling" to get extra credit. (This step is important. It will help you recall what you already know and will force you to think and sort out the information.)

Using your textbook as a dictionary, look up the answer to your question and "grade" yourself. How well did you do? If you find new points to add to your answer, put them in your Key Word Diagram.

Bring to class:
1. Key Word Diagrams you've written from exam questions you predicted; and
2. Your completed (and marked) essay exams, including the Key Word Diagrams you wrote in your exam booklets.

STUDENT SAMPLE
Key Word Diagrams

Here's a student-written essay exam questions and matching Key Word Diagrams on the causes of World War I.

what were the 4 factors that led to war between
the Allies + the Central powers? How did those
factors cause WWI?

Nationalism	Imperialism	System of Alliances	Militarism
European ethnic groups wanted: -freedom -self-determination	British + French vs. Germans V Africa Middle East V Balkans	Triple Entente + Triple Alliance	- arms stockpiled - naval arms race

Nationalistic Black Hand Society → assasination of
⠀⠀⠀⠀⠀⠀⠀⠀⠀⠀⠀⠀⠀Archduke Ferdinand
⠀⠀⠀⠀⠀⠀⠀⠀⠀⠀⠀⠀⠀⠀⠀↓
⠀⠀⠀⠀⠀⠀⠀⠀⠀⠀⠀⠀Austria-Hungary
⠀⠀⠀⠀⠀⠀⠀⠀⠀⠀⠀⠀⠀vs.
⠀⠀⠀⠀⠀⠀⠀⠀⠀⠀⠀⠀Serbian
⠀⠀⠀⠀⠀⠀⠀⠀⠀⠀⠀⠀nationalism
⠀⠀⠀⠀⠀⠀⠀⠀⠀⠀⠀⠀⠀↓
⠀⠀⠀⠀⠀⠀⠀⠀⠀⠀⠀⠀A-H war vs.
⠀⠀⠀⠀⠀⠀⠀⠀⠀⠀⠀⠀Serbia
⠀⠀⠀⠀⠀⠀⠀⠀⠀⠀⠀⠀⠀↓
⠀⠀⠀⠀⠀⠀⠀⠀⠀⠀⠀⠀alliances:
⠀⠀⠀⠀⠀⠀⠀⠀⠀⠀⠀⠀3 All./3 Ent.

⠀⠀⠀⠀⠀⠀⠀⠀⠀⠀⠀⠀⠀↓
⠀⠀⠀⠀⠀⠀⠀⠀⠀⠀⠀⠀Eur. War
⠀⠀⠀⠀⠀⠀⠀⠀⠀⠀⠀⠀WWI

Empower Yourself
Attaining Goals With Key Word Diagrams

Key Word Diagrams can play an important part in problem solving because they help you "see" the problem and its possible solutions.

Pro/Con T. For example, you can use a Pro/Con T to help reach certain goals. Imagine that you've been out of high school for many years, and you'd like to be a full-time college student. Your Pro/Con T could clearly show you the *helps* and *hindrances* to your going back to school:

Helps	*Hindrances*
spouse is supportive	*time*
spare bedroom (study)	*kids need attention*
	money

Looking at your Key Word Diagram can help you plan. Which side are you in control of most? How can you increase the helps, or decrease the hindrances?

Cause/Effect. A Cause/Effect, or "If.../then..." diagram can also help in problem solving and decision making. Putting all the information you have on a problem into a Cause/Effect Key Word Diagram can help you see the parts of the problem – and where they come from – more easily.

Compare/Contrast. Once you've defined the problem by creating a Cause/Effect Key Word Diagram, a Compare/Contrast Key Word Diagram will help you see the different impacts of your several possible solutions to the problem.

Chain of Events. A Chain of Events Key Word Diagram can also help you find problem solutions. By starting from your goal – what you want to achieve – you can *work backwards from your goal,* seeing the steps that would be needed to reach the goal. If needed, you can *rearrange some of the steps* and come up with a new solution.

In Your Words:
Attaining Goals With Key Word Diagrams

Working with another student, think of a problem you'd like to solve, using a combination of Key Word Diagrams (either the ones suggested, or your own) and different question types to find a solution to it.

Write your problem-solving Key Word Diagram here:

WRITING MOCK EXAMS

Practice taking exams: Make up and take your own "exams" before you're tested in class. By taking Mock Exams, you'll feel more confident when you come to the actual exam. You'll be used to the exam format; and you'll have practice writing essay answers based on your Key Word Diagrams. Because you've taken a Mock Exam in a safe environment, you'll feel less pressure when you're in the survival environment of a real exam.

Steps for Writing Mock Exams

1. Write your questions in the form you expect them to be on exams.

   ◆ If you expect short-answer questions, you can use most of the questions you've written from lecture notes and readings.

   ◆ If you expect essay questions, combine a few lecture-note and textbook questions into exam questions.

   ◆ If you expect multiple-choice questions, make up some multiple-choice questions from your Question Charts.

2. Approximate the exam situation. Put yourself under *time pressure* when you take your Mock Exams. You'll find out what kinds of information you go "blank" on when you're under time constraints.

3. Test yourself on your own exam. Unless you do so, you won't be able to tell what you really know from what you *think* you know.

Hints:

◆ Pay attention: Did your instructor often refer to any special material?

◆ Make up questions about parts of your textbook – like diagrams or illustrations – that your instructor mentions.

◆ Will the test cover information you learned early in the semester?

◆ Was there a lecture near the exam where the instructor covered so much information that you could hardly take it all down? *Study notes from that lecture carefully.* Professors often rush through information in this way to make sure that everything they plan to cover on an exam was covered in class.

STUDENT SAMPLE
Mock Exam

Here's a student's mock exam for an economics course.

1) Suppose Mr. Johnson attaches the following total utility to various quantities of hamburgers consumed per day:

Number of hamburgers	Total Utility
0	0
1	5
2	12
3	15
4	17
5	18

Between 3+4 hamburgers, what is the marginal utility of a hamburger? Between 4-5 hamburgers? Do these results conform to the law of diminishing utility?

2. A tool & die shop has 3 kinds of inputs: labor, machine, & materials. It can't obtain additional machines in less than 6 months. In the next month, do you think that labor is fixed or variable input? Are machines fixed or variable input? Explain.

WRITING ESSAY QUESTIONS

Imagine that you're reading a chapter on "Motivation" in a textbook on psychology in the workplace. Here are the chapter's major headings and sub-headings:

What motivates people?
> The power motive
> The need to achieve
> Financial rewards
> The power of positive reinforcement

Effective supervision
> The importance of recognizing strengths
> Making teams work

In Your Words:
Writing Essay Questions

1. Pretend you're an instructor writing a final exam question. Write a question that would ask your students to discuss the major points of the chapter outlined above.

   _____

   _____

   _____

   _____

2. Open your notebook and textbook for one of your courses. Write two or three questions that you think are important to the course.

   _____

   _____

   _____

   _____

   _____

   _____

   _____

Assignment
Bring your essay questions to class. Underline the key words in your questions, and write matching Key Word Diagrams.

Make up complete mock exams for two of your content courses. Ask questions similar to those your instructors ask. Bring your mock exams to class next time.

PICTURING IDEAS

It's often hard to learn new technical terms – especially those which are defined by *other* technical terms. Instead of memorizing all the technical words, try the "Picturing Ideas" method.

STUDENT SAMPLES

The illustrations below were done by a biology student who drew simple pictures to remember these technical terms:

Bioluminescence: The emission of light by living organisms.

Photoautotrophs: Organisms that use light as an energy source, like plants and flowers.

If you tried to remember this term by a word example (e.g., flower), you'd have missed the general meaning of the term.

Picturing Ideas 1

Working with another student, draw simple word pictures of the following terms.

Don't worry about being "correct." Your drawing is just a reminder, another way of thinking about the term besides the words. Drawing a simple picture of an *idea* will help reinforce a term's meaning for you.

ceolem: *Body cavity of roundworms and higher animals in which the internal organs are suspended.*

synapse: *The junction between a neuron and an adjacent cell across which an impulse is transmitted.*

radiation: *The traveling or transference of heat from one object directly out into the air.*

decision variables: *Factors under the decision maker's control that, if changed, can result in different outcomes.*

In Your Words:
Picturing Ideas 2

Working with another student, draw simple pictures "defining" four technical terms from your content courses.

Do your work here:

In Your Words:

Picturing Ideas 3

Simple drawings can also be used to help you learn other things that are hard to understand and remember. These include *processes in the sciences*, or even a sequence of *events or terms of a treaty in a history course*. For example, let's look at an imaginary set of rules drawn up between a prince and his subjects in the Middle Ages:

a. A peasant's land reverts to the landlord on the death of the peasant.
b. The landlord's oldest son inherits his father's land.
c. The peasant pays the landlord 10 pieces of silver a year for the use of the land.
d. The landlord pays the prince 100 pieces of silver a year for the use of the land.

You might draw a picture like this to represent the first of these rules:

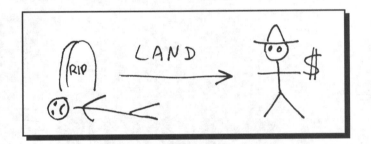

Working with another student, draw a set of simple pictures to represent rules b – d of the imaginary principality we've just described.

Do your work here:

Assignment
Find a number of terms, processes, and lists that might be hard to understand or remember, and "define" them using word and picture examples. Bring your work to class.

READING ESSAY EXAM QUESTIONS

You've predicted exam questions; self-tested; prepared and reviewed Question Charts and Key Word Diagrams. But when you get to the exam, you don't understand the essay exam questions. The way they're written, you don't know how to relate them to what you've studied.

Practice "translating" these complex essay questions into the major topics your course has dealt with.

Essay exam questions *always* cover topics discussed in class. In fact, they usually deal with topics that were the subjects of many class meetings. Your task is to *recognize the familiar aspect* of the essay question. For example, imagine that you wrote this question from your lecture notes in a political science course:

> *Compare and contrast the following communist ideologies: USSR under Stalin; USSR under Krushchev; China under Mao Tse Tung.*

To prepare for this question, you wrote a Question Chart with these items and questions:

	Stalin's USSR	Krushchev's USSR	Mao Tse Tung's China
What was the policy towards internal dissent?			
What was the policy on exporting communism?			
What was the policy on domestic economic development?			
Etc.			

But when you go to the exam, you see this question:

The Chinese Communists under Mao had a higher opinion of Stalin than Krushchev did. Show that this is compatible with broader ideology between the two regimes. List a few of the causes of these ideological differences.

You panic. This doesn't look at all like the question you wrote.

Look closer. You'll see that your Question Chart would have contained the parts of this answer. If you'd prepared a Key Word Diagram listing parts of all three versions of communism, you'd be able to jot it down *as soon as you saw the essay question.* Then you'd be free to organize the information (from your Key Word Diagram) to fit the question asked.

This brings us to Rule #1 in taking essay exams:

Before you panic, find the familiar parts of the question – they're what's important.

In Your Words:
Reading Exam Questions

Match the essay exam questions on the next page with student-generated questions. One of the student-generated questions is a very good "translation" of the essay question.

For each exam question:

1. Read the question. <u>Underline</u> words that look important to you in the question.

2. <u>Circle</u> the *one* student-generated question that best matches the information in the exam question.

Exam question 1:   *Most historians agree that by 1558 (the death of Queen Mary) the ultimate victory of Protestantism in England was assured.   Taking into account the progress of the Reformation from its inception under Henry VIII, what reasons would you give to support this view?   In answering this question, attention should be paid not only to the positive attractions of Protestantism, but also to the weaknesses and mistakes of the Catholic party during this period.*

Student questions: a.   Compare the Protestant Reformation to the power of the Catholic church in the 1500s.

b.   What did Henry VIII do to encourage the Reformation in England?

c.   How did the strengths of Protestantism and the weaknesses of Catholicism affect the growth of British Protestantism in the 1500s?

d.   What effect did Queen Mary and Henry VIII have on the dominance of Protestantism during the 1500s?

Exam question 2:   *Marx regarded religious institutions as reflecting economic realities, but not as causative of them. What sort of evidence could one draw on to support the "reflecting" aspect of his position? What sort of evidence might undermine his denial of causative power?*

Student questions: a.   How do religious institutions and economic conditions affect each other?

b.   Discuss why Marx felt that religion was "the opiate of the people."

c.   According to Marx, what are some of the causes of the conflict between the church and state?

d.   Why is religion often seen as totally separate from economic reality?

Empower Yourself
Getting Past The Anxiety Cycle

One of the hardest things about taking tests is getting past the negative messages you may be giving yourself. There's a kind of anxiety cycle: You tell yourself that you won't do well, and you then begin to get physical symptoms of anxiety – your breath gets short, your palms are sweaty, your stomach feels tense. These physical reactions confirm your anxiety – "Boy, if I'm feeling this bad, I must be right. I'm *not* prepared. I'm going to fail." This negative mental self-talk results in greater tension – and your fears worsen.

Because you failed in the past – before you had the LTL tools – there is no reason for you to believe that the situation is the same, and you will fail again. The setting and difficulty of the exam might be the same – but *you* are different. Before, you had a liability. You now have an advantage – not only an affirmation, but also an advantage based on reality.

Be proactive. When you feel the anxiety cycle beginning, attack it before it attacks you. First, recover your physical and emotional balance by doing the 30-second Stress Reduction exercise in Chapter 10 (page 222). Next give yourself new messages based on the new realities of having new, effective tools:

◆ There are students like me in those "Student Voices" quotes. If they can do well in school, so can I.

◆ This time taking exams will be different, like a game. I'll see just how close my questions are to the real exam questions.

◆ I'm going to start my essay exams by jotting down my Key Word Diagrams. Then I'll relax and just use the Key Word Diagram as an outline to write my essay.

◆ Visualizing my Question Chart will really help me answer objective questions.

Positive, reality-based self-talk like this will get you past your exam fears. And LTL skills will take care of the practical side of taking exams. Your confidence will not be based on wishful thinking – but on the new *competencies* you've acquired.

COMPUTING YOUR GRADE POINT AVERAGE

Now that you'll be getting the grades you've always wanted, let's see how to compute your grade point average.

Grades at most colleges are based on a 4-point scale, where numbers are assigned to each grade:

$$A = 4 \quad B = 3 \quad C = 2 \quad D = 1 \quad F = 0$$

Steps for Computing Your GPA for a Semester

1. Multiply the number assigned to each grade by the number of credit hours for each course.
2. Find the total number of points earned for the term by adding the points for all courses.
3. Divide the total number of points by the number of credit hours.

For example, imagine you earned the following grades:

Economics 101 B+ (3 credits)	= 3.5 x 3 = 10.5
World History A (3 credits)	= 4 x 3 = 12.0
Intro to Psychology B (3 credits)	= 3 x 3 = 9.0
Inorganic Chemistry B (4 credits)	= 3 x 4 = <u>12.0</u>
	43.5

Semester GPA: 43.5 ÷ 13 credits = **3.35**

CALVIN AND HOBBES © 1992 Bill Watterson. Dist. by UNIVERSAL PRESS SYNDICATE. Reprinted with permission. All rights reserved.

Self-Evaluation Checklists

Building Question Charts

1. Did you draw a grid, placing comparison items across the top and questions down the left side?	Yes/No
2. Did you use comparison items from the same category?	Yes/No
3. Did your questions apply to all items to be compared?	Yes/No
4. Did you avoid questions answered by Yes or No?	Yes/No
5. Did you ask complete questions?	Yes/No
6. Did you write one question that summarizes the Question Chart at the top of the chart?	Yes/No

Preparing for Objective Tests with Question Charts

1. Did you construct Question Charts to compare and contrast facts and ideas that will be tested by objective exams?	Yes/No
2. Did you test yourself on your Question Charts?	Yes/No

Preparing for Essay Exams with Key Word Diagrams

1. Did you write essay questions from your lecture notes and readings?	Yes/No
2. Did you list key words that answer your questions?	Yes/No
3. Did you construct diagrams that help you see the connections among the key words and help you recall whole answers?	Yes/No
4. Did you test yourself on your Key Word Diagrams?	Yes/No
5. Did you use your Key Word Diagrams while taking essay exams?	Yes/No

THE QUESTION CHART GAME

Choose a Question Chart topic everyone in the class is familiar with. (For example, you might choose people and events at your college.)

Two teams compete. Each team has a Part 1 Squad and a Part 2 Squad. There are no more than 5 members of each team on the Part 1 Squads. During Part 1, both Part 2 Squads leave the room.

Part 1 (5 minutes)

Pairs of contestants from each team compete: Who is quicker at generating questions for the Question Chart?

Part 2

Part 2 Squads enter the room after Part 1 Squads have completed the Question Chart shell. Contestants are now drawn from Part 2 Squads. Who is quicker at coming up with the answers to the questions in the Question Chart?

THE READING ESSAY EXAMS GAME

Working in pairs, write complex exam questions. Throw them into a jar. You'll also need 2 bells.

Form 2 teams. Contestants from each team compete. Whoever "translates" the question into simple English first wins. (A contestant rings a bell to signal that he/she has an answer.)

Discussion and Review

How do this chapter's LTL skills illustrate the Four LTL Thinking Tools?

The LTL Journal

Continue your journal of your thoughts and feelings. How can Question Charts and Key Word Diagrams help you visualize your personal choices more clearly?

Chapter 7:
WRITING, RESEARCH, & THE INTERNET

I can understand why this book has a chapter on the Internet.
But why does a freshman seminar text contain a chapter
on writing and research skills? Aren't those topics
covered by other courses?

The Four LTL Thinking Tools – especially the *questioning* techniques – have unique applications for two areas of writing: writing well-organized paragraphs and writing research papers.[1] LTL's *Writing to Answer Questions* techniques offer solutions to writing problems that you won't find in a standard writing course. You'll learn a simple and powerful method to check the organization and clarity of your paragraphs – without using the complex terminology of syntax and grammar. And our research paper methods will save you time, give your writing focus, and help you get past the "writer's block" that afflicts writers at all levels of proficiency.

These days, there are many places to look for answers to your questions. The Internet and your college library's electronic card catalogue are wonderful resources for doing research. They're new enough that you may need instruction in using them. LTL questioning techniques can help you use these electronic research tools in a more focused way.

In this chapter you'll learn to write papers – and use the new electronic research tools – without panic or exhaustion.

---

[1] There are many other writing skills you'll need to master in college, such as description, argumentation, comparison/ contrast. These and other writing skills will be covered in your writing courses.

WRITING TO ANSWER QUESTIONS

Many students have a hard time expressing what they've learned on paper in an organized way. In this chapter, you'll learn to apply some of the LTL skills that you've been practicing to improve your writing skills.

You've begun to see your lecture notes and books can be viewed as a series of answers to questions. This also applies to your own writing. Everything you write – in fact, all consecutive thought – is a series of answers to implied questions. Questions will help you get "unstuck" when you're trying to write something that's difficult for you; they'll help you organize information and break up writing assignments into manageable tasks.

USING QUESTIONS TO WRITE GOOD PARAGRAPHS

Well-written paragraphs have a single main idea, stated in a topic sentence. The main idea is actually an answer to an *implied question*. We call it a *Topic Sentence Question*.

For example, in the paragraph below, the main idea concerns social mobility. The paragraph answers the implied question, *"What is social mobility?"*

> *Social mobility is a change in a person's economic position. The change may be either upward or downward. For example, if a rich heiress becomes a poor sanitation worker, she has become socially mobile in a downward direction. However, if a man whose father was a janitor becomes a doctor, he achieves upward social mobility.*

Topic Sentence Questions

While there are many kinds of questions, most paragraphs answer the questions *Who? What? Why? How?* Here are some examples of this:

Who?
Jack Hammer was the greatest detective of all time. *(Who was Jack Hammer?)*

What?
A present is something given voluntarily without compensation. *(What is a present?)*

Why?
Networking is a useful career-search skill because... *(Why is networking a useful career-search skill?)*

How?
To obtain a driving license, you must pass both a driving and a written test. *(How do you obtain a driving license?)*

Paragraph Structure

How is paragraph structure related to Topic Sentence Questions?

◆ *Every well-constructed paragraph answers one major question.*
◆ Most paragraphs answer *Who? What? Why? How?* questions.

After you've found your Topic Sentence Question, you'll need to fill in the details that *answer* that question. For example:

◆ If your topic sentence says you're going to talk about how an internal combustion engine works, your paragraph will give the details of that process.
◆ The paragraph *won't* discuss the differences between an internal combustion and a rotary engine – that's another question, which requires another paragraph. *("What are the differences between an internal combustion and a rotary engine?")*

Most poorly written paragraphs include information that doesn't answer the topic sentence/question. The writer tries to fit too much information into one paragraph. For example, imagine you're writing a brief paper on how you spent your summer vacation. In one paragraph, you're answering the question, "What I like about summer." You start by talking about your activities in the summer, then say that you also like summer because you don't go to school then. You continue by saying what you don't like about school. *In the "paragraph," you tried to answer two questions: What you like about summer and what you don't like about school. Since you're writing about two questions, you'll need two paragraphs, not one.*

Some Topic Sentence Questions can only be answered by asking and answering a series of smaller questions. For example, if you were writing a paragraph about Abraham Lincoln ("Who was...?"), you might find it useful to ask and answer minor questions like: *What did he do? Where did he do it? When did he do it?* The main point is to *identify the major question you're asking in a paragraph and stick to information that answers the question.*

Concluding Sentences

Not all paragraphs need a definite end. But the *concluding sentence* (the last sentence) of a paragraph can serve two purposes:

◆ It *summarizes* the paragraph's main idea.
◆ It can provide a useful *transition* to another paragraph.

Examples from Paragraph Skeletons

1. ***Concluding sentence summarizing the main idea:***
   <u>First sentence</u>:
   M. Smith's book on Chinese cooking will certainly become a classic in its field.

   (The middle of the paragraph has details showing why the book is so good.)

   <u>Concluding sentence</u>:
   This fresh approach to cooking will be an inspiration to cooks everywhere.

   In this paragraph, the concluding sentence *summarizes* the paragraph's main idea.

2. ***Concluding sentence used as transition to the next paragraph:***
   <u>First sentence</u>:
   The teacher who is unaware of her student's hearing or visual problems can damage the child's ability to learn.

   (The middle of the paragraph has details showing how an unaware teacher can damage these students.)

   <u>Concluding sentence</u>:
   This instructional practice can lead to the child's becoming a "behavior problem."

   The *concluding sentence* provides a *transition* to the next paragraph in this essay – which might then define a "behavior problem."

NOTE: Each of these concluding sentences starts with "this," which refers to ideas presented in the paragraph. (Notice that each "this" does not stand alone: We wrote, *"This fresh approach"* and *"This instructional practice."* Using "this" alone creates a vague reference and can confuse the reader.)

Steps for Writing Good Paragraphs

1. Write a Topic Sentence Question.

2. Write sub-questions if needed.

3. Write the key words (one key word or phrase for each point you plan to make) that will answer your question.

4. Using your sub-questions and key words, write the paragraph.

5. Write a concluding sentence.

6. Check your paragraph: *Does the information answer your Topic Sentence Question?* If you've begun to answer another question, you'll need a new paragraph.

    a. Modify your paragraph. (Take out the information that doesn't answer your original question.)

    b. Write the Topic Sentence Question that covers this information. You can use it as the first sentence of your next paragraph.

STUDENT SAMPLE:

A Paragraph That Answers One Central Question

Here's a well-written paragraph, where all the information answers the paragraph's main question. Underline three key word points in this paragraph that are the major answers to this question:

What will participation in organized sports do for a child? First of all, the child will develop a sense of discipline. The fact that the child shows up on time every day for practice shows some amount of discipline, and taking orders from coaches and doing things that he basically doesn't want to do develops this sense of discipline more fully. Participation also develops a sense of teamwork. Assuming the coach is competent, he will stress the importance of working together as a unit. Perhaps the most important trait that a child can carry with him from sports to adulthood is a sense of pride! Nobody wants to be on a losing team and the child's pride will force him to work harder, so that even if the team does lose, the children can take pride in the fact that they gave their best effort. Discipline, teamwork, and pride. These are not the only elements needed for a productive adult life, but they are a step in the right direction.

A Paragraph That Does *Not* Answer One Central Question

Contrast the paragraph you just read with the one below. As you read this "paragraph," you'll notice that the student began to raise a series of questions but did not develop them. Each implied question has been numbered by the instructor correcting the student's writing. The student tried to answer the question, *"What effects did the shuttle disaster have on the future of NASA?"*

[1]*Man must learn from trial and error. A contemporary example of such a fact is the NASA crash.* [2] *This crash shocked the world as well as myself. My disbelief pressed my curiosity to learn more about it. I listened to the news with uninterruptable attention, but when my curiosity was satisfied, I sat back realizing the fatal consequences for future missions.* [3] *The pressure on NASA officials to explain and prove the accidental mistake will push their potential to the limit. The press snatches and sniffs for untold information in order to gain viewers; they will question anyone anytime to complete such a task.* [4] *The press will even put more attention on future missions waiting for the next opportunity to do it all over again. But for now, the press will focus the attention on the families of the dead astronauts. The world suffered for such pioneerism, but* [5] *the families suffered in ways we cannot know. Their grief cannot be helped by the idea of missions in space.*

In Your Words:
Finding "Buried" Topic Sentence Questions

I. Working with another student, write the questions that are buried in the "paragraph" on NASA:

1. _____

2. _____

3. _____

4. _____

5. _____

II. Read the paragraph below and insert numbers when a new "buried" question is raised.

People work harder on meaningful activities. They become creative and look for solutions to problems they consider worth solving. Have you ever tried to work on something you did not like and thought was not worth your time? But paying people well also has an effect on their work. Of course, money is not so important to many people. Some people get their rewards from helping others. Many people think that teachers and social workers can be paid less because they just enjoy helping others. They do not understand that teachers and social workers have bills to pay, too.

In Your Words:
Finding "Buried" Topic Sentence Questions

II. Working with another student, write the questions that are buried in the above "paragraph".

1. _____

2. _____

3. _____

4. _____

5. _____

Assignment

1. Take five Topic Sentence Questions that you wrote in class *(Who? What? Why? How?)* and develop them into paragraphs. Bring all your work to class.

2. Look over the papers you've received from other courses. If your instructors tell you that there's a problems with your writing, re-read your papers and write the questions that each paragraph answers in the margins of your paper. If a paragraph has been marked "confusing," check to see if you're trying to answer more than one question in it.

If you find "buried" Topic Sentence Questions, write them out and list the key words, and use them to answer each question – that is, to develop new paragraph(s). Bring your work to class.

> ✔ **THINK ABOUT THIS**
>
> If you find it hard to write a specific paragraph, it may be you're trying to fit too much information into that paragraph. You may need to break it up into two paragraphs, each answering a sub-question of your original topic question.

WRITING TERM PAPERS

> *When Ron is assigned a term paper, he usually goes to the library and finds as many books as he can on the topic. When reading books, he reads diligently, taking notes as he reads. But when he begins to write, it's hard to fit all this information into the paper.*

Ron uses a *traditional* approach to writing term papers. On the following pages we'll describe the LTL approach – an easier, more effective way to write term papers. The method has four steps: *Choosing a Topic, Writing Questions, Going to the Library,* and *Writing the Paper.*

Steps for Using LTL to Write Term Papers

1. Write questions and sub-questions.
2. Guess at possible key word answers.
3. Put your questions and matching key words on 5″ x 8″ cards.
4. Go to the library to verify your key word answers.
5. Begin writing.
    a. Arrange your 5″ x 8″ cards in a logical order.
    b. Find a sub-question you want to answer (not necessarily the beginning of the paper).
    c. Write a paragraph from this sub-question and your key words.
    d. Find the next sub-question you want to answer.
    e. Take a Creative Break. (See page 108.)
    f. Write the next paragraph, using questions and key words.
    g. Etc. (Repeat the process until your paper is completed.)

In more detailed form, the process looks like this:

1. Choosing a Topic

It's important to choose a topic that you know something about, can find information on, and get credit for. First, write a series of major questions, each of which could be a topic for a term paper. How do they score on the criteria we've mentioned for choosing a topic?

Once you've chosen a general topic, narrow it until you have a question that can be answered in 10–15 pages. For example, imagine that you decide to write a paper on drugs. You'll need to limit your topic: A paper on drugs may be too broad. But a paper on one part of the topic – for example, the abuse of drugs by some groups – may fit within a term paper.

If you used a Question Chart like this one, you'd be able to limit your paper to a topic you could handle.

	Prior Knowledge	Availability of Information	Interest in Subject	Uniqueness of Subject
Why do different drugs attract different people?				
How have different civilizations used psychedelic drugs?				
What is the relationship between street crime and drug use?				

In Your Words:
Choosing a Topic

Pretend you're choosing a topic on this paper. Each potential topic is represented by one of the three questions. Write numbers in each cell: 4 for "most", 1 for "least." Add up the numbers. The question with the highest numbers across all categories is the topic you should choose for your paper.

After you've chosen your topic, the preparation and writing process really begins.

2. Writing Questions

1. Write several major questions which your paper will have to answer. For example, a paper on drug abuse might ask such major questions as *"What are the effects of different drugs when they are abused?" "Which groups of people tend to abuse different drugs?"* (e.g., marijuana, cocaine, heroin, barbiturates)

2. Take a Creative Break. Do something else – different work or whatever relaxes you.

3. When you come back to your term paper questions, write sub-questions under the main questions. For example, you might write, under the effects of drug abuse, "What *are the physiological effects of drug X?" "What are the effects of abusing drug X on a person's relationship with others?"* Write as many sub-questions as you can. Take a break, come back, and write some more sub-questions.

4. If you think you know some partial answers to these questions, write them down in key words and phrases.

5. Put all your questions and key words on 5" x 8" cards.

3. Going to the Library

Since you know what you want to find out, your job is fairly easy. Check with the reference librarian, look at the index to your field of study, or do a computer search for a relevant topic. When you find the right section of the library, don't just take out a pile of books. *Look in the index of each book to see if the book answers questions you've asked.*

4. Writing the Paper

You should have 5" x 8" cards with questions and key word answers – some from your own ideas, others referring to what you've read. The writing process looks like this:

1. *Take a sub-question* (not necessarily the first – leave the introduction until later) and the key words you generated. Write a paragraph answering your question.

2. *Find the question you think should be answered next.*

3. *Take a Creative Break.* You'll be thinking about your answer – without consciously trying – during your break. If you start your break with a question in mind, your subconscious will sort out and create connections between the different items without effort on your part. So when you come back from your break, you'll not only save time, but you may also have a new vision of the project.

4. *Write a paragraph answering the next question.*

5. *Continue in this way until the paper is finished.*

Writing The Paper

Imagine you're writing a paper on the media (TV, radio, newspapers) for a communications course. What are some of the main questions you'll need to answer in this paper? Working with another student, write your questions in the space provided:

1. _____
   _____
   _____
   _____

2. _____
   _____
   _____
   _____

3. _____
   _____
   _____
   _____

Write sub-questions between your main questions.

One or more of your questions might call for a Question Chart. For example, if you asked *"How has the media influenced American life?"* you might want to compare different kinds of media. Your chart would then look something like this:

	TV	*Radio*	*Newspapers*
What kind of entertainment is provided by this medium?			
?			
?			

Write additional questions in the spaces provided in the left-hand column boxes. Add key words if you know some of the answers now.

Empower Yourself
Finding What You Need When Writing Term Papers

Imagine these scenarios:

Scenario one:

You're a diligent, motivated student. You take initiative and find lots of information on your topic in the stacks of the library. You put in an enormous amount of time and hard work. With good intentions, you really cover a lot of ground. You read many articles, and even a couple of books. But when you read, you're on "automatic pilot": You're under time pressure, feel like you don't have time to think, and rush to read all you could find on the topic – without actively looking for answers to your own questions.

When you try to write your paper, you run into a road block. There's too much information, and you can't fit it together. You feel frustrated, thinking that all your hard work was wasted. In fact, you feel penalized for being good. How motivated will you be to start your *next* paper?

Scenario two:

As an LTL student, you have a method to be conscious and deliberate about decisions of what's right in a given situation, and what doesn't fit. When you do research for a paper, you start by generating questions and use the questions to make choices about what's relevant. You check to see if you've answered all the questions. You take feedback, noticing which questions distract from your goal; you correct or eliminate them accordingly. You might add new questions, and then decide to change or shift the direction of the whole paper, but in any event you are *conscious* of the pros and cons of your decision. If more is needed, your search is focused on that need. If you start going in the wrong direction, you can retrace your steps and re-start from where you digressed – so that you can always progress along the line of greatest advantage.

Finding What You Need When Writing Term Papers

Have you ever had a frustrating research and writing experience, as in scenario one? If so, describe it here:

_____
_____
_____
_____
_____
_____
_____
_____

What would you have done differently if you had known about LTL?

_____
_____
_____
_____
_____
_____
_____

Student Voices

Debra Clavenger

Learning to Learn? I love it. I think it's done me a world of good. When I was in high school I could never get over a C in anything. I studied and studied and just couldn't get it. When I started in college this semester, I was scared. I'm taking two hard courses, and I didn't think I could handle it. Well, in the first week of school I went to my teacher – he's teaching both these courses – and told him I wanted to drop one of them. He said I should just try keeping both of them for awhile and see how I did. I was enrolled in LTL, so I decided to give it a chance, and I started putting all the LTL tactics together. I got a 98 on my first test, and I've been averaging A's in both of these classes all semester.

Last week the teacher came to me and asked me to be a tutor. I said yes, and asked if there was anything in particular he wanted me to start with. He was going to give me an outline of the chapter for this girl to use, but I said, "No. I'm going to get her to make her <u>own</u> outline – with questions. I'm going to teach this girl what I'm learning in LTL."

Using a Writing Flow Chart

The flow chart below will help you through the writing process. It will show you what progress you're making on your paper as you write it, using the LTL steps to guide you.

Preparing to write the paper:

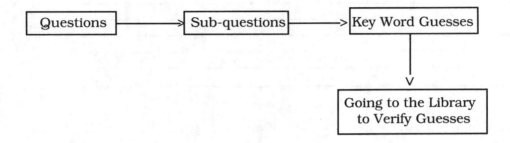

Writing the paper:

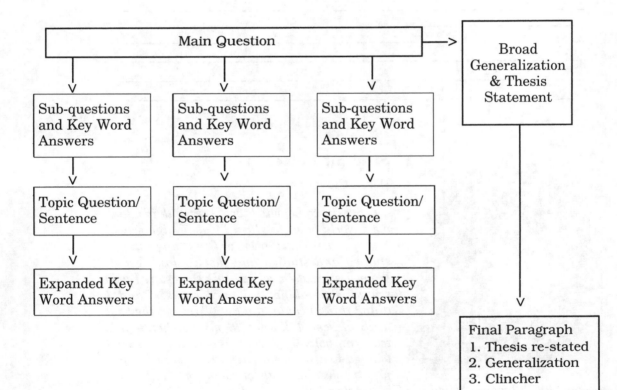

THE EDITING CHECKLIST
FOR REVISING ROUGH DRAFTS

After you've written a rough draft, review it to check:

Organization

◆ Do you use an introductory paragraph that contains your paper's thesis – the broad concepts and a summary statement of your paper's main idea?

◆ Does the first paragraph arouse the reader's interest?

◆ Does each paragraph answer only one main question and its sub-questions?

◆ Do you give supporting evidence, details, and examples in all paragraphs?

◆ Are there concluding or "bridging" sentences at the end of each paragraph?

◆ Is the main idea restated in the final paragraph?

Sentence Structure

Read your paper aloud to answer these questions:

◆ Does each sentence make sense?

◆ Does each sentence contain one complete thought?

◆ Are there any missing words?

◆ Are there unnecessary, repeated words?

◆ Can you simplify your writing? Can you eliminate some words and still convey your message?

◆ Are sentences short and choppy? If so, can any sentences be combined?

◆ Are any sentences too long? If so, can they be broken down?

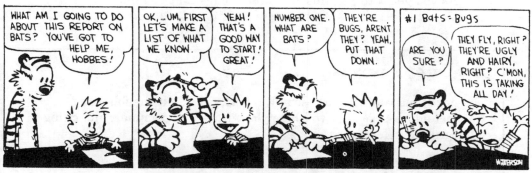

CALVIN AND HOBBES © 1992 Bill Watterson. Dist. by UNIVERSAL PRESS SYNDICATE. Reprinted with permission. All rights reserved.

EDITING CHECKLISTS

Editing checklists are a list of errors you often make. Use your checklists to edit your writing.

Steps to Better Grammar
Look for *patterns of grammatical errors* in your writing. For example:

1. Do you often use overrun sentences? Double negatives? Do you use "be" incorrectly? ("I <u>be</u> thinking" instead of "I am thinking.")

2. Do you write "it's" when you mean "its?" "Your" for "you're?" Do you write "the students work", instead of "the student<u>'s</u> work?"

3. If you use a pronoun, does it agree with the noun it refers to? ("The student said... ~~They~~ He meant that...")

4. Did you insert periods and commas where needed?

Steps to Better Spelling
1. Look for spelling-error patterns in your writing.

2. Use your own spelling checklist when you write.

3. When you write on a computer, make sure to check your writing with a Spell-Check program.

4. If you spell phonetically (the way words sound), try this:

   ◆ Find the correctly spelled lyrics of a song you like.

   ◆ Memorize the words to the song until you can "see" the words in your head as you sing, hum, or think of the song.

   ◆ Compare the spelling in the words you write to the words in the song.

   ◆ Use these words in your writing by picturing them in your mind.

   ◆ As you get better at this, add other songs that you like.

Internet Exercise

The next time you write a research report, check out the following Internet addresses. They will help you with style, grammar, and citing bibliographic references.

Modern Language Association:
`http://155.43.225.30/mla.html`

Elements of Style (Strunk):
`http://www.columbia.edu/acis/bartleby/strunk`

Solving Personal Problems With Editing Checklists

We've just talked about using Editing Checklists to improve grammar and spelling. We mentioned that everyone has a different pattern of grammatical and spelling errors – so everyone has a different Editing Checklist for grammar and spelling. In the same way, no two people make exactly the same kinds of mistakes in daily living.

A problem is easier to solve if it's predicted. You might have an area in your personal or work life where you often make your own kind of mistakes.

In Your Words:
Solving Personal Problems With Editing Checklists

Working with another student, brainstorm your own Editing Checklist of errors that you tend to make in your personal life or on the job. Make up an Editing Checklist of these errors.

Use the space below for your checklist.

WHAT IS TRUE?
THE ISSUE OF VERIFICATION

The issue of verification is important – for doing research and for your own writing. When you research information, ask yourself questions about whether the author provided enough evidence to support his/her conclusions. (And ask yourself the same questions about your own writing.)

What evidence does the writer present?
What kinds of support or evidence does the author present? Look for: *historical facts; statistics; observations; reasons; explanations; analogies; examples; scientific evidence.*

How valid is the evidence presented by the writer?
Is the author's support or evidence valid (just, sound)? Look for faulty evidence or support. Based on your own knowledge of the subject, decide if the author's evidence is valid. Do you see any places where the author's evidence is faulty? If you don't know enough about the subject, do you see places where the author did not present enough information to make his/her case?

WHAT IS *NOT* VALID RESEARCH?
THE ISSUE OF PLAGIARISM

Plagiarism is taking another person's words or ideas and passing them off as if they were your own. Plagiarism is another form of stealing – in this case, it's called "intellectual theft." Like other forms of theft, plagiarism has serious consequences. In college, a student caught plagiarizing will fail the course, or will be expelled from the college. There are even federal laws against plagiarism: A person who prints another person's words and ideas without permission may be subject to prosecution under federal copyright laws.

Does plagiarism apply to all academic products? No. It's okay to write ideas from someone else without referencing them when you're taking a test. But when you're writing a paper, if you're using another person's ideas, you must cite the author and text where that information came from. If you're quoting someone's actual words, it's important to use quotation marks, or set off the quote by indenting it, and cite the specific bibliographic reference, including the page number.

Cheating can have important personal consequences, too. If you submit work that's not your own, it will hurt your academic growth. Writing is one of the most important skills you will gain at college; learning to write well will help your entire career. If you don't do your own research and writing, you're hurting yourself, academically and personally. Not only that: If you establish a pattern of trying to "get away with it," it will catch up with you later, in graduate school or on the job, in a way that can ruin your future.

Using The Internet

What is the Internet?

The Internet is hundreds of thousands of computers that are connected by telephone lines. The Net is used to communicate with others and to find or provide information.

The Net is an extremely important source of information if you're doing research on any topic.

Where can I find an Internet connection?

Your college or university probably has access to the Internet. If so, log on. Use of the Internet is free.

Can I find information on the Internet as easily as I can in the library?

1. **Information is often easier to find on the Internet.***

   In most libraries, information is organized either alphabetically or through the Dewey decimal system. In a conventional library, a book can be on only one shelf at a time. A book about mental health, for example, is shelved under medicine or psychology, and can't be in both places at the same time.

   On the Internet, information is organized in terms of its relationship to other information. In fact, the same set of information may be arranged in multiple ways at the same time. Suppose that you're interested in what influenced a particular historical person. You can begin by looking at her basic biographical information: Where and when she was born, the names of her parents, her religion, etc. Then you can expand on each fact by finding out what else was happening at that time in her part of the world, what was happening in other parts of the world, and what influence her religion may have had on her. You draw a picture by pulling together all these aspects and understanding their *connections*.

2. **The latest information is available on the Internet.**

   Suppose you're doing a research paper in perceptual psychology. The library will contain articles published in your area of research last year. The Internet may contain articles presented at an international conference on your topic *last week*.

---

* Information in this paragraph is reprinted with permission from *The Internet for Dummies,* 5th Edition, John Levine, Margaret Levine Young, and Arnold Reinhold. IDG Books Worldwide: Foster City, CA, 1997.

DOING RESEARCH ON THE INTERNET

Learning to Learn® and Internet Research

Remember, when doing any kind of research, *begin by generating questions.* If you're *looking for answers to your own questions,* the information you find will fit together more easily and your search will be more focused.

The Internet information in this section is condensed and reprinted with permission from *The Internet for Dummies,* 3rd edition.*

Uniform Resource Locators (URLS)

One of the key advances that Web technology brought to the Internet is the Uniform Resource Locator (URL). URLs provide a single, standardized way of describing almost any type of information that is available in cyberspace. The URL tells you what kind of information it is (such as a Web page or an FTP file), what computer it's stored on, and how to find that computer.

Here's an example of a URL:
`http://world.std.com/~reinhold/papers.html`

◆ **http** indicates a Web page.
◆ **world.std.com** is the host computer on which the Web page is stored.
◆ `/~reinhold/papers.html` is the name of the file containing an index to Arnold Reinhold's papers.

Be careful to enter URLs exactly as they are written, being especially careful about the upper case and lower case letters.

Browsing the Web‡

America Online has a built-in Web browser. Other service providers may send you a Web browser. Or you may have to go out and buy one. Getting on the Web is simple. For example, if you have America Online, first sign on, choose the Internet Connection from the Channels window, and then click the World Wide Web icon. You will then see the AOL Web browser window.

When you first start the AOL browser, it displays a home page. Initially, this is AOL's own home page at `http://www.aol.com`.

You can change the home page location to any Web page:
1. Choose Members Preferences. You see the Preferences window.

2. Scroll down on the left-hand window until you see the Web or WWW icon. Click it.

---

* *The Internet for Dummies,* 3rd Edition, John Levine, Margaret Levine Young, and Arnold Reinhold. IDG Books Worldwide: Foster City, CA, 1997.

‡ We've provided an example from America Online. Procedures for browsing the Web differ somewhat for other service providers.

3. If you see tabs across the top of the window, click the Navigation tab.

4. In the Your Home Page or Address box, type the URL of the Web page you want AOL to start with.

5. Click OK to close the Preferences window.

Going to a URL

Type the URL you want into the Address text box (or use cut and paste to copy it in from another window) and press Enter. You may have to wait a while. At the bottom of its window, AOL tells you how things are going.

If you want to give up, click the Stop icon.

If you click the Address button, you see a list of URLs you visited in this session.

*Using Bookmarks**

A Bookmark is a your list of Internet addresses that you would like to return to. Clicking on an address stored in a Bookmark allows you to bring up the address without typing its URL.

When you find a site you like, you can add it to your to your Favorite Places list, AOL's name for bookmarks:

1. Click the little heart button on the upper-right corner window. Or choose Window ⇨ Add to Favorite Places.

2. When AOL asks what you want to do, confirm that add it to your list of favorite places.

3. To go to a Web page on your favorite places list, click the Favorite Places icon on the toolbar (the heart in a folder), or select Go To ⇨ Favorite Places.

Directories

Web directories are hierarchical catalogs of the World Wide Web – major topic headings are broken down into smaller areas which, in turn, are broken down still further. Web directories work like the card catalog in an old-fashioned, paper-book library.

When you visit a directory site, you see a list of major categories along with selected subcategories. Popular catalog sites include:

◆ Yahoo!: http://www.yahoo.com
◆ Galaxy: http://www.einet.net/galaxy.html
◆ Infoseek: http://www.infoseek.com
◆ Lycos: http://a2z.lycos.com

A more complete list of directories can be found at http://net.dummies. net/search.

---

* We've shown you the AOL Bookmark system here. Other Internet providers have similar Bookmarks.

Clicking on any category or subcategory takes you to another page with more entries. For example, at Yahoo!, clicking the subcategory Diseases under Health displays an alphabetized list of some 138 catalog pages on specific diseases – from Acoustic Neuroma to Yeast Infections – followed by a second list of individual pages. When you find what you are looking for, just click it.

Indexes and Search Engines

Several organizations have taken on the formidable task of indexing the entire World Wide Web. Their electronic scouts visit Web sites every few weeks, analyze the text for key words, and follow every link they find to discover new pages.

The information they gather is available to anyone at special Web sites called search engines (a computer program that collects Web page information, indexes it, and lets you search the index).

Popular search engines include
- Digital Equipment's AltaVista: `http://altavista.digital.com`
- Infoseek: `http://www.infoseek.com`
- Excite: `http://www.excite.com`
- Lycos: `http:// lycos.cs.cmu.edu`
- Webcrawler: `http://webcrawler.com`

To use these services, which are usually free, do the following:

1. Pick a search engine and go to its Web site.

2. Think of a few words that describe the information you're looking for.

3. Type your search words into the text area on the search engine's page.

4. Click the Search button or hit the Enter key.

   The search engine eventually returns a list of Web pages that it thinks match your request. The pages are ranked by how good the match appears to be, with the best match listed first.

5. Look over the list. If an item seems interesting, go to that site by clicking the item.

6. If the page you visit doesn't meet your needs, return to the search engine's page using your browser's Back button.

7. If none of the items listed has what you want, either ask to see more pages that match your search words or alter the search words and try the search again.

Keys to Effective Searching

Here are some ways to sharpen your search request. These tips work on AltaVista, but most search engines are similar.

◆ Only capitalize words when you're sure that they would be stored that way, for example, proper or place names. Search words must match exactly if they have any capital letters or accent characters. Lower case search words will match any capitalization.

◆ Put double quotation marks (") around words that you expect to see right next to each other. Words connected by punctuation – including URLs – are treated the same way. For example, `"run of the mill"` and `run-of-the-mill` are both treated as a single phrase in a search.

◆ Put a plus sign (+) in front of a word that must appear in any document that AltaVista finds for you.

◆ Put a minus sign or hyphen (–) in front of a word that should not appear in any document that AltaVista finds for you. This delimiter is very handy when you get flooded with responses you did not expect.

◆ Make sure that you put a space before the + or – and no space between it and the word.

◆ AltaVista treats any string of letters or numbers separated by a space or punctuation as a word. `USA` and `Year 2000` are single words, Year-2000 is a two-word phrase, and U.S.A. is a three-word phrase.

◆ AltaVista does not index punctuation.

◆ Don't direct your simple search with words like `AND`, `OR`, and `NOT` or parentheses. AltaVista has an advanced search mode in which you can use these commands.

◆ Use the wildcard character * to search for variant spellings. For example `Dumm*` matches Dummy, Dummy's, and Dummies. AltaVista requires at least four characters before the *.

◆ If you don't like the answers you get, check your spelling and remove unneeded capitalization; then try to express your search in different words.

Examples of search-word syntax are

```
repair "fax machine" +Chicago
"word processor" - Windows - DOS
job Mass* internet writer
```

More Searching Tips

◆ Start with the most naive search you can think of. For example, if you want to rent a car in Madrid, enter `car rental Madrid`.

◆ If you don't find what you want in the first page or two of search results, refine your search instead of looking at more pages of results.

◆ Keep trying. It often takes several searches to find what you want. Persistence pays off.

◆ If you get many similar, irrelevant responses, find a word they all have in common and use the minus sign (–) feature. For example, looking for computers, you search for `powerful processor`. Getting a dozen Cuisinart sites, you change your request to `powerful processor - food`.

◆ Be ingenious in thinking up search words. A thesaurus can help.

In Your Words:
Finding Information on The Internet

Imagine you're writing a paper on genetic engineering for a biology course. What are some questions you'd want to answer?

_____

_____

_____

_____

_____

_____

What are some key words you might use to do a search to find the answers to these questions?

_____

_____

_____

_____

_____

_____

Assignment

Complete this exercise by finding answers to your questions on the Internet and bringing the information to class.

DOING COMPUTER-BASED RESEARCH IN THE LIBRARY

In years past, library research involved searching through a card catalogue – thousands of 3″ x 5″ cards, filed alphabetically by Author, Title, or Subject.

Things are different today. Computers have made library research a lot faster and more thorough. But in order to use these new research aids, you'll need to use an *electronic card catalogue* – which may seem confusing if you're not yet comfortable with computers.

What kinds of computers are used?
Most library-based computers are DOS-based. In order to find information, you may have to type in requests on a keyboard.

Do I have to know how to type to use these computers?
No. You can use two fingers to type your requests. Most complex searches can be accessed by hitting a single key.

Go to the library before you have to do research, just to get familiar with the most important keys – where they are on the keyboard and what they access.

What information do the important keys access?

Return *or* **Enter**   Most search programs ask you to press the **Return** or **Enter** key after you type in any request. The **Return/Enter** key tells the computer to do the work – to find what you're looking for.

Author   Press the **Author** key or the key marked "**A**" + the **Return/Enter** key.

  This brings up a screen where you type the name of the author you're looking for. After you type the name, press the **Return/Enter** key. This will bring up a screen listing the author's books.

Title   Press the **Title** key or the key marked "**T**" + the **Return/Enter** key.

  This brings up a screen where you type the title of the book you're looking for. After you type the title, press the **Return/Enter** key. This will bring up a screen listing the title and where it can be found. (Your campus library? Or in another library which has an interlibrary relation to your campus library?)

Subject	Press the **Subject** key or the key marked "**B**" + the **Return/Enter** key.
	This brings up a screen listing titles related to your subject. After you type the subject, press the **Return/ Enter** key. This will bring up a screen listing titles related to the subject – *if the subject is listed on the computer.*
	*If your subject is not listed on the computer, try a **Keyword** search.*
	For example, suppose you're looking for titles under the subject "Management training." You'll probably find "No titles listed" under this **Subject** search.
	But using a **Keyword** search, you'll find 173 titles listed under "Management training."
Keyword	Press the **Keyword** key or the key marked "**K**" + the **Return/Enter** key.
	This brings up a screen listing titles related to your keyword. After you type the keyword, press the **Return/Enter** key. This will bring up a screen listing titles related to the keyword – *if the keyword is listed on the computer.*
	*If your subject is not listed on the computer, try an **Expert keyword** search.*
	For example, suppose you're looking for titles under the keyword "Outsourcing." You'll probably find "No titles listed" under this **Keyword** search.
	But using an **Expert keyword** search, you'll find the following title:
	Lacity, Mary Cecilia *Information Outsourcing* J. Wiley, 1993
Expert keyword	Press the **Expert keyword** key or the key marked "**E**" + the **Return/Enter** key.
	This brings up a screen listing titles related to your expert keyword. After you type the expert keyword, press the **Return/Enter** key. This will bring up a screen listing titles related to the expert keyword.

Once I get a screen with titles I want, how do I look further?

Author search   Suppose you typed "Thoreau" under an **Author** search. You might get a screen that includes these items

1   5   Thoreau, David
2   188 Thoreau, Henry David 1817-1862

This means that the database lists 5 works under "David Thoreau" and 188 works under "Henry David Thoreau."

If you want to find titles written by the 19th century writer, **press 2 +** the **Return/Enter** key.

Title search   If you typed "Walden" under a **Title** search, you might get a screen with these items:

1   Walden, or life in the woods, and on the duty of civil disobedience

2   Walden, la vie dans les bois (Walden, life in the woods)

3   Walden Pond State Reservation

A screen prompt will tell you to **press a number**.

If you press 1 + the Return/Enter key:

The screen will tell you where to find the book in your library.

If you press 2 + the Return/Enter key:

The screen will probably say, "No holding at this location." A prompt will tell you where to find the book.

If you press 3 + the Return/Enter key:

The screen will probably tell you the location and telephone number of the Walden Pond State Reservation.

Press the **Return/Answer** key if you want to see **more items** than are listed on the screen or if you want to scroll to the next page.

What about research using journal articles?

The database and computer program for accessing journal articles is different from that for accessing book titles. This information will probably be on a different computer in the reference section of the library.

Journal articles are usually easy to access. Here are some key points:

◆ Type in your **keyword + Return/Enter** key and get a list of articles relating to your keyword.

◆ If you want to find additional information, press **E + Return/Enter** for **Extended search**.

◆ In many cases, abstracts of the journal articles are available. If the computer is connected to a printer, you'll be able to print out both the journal references and abstracts.

◆ Talk with the reference librarian. Some computer databases may contain special information, referring to journals in specific subject-areas. The database may not include information from older journals. You may need to get some information from indexes of periodical journals.

In Your Words:
Finding Information in an Electronic Card Catalogue

Imagine you're writing a paper on President John Kennedy for a political science course. What are some questions you'd want to answer?

_____

_____

_____

_____

_____

_____

What are some key words you might use to do a search to find the answers to these questions?

_____

_____

_____

_____

_____

INFORMAL WAYS TO USE THE LIBRARY

Spend some time in the library when you don't have to be there.

◆ Explore. Wander around the stacks in different sections, browsing through books in the same way you would in a bookstore.

◆ Are there listening booths where you can sit back and listen to jazz?

◆ Find corners of the library where you feel comfortable – where you'd like to study or write, or just be alone with yourself.

◆ Are there conference rooms where you can get together and study with friends?

◆ Do you know where the photocopy machines are?

◆ What are the library hours?

In Your Words:
Your Questions About The Library

What are some ways you'd like to explore the library? What questions do you have about what's available in your college's library?

_____

_____

_____

_____

_____

_____

_____

_____

_____

_____

_____

_____

PUTTING IT ALL TOGETHER

Using The Internet and The Electronic Card Catalogue to Help You Write a Term Paper

1. Write some major questions and sub-questions you'll need to answer for a term paper you plan to write this semester.

2. What are some Internet addresses that might have information answering these questions?

3. What are some Electronic Card Catalogue sources that might have information answering these questions?

THE LEARNING TO LEARN® SCHOLARSHIP CONTEST

1. Write an essay of 800 words or less on the topic, "How the Four LTL Skills Made a Difference in My Life."

2. All essays must be accompanied by a list of the Topic Sentence Questions and key word answers which you used to construct your essay.

3. The deadline for submitting essays to your instructor is December 10.

4. A winning essay will be chosen from each college where LTL is used for freshman seminar classes. The author of the winning essay at each college will become a contest Finalist and will receive an LTL Achievement plaque.

5. Finalists' essays will compete for the National LTL Scholarship Award.

6. Three national winners will be chosen from among the Finalists' essays. Each winner will receive $1000 in tuition expense reimbursement. Winners will be announced in March.

THE WRITING GAME

As a class, choose a topic from the news that all class members are familiar with.

Form two teams and a panel of 5 judges.

Each team generates questions and key word guesses which might form the basis for a term paper.

The winning team is judged best in question quality and interesting key word guesses.

Discussion and Review

How do this chapter's LTL skills illustrate the Four LTL Thinking Tools?

The LTL Journal

Continue your journal of your thoughts and feelings. How can the skills in this chapter help you reach your personal goals?

Chapter 8:
BEING ALL THAT YOU CAN BE

It's important to feel good about yourself as you begin the adventure of higher education. In this chapter we'll give you some tools to enhance your motivation and self-esteem.

You'll be introduced to the concept of a "Private Laboratory" – a place where you can safely consider past events that influence your self-image and affect the way you feel and act. You'll learn how to use your time in your Private Lab to build a new vision, with new hope, around personal problems you have struggled with.

You'll move on to the Success Inventories, where you'll be given a chance to assess your present and see what you want to do about it. These self-quizzes will give you a picture of who you are at this time in your life. Seeing yourself clearly will help you focus on your goals, see what's important, and prioritize.

You'll assess how well you take initiative, your feelings of personal competence; and you'll explore alternatives to a common barrier to success, "the blame game." You'll look at your current learning habits, and take a "personal snapshot" of who you are now. Throughout this section, we'll discuss ways you can improve areas that need work. Finding what you're good at and working on areas that need improvement will give you a sense of direction and accomplishment.

You'll learn how to become your own best friend. In this section we'll discuss issues of self-esteem – and suggest ways to build a new self image. We'll help you acquire a future-oriented view, and let go of past failures. You'll really see that the future is bigger than the past.

Finally, you'll explore your values. You'll have a chance to look at what's important to you at this stage in your life.

Turn the page, and enter your Private Laboratory.

Your Private Laboratory

1. Sit comfortably in a quiet place, with both feet on the floor and your hands resting on your thighs. (Don't sit at an angle, hold a pen, etc.)

2. Stretch your arms out, then let them drop. Let your head drop; move it slowly from left to right and back again.

3. Slowly sit up with your back straight. Close your eyes, and count backwards from 20 to 1. Breath deeply into the abdomen.

4. Stop all movement. Freeze. Hold your posture effortlessly, like a stone statue.

5. Notice your sensations and feelings inside your skin. (Do you feel warm? Are your stomach muscles relaxed? Tight? Are you restless? Sluggish? Heavy? Light?) Ask yourself: Where do these feelings come from?

6. Don't try to control your thoughts. If you think about consequences of your recent actions, let the thoughts pass, without "commenting" on them to yourself. Turn your attention to your bodily feelings and sensations.

7. You are in your "Private Laboratory." Experiment with your breathing. Gently accelerate, then slow down your breathing: Notice what happens in each case.

8. Observe what you're thinking about. The more important the consequences, the stronger your emotional response. Let emotions pass over you, like a wave, without thinking deeply or trying to solve the problem. Keeping your posture still, stay with your emotions for a few moments.

9. Choose a "thought topic" from Step 8 that elicits strong feelings. Can you see others as resources? Can you see yourself responding in a way that can bring about the desired results? If you can't, focus again on your bodily sensations.

   What is blocking your imagination? Do your feelings show that you still can't let go of your old view? Ask yourself: *"Which fears sabotage my vision. Why? How do they keep me from finding other ways to act?"*

10. Conclude with a slow count backwards from 5 to 1, gradually moving from "thought experiments" to reality, feeling calm, ready to implement your new vision.

➤ *This exercise will be the foundation for later work in the chapter. We'll refer to it throughout this chapter.*

SUCCESS INVENTORIES

In this section, you'll find out more about who you are now – how you see yourself, good and bad. Be honest with yourself in doing this self-assessment. You're the only person who needs to look at what you write here.

To be a self-starter, it's good to know when to take action. The first step is to feel that you are a person who *can* do a good job. How much of a self-starter are you now?

Check each statement 1 to 5 on how well it describes you at this time.

> To guide you:
> **1** = hardly ever
> **3** = sometimes
> **5** = nearly always

TAKING INITIATIVE

1.	I work well independently.	1	2	3	4	5
2.	I correct a problem if I find an error.	1	2	3	4	5
3.	I break complicated tasks into smaller parts.	1	2	3	4	5
4.	I look for solutions to problems.	1	2	3	4	5
5.	I find ways to monitor my own progress.	1	2	3	4	5
6.	I'm not afraid of trying new ideas or methods.	1	2	3	4	5
7.	I'm not afraid to offer my own opinion.	1	2	3	4	5
8.	I'm a self-starter; I need little direction once work begins.	1	2	3	4	5
9.	I pay attention to the work at hand and see a project through to completion.	1	2	3	4	5
10.	Others view me as highly motivated.	1	2	3	4	5
11.	I find ways to monitor my own work.	1	2	3	4	5
12.	I'm interested in learning new things.	1	2	3	4	5
13.	I'm very goal-directed.	1	2	3	4	5
14.	I like challenges.	1	2	3	4	5
15.	I volunteer to find solutions to problems.	1	2	3	4	5

What's your score?

If your score is 60 or more, you're a real self-starter. That will help you get to where you want to be. If you scored 35 – 50, work on the areas where you scored poorly. If you scored 15 – 34, you need work in this area: The inability to take initiative can hold you back.

To improve your skills in the area, give yourself a personal assignment: Begin a small project of your own creation. Using a Task Management Checklist, list the sub-tasks needed to complete the project. Monitor your progress: Check off each item, and date it, when it's completed. Give yourself several of these "assignments" until you feel more comfortable in this area.

FEELING PERSONALLY COMPETENT

Remember, the only confidence worth having is confidence based on competence.

1. I know where to look for information I need.	1	2	3	4	5
2. I know the technical side of the work at hand.	1	2	3	4	5
3. I take pride in good work.	1	2	3	4	5
4. I'm competent in my work.	1	2	3	4	5
5. I can be counted on to turn in good work.	1	2	3	4	5
6. I'm aware of and take care of important details when I do a project.	1	2	3	4	5
7. I do assigned tasks on time.	1	2	3	4	5
8. I "own" my actions. I do not "pass the buck."	1	2	3	4	5
9. I handle personal problems easily and well.	1	2	3	4	5
10. I'm organized, and can find what I need.	1	2	3	4	5
11. I feel confident that I'll do well in college.	1	2	3	4	5
12. I've always felt that I will be successful.	1	2	3	4	5
13. I'm good at applying new information.	1	2	3	4	5
14. I like figuring out how to use new technologies.	1	2	3	4	5
15. When I complete a job, I check it for errors before I hand it in.	1	2	3	4	5

My self respect is highest when I *(Number in order from highest to lowest.)*

❑ win a game　❑ help others　❑ am praised by my superiors

❑ do a good job　❑ get good grades

When I do poorly, who or what do I blame? *(Number in order from highest to lowest.)*

❑ my professors　❑ my notes　❑ my physical state (exhaustion, etc.)

❑ my lack of preparation　❑ my poor memory

What's your score?

If your score is 60 or more, you feel very confident that you'll succeed at whatever you do. That will help you get to where you want to be. If you scored 35 – 50, work on the areas where you scored poorly. If you scored 15 – 34, you need work in this area: Feeling incompetent can hold you back.

Improving self-confidence is a complicated process: Your feelings may be based on a long history of failing to reach your goals, large and small. Many of the exercises in this chapter will help. And using LTL skills will improve your grades, so you'll begin to feel academically confident. But it will also help to give yourself "homework" in this area. For starters, work on the following:

1. When you begin a new project, ask yourself questions, and ask questions from an expert source, so you know what information you need.
2. Give yourself enough time to get the project done well. When you start the project, list its steps. If you don't have enough time for the project as planned, scale it back to a more reasonable size before you get too far.
3. Use a Task Management Checklist to keep yourself on track.
4. Check for errors as you complete parts of the project.
5. Keep the parts of the project in a place where you can easily find them.
6. Ask for feedback from an outside source as you work through the project.

If you tend to blame others for your failures, our next skills should help.

AN ALTERNATIVE TO THE BLAME GAME

What do you say to yourself when things don't work out – you fail a history exam, or you have a big fight with a good friend?

Do you ask yourself, *"Why did it happen to me?"* Meaning, *"I don't like what happened to me. I don't care why or how it happened. Maybe I'm to blame, maybe I'm not to blame. Some people get away with it. Why not me?"* You react with hostility and denial.

Do you say to yourself, *"How could this happen? Oh, why didn't I act differently?"* You spend time and effort blaming yourself.

Or do you ask yourself, *"I didn't judge the situation correctly. Looks like I made a mistake. How can I correct that next time? What are the possibilities?"* In this case, you don't view the situation as punishment for doing the wrong thing; instead it's an occasion for self-improvement, where understanding how things work will help you change outcomes. Your mistakes provide information for making things work better next time. You recognize that you're in a learning environment, where you have the luxury of making mistakes in order to grow. And where no one mistake can cause a disaster. You tell yourself, *"I can stand a few blows like that. Let me figure out what happened so I know what to do next time."*

Adopt this approach, and you can turn knowledge into power for change: What you learn from this mistake will make you more informed – better prepared to face obstacles and reach your goals. You'll also feel good about your mature emotional response: You didn't waste time on blame, self-pity, regrets. You had the courage to look at what happened and learn from negative feedback. Looking at the truth of what happened – however painful – helped you profit from what otherwise may be considered failure.

In Your Words:
Learning From Feedback

The next time you fail – at school or in your personal life – look at what happened. Make a Pro/Con T (Chapter 6) to see if you'll gain more than you lose by correcting your mistakes. Be honest with yourself. Be brave enough to face failure as feedback: *How did you contribute to the negative outcome? Are there behaviors you need to work on?* Go to your Private Laboratory, and work through Steps 1 – 8. What are some changes you'd like to make?

_____

_____

_____

_____

   List some behaviors you need to work on that may have caused this loss:

_____

_____

_____

_____

Read this list when you get up in the morning or when you go to sleep at night. Give yourself feedback: Look for results of changes in your behaviors, and write about them in your LTL Journal.

WHAT ARE YOUR LEARNING HABITS?

Look at your learning habits. Don't worry if you score poorly on this questionnaire. Take the feedback you get from this questionnaire, and work on areas where you scored low. After a few weeks, score yourself again and see how much better you're doing.

Please circle the answer which best fits your current use of learning skills.

		NEVER	SOMETIMES			ALWAYS
1.	Write questions from notes.	0%	25%	50%	75%	100%
2.	Use questions as guides in reading.	0%	25%	50%	75%	100%
3.	Focus on reading to solve problems when reading math-based material.	0%	25%	50%	75%	100%
4.	Read for examples.	0%	25%	50%	75%	100%
5.	Use checklists to break tasks into smaller parts and plan work.	0%	25%	50%	75%	100%
6.	Use models when problem-solving in math or science.	0%	25%	50%	75%	100%
7.	"Translate" diagrams into words.	0%	25%	50%	75%	100%
8.	Use charts to format information.	0%	25%	50%	75%	100%
9.	Use key words to help organize and recall information.	0%	25%	50%	75%	100%
10.	Generate questions before writing.	0%	25%	50%	75%	100%
11.	Predict test questions effectively.	0%	25%	50%	75%	100%
12.	Edit your own writing errors.	0%	25%	50%	75%	100%
13.	Break down large projects into small tasks.	0%	25%	50%	75%	100%
14.	Think of questions about the subject while you're in class.	0%	25%	50%	75%	100%
15.	Set goals and monitor your progress towards reaching them.	0%	25%	50%	75%	100%

A PERSONAL "SNAPSHOT"

The next group of items will show you areas of strength and those you need to work on:

Agree ←——→ Disagree

1.	Monday morning always makes me blue.	1	2	3	4	5
2.	I don't get enough sleep.	1	2	3	4	5
3.	I feel anxious if I have to speak in public.	1	2	3	4	5
4.	I often feel that I'm treated unfairly.	1	2	3	4	5
5.	I don't get the credit I deserve.	1	2	3	4	5
6.	There are certain things I just can't stand.	1	2	3	4	5
7.	People just don't understand me.	1	2	3	4	5
8.	I think that luck determines a lot of what happens to a person.	1	2	3	4	5
9.	Rainy days get me down.	1	2	3	4	5
10.	You can't trust most people.	1	2	3	4	5
11.	I often think about past mistakes I've made.	1	2	3	4	5
12.	I don't feel in control over my future.	1	2	3	4	5
13.	I feel very uncomfortable with people I haven't known for a long time.	1	2	3	4	5
14.	I'm easily discouraged by others or by failure.	1	2	3	4	5
15.	People can easily persuade me to do things they want and not to do things I want.	1	2	3	4	5

What's your score?

If your score is 60 or more, you feel positive and in control of your life. That will help you get to where you want to be. If you scored 35 – 50, work on the areas where you scored poorly. If you scored 15 – 34, you need work in this area. The information on the next pages can get you started.

Student Voices

Christie Nicolaides

With LTL, I understand exactly what everything is, because my work is so well organized, and the questions I generate really help. And I know how to use my time better, so that I'm not wasting it. Also, with the LTL methods, I get a lot more done in less time.

In all, LTL has really helped improve my confidence as a student. Even though the competition is intense in the School of Management, I go into exams and tell myself that there's no reason why I won't do well. And I feel that I have a much better shot at graduate school since I've taken LTL.

Empower Yourself
A Positive "Personal Snapshot"

Everyone spends time in self-talk. If you've failed in the past, you might tell yourself that nothing you do is right, and that you're likely to fail.

We'll help you change that. You'll learn to focus on future possibilities, turn your failures into learning opportunities, and notice your past successes. Finding new opportunities will improve your morale, and your successes will provide a model for reaching your goals.

The "Personal Snapshot" Inventory you've just completed includes items like, "Monday morning always makes me blue;" "There are certain things I just can't stand;" and "Rainy days get me down." These are all examples of giving yourself a message that you're a victim; the *language* in your self-message imprisons you.

After all, some people love rainy days; others who don't still find things to do that make rainy days productive. That means that rainy days are neutral. You assign the value. Why not assign values that make you free to act? It's not the *rainy day* that gets you down. You're *letting* the rain get you down. The first step in changing these negative self-messages is to state them as they really are – neutral. Translate *"Monday morning always makes me blue"* into *"I let myself feel blue on Monday mornings."* Something you "just can't stand" may be something you have no control over, cannot avoid, run away from, or destroy. It's something you think you have to put up with. *Be free to assign values that make you active. Don't jail yourself in the prison of negative self-messages.*

Rise above the negative. Don't make things worse for yourself. If you *let* yourself get upset, you're acting against your self-interest. Go beyond the negative result. See "mistakes" as feedback and use language for, not against, you. This will give you a chance to do things you enjoy and can be proud of. If you often think about past failures as mistakes, you're cheating yourself out of the opportunity to act and enjoy what's good about *this moment in time, the present* – the chance to act toward your goals, according to your values.

You can turn past failures into future opportunities for action. Think of the many new successes you'll have by capitalizing on past failure. The future is always bigger than the past. If a mistake helps you find a better way to act, you paid a small price – a bargain – for failing.

Of course, you can complain, blame, and suffer. Or you can react in a different way. True, you can't just wish away past feelings. You have to exercise your choice by *practicing* new responses. *(You'll begin practicing this on the exercise on the next page.)*

In Your Words:
A Positive "Personal Snapshot"

Look back at a situation where you previously failed. Using the information on page 192, list new responses you need to practice to prepare for the next time you face a similar situation.

_____

_____

_____

_____

_____

_____

_____

✔ **THINK ABOUT THIS**

◆ *Is there some humor in the situation?* It will help to see alternative approaches. One of them is humor – which may diffuse your negative emotions and loosen the grip of fear.

◆ *Can you learn from it?* Can you use past failure to exercise your freedom of choice, and translate negative self-messages into future oriented action plans?

◆ *Is there anything you can do to make it better?* If Monday morning makes you blue, make it better by getting up a little early and doing something different. For example, start your day at a special coffee spot you've been meaning to visit. Or work on project you've been hoping to begin.

◆ *Remember that you're in a growth environment,* where you can afford to make mistakes. Mistakes are not fatal in a learning environment.

◆ *The future is always bigger than the past.* See the result of a mistake as a small price you paid for future success.

◆ *Instead of focusing on the negative as a substitute for change, do something about it.* You've already paid the price for the mistake. So don't complain. The hard part is over. Use what you've learned from this "mistake" to change your actions in the future.

What can you do in the future?
◆ Practice changing your negative messages into factual descriptions of what you're facing.
◆ Keep in mind what you're good at.
◆ View negative outcomes as strong feedback or as payment you've already made. Write down what you "bought." Make a list of things you can buy with the lessons from negative outcomes.
◆ Build on your strengths and focus on what you can do. Don't get upset or indulge in wishful thinking. This kind of effort leads to nothing but regrets.
◆ Dwell on the good. When you do something well, think about it. Use it as a model for future action.

BEING YOUR OWN BEST FRIEND

The central message of this chapter is: You have a *choice* about how you react to what happens to you. You'll feel better about yourself if you:

◆ take feedback, and use it to do better next time, and

◆ practice giving yourself positive messages.

If you feel good about yourself, you're more likely to take initiative. Also you're more likely to find solutions when you run into problems – instead of dwelling on what you wish you *could* do and *can't* do.

Let's say that your computer broke down. You might tell yourself, *"Why did this happen to me? If I only could fix the computer."* Feeling good about yourself would help you think of alternatives: *"When is the campus computer lab open? In the meantime, what else can I do?"*

If you're feeling low, whatever the source of this feeling, start generating positive experiences. Orient your action towards achievement.

Feelings of Low Self-Esteem

Thinking about what you can't do promotes wishful thinking or moodiness – which distract you from positive action. You tell yourself, *"If I only had X, I'd reach the goal. But I don't have it."* You're giving yourself an excuse to be passive. You're setting yourself up for failure.

This is like saying, *"Oh, I can't do this. I'll make mistakes. The situation isn't right."* People who look for perfection are beaten before they start: They can't take negative feedback – it's too painful. They can't adjust their actions to their goals. All they do is redefine the goal: *"My goal is to find an excuse for not doing it now."*

Everyone has a specific source of personal pain and insecurity. Whatever the source, the *experience* of low self-esteem is the same: You feel that nothing you do is good enough; that anyone who knew the *real* you would reject you; that all criticism of you is justified.

There are times when everyone feels that way. Don't be discouraged. You're on a journey – going from where you are to where you want to be.

Building a New Self-Image

Why is self-image important? Because your self-image is a summary of all your experiences: It limits or expands the range of what you consider possible, available, and permissible. Surprisingly, your self-image is mostly imposed on you by other people's responses to you and your efforts. A mirror image is always a reflection from outside; it is the feedback you get from reality, mainly from others.

Your self-image is your perception of what you think you can do. Under what circumstances do you succeed or fail? From there you can "revisit" your past with a new understanding. For example, if you think you have no capacity for math, retrace your experience. You might discover that your fifth grade math teacher gave timed math exercises that you never finished on time. In your Private Laboratory, "revisiting" this experience, revise your self-image in this area. Tell yourself, *"Under those circumstances, sure I did badly. But I'm not a child, and circumstances have changed. I like to figure out puzzles, and I might be good at math now."* Your revised self-image may be the perfect starting point for success in this area; it doesn't limit you, but supports your efforts. Reinterpreting your past will help apply your *present* resources for success.

To work on change, go to your Private Laboratory (page 186). Consider an experience that holds you back, and go through Steps 1 – 8. Then try to "revisit" it again and see if your feelings have changed.

If you still have negative feelings:

◆ Imagine that this experience happened to another person.

◆ Looking objectively, imagine the person's response to the incident.

◆ Now go back and find or construct an experience that is related to your negative experience, but had a positive outcome.

◆ Replay this experience in your mind, and put it consciously into the inventory that will make up your revised self-image.

◆ With your new understanding, replace the old conclusion that caused you pain. (You'll get better at this with practice.)

◆ Keep a hard copy of the results of each practice session. Write them in your LTL Journal. Write in positive terms about how close you got towards reaching your goal.

In Your Words:
Continue Building Your New Self-Image

Let's begin by looking at what you've done right.

There is at least one incident in your life that makes you feel proud. You acted according to your ideals – even when you were afraid to, even when it was hard to do so. Or it might be that you accomplished something you thought would be hard to achieve.

Describe something specific you did that you feel good about. Can you apply what you did then to other areas of your life?

_____

_____

_____

_____

_____

_____

_____

_____

_____

_____

_____

_____

_____

_____

_____

_____

Go to your Private Laboratory (page 186) and work through Steps 1 – 8. Visualize yourself in a situation where you've admired your own behavior. How did this success make you feel, physically and emotionally? When you have this picture clearly in mind, lightly touch a finger with your thumb and press down.

If you practice this technique, you'll "teach" your body and mind new responses. With practice, you'll feel better about yourself just by touching your finger and thumb.

Practice this visualization until you can easily "see" it when you feel unsure and afraid. Then take the next step towards achieving your new goal.

In Your Words:
Looking at The Best in Yourself

Look at what you've done right. Ask yourself and answer the questions below:

◆ *What makes you a good friend?*

_____

_____

_____

_____

◆ *What do you do well?*

_____

_____

_____

_____

◆ *In what ways are you creative?*

_____

_____

_____

_____

_____

◆ *What are your best personal qualities?*

_____

_____

_____

_____

_____

_____

◆ *What makes you a unique person?*

_____

_____

_____

_____

_____

_____

You don't have time to waste thinking about things you can't do. Instead, "reorganize" the past so that it will provide a starting point for future achievements. The future, unlike the past, is open-ended.

Looking Towards The Future

Now look at yourself in the future. Picture your life as you'd like it to be.

What parts of the externals of your life would you like to change? Picture a job, your home life, personal relationships – even your surroundings. Describe what they would look like in ten years if you accomplished the goals you set for yourself. Look for as much detail as you can find in this future picture. (Write more in your LTL journal if you run out of space.)

_____

_____

_____

_____

What parts of your internal life – your character – would you like to change? Imagine a situation that you would now find very stressful. Putting yourself in the best light, how would you handle that situation? (Remember, guilt will only hold you back from what you can be – from realizing your potential.)

If you can't bring yourself to visualize yourself handling the situation you just described, *how would your hero handle it?*

_____

_____

_____

_____

_____

_____

Getting There

People who set clear goals for themselves are more likely to achieve their goals. Set out a plan of action to attain the life you want – both external (your goals) and internal (your values).

What are some of the steps between where you are now and where you want to be?

_____

_____

_____

_____

_____

_____

On Your Journey

To help you on your way towards a better life, try the following:

◆ *Start by working on one part of your life.* Choose an area – internal or external – where your goals are most clear and where you can see progress in a fairly short period of time.

◆ *Make short-term and long-term Task Management Checklists* (see Chapter 5) for reaching your goals. Reward yourself as you accomplish your sub-goals – and when you see yourself breaking a negative pattern you've carried from your past. (Make sure your self-rewards carry you forward, not back. Do something special for yourself that you've been waiting for someone else to do for or with you – get flowers, see a movie or a baseball game, ride a bicycle in the park, call an old friend, visit the zoo.)

◆ *Keep a journal* of your progress.

◆ *Write positive statements about yourself* and what you're reaching towards. Read and recite these affirmations at the start of every day.

◆ *Find the parent you always wanted to have inside yourself.* Find the wise, helpful, caring part of you, and reach out to it. Look to this "internal" parent for advice and comfort.

◆ *Share what you're doing with a special friend.* (If you don't have such a friend, turn to the "Friends" section of Chapter 9. Use our suggestions to help find one or more people you can share your *real* life with.)

◆ *Don't try to be what other people want you to be.* It's your life. Be what *you* want to be.

---

*How would you use the **Four LTL Thinking Tools** to solve problems you have in this area? If this is an area where you'd like to make some changes, turn to the Four LTL Thinking Tools exercise at the end of this chapter.*

Empower Yourself
Picturing The Future

Picture yourself in ten years. Put in the details – not just that you'll have X job, or you'll be married, etc. Instead, imagine a whole day in the future: What your room will look like when you wake up in the morning, who (if anyone) else will be there with you, what you're thinking about traveling to work, what specific things you do at work – parts of the job which you like and dislike, what dinner is like, etc.

Put your picture aside, and come back to it in a couple of days. If it looks too good to be true, imagine problems that might arise. If it doesn't look like a happy life, what would need to be changed?

When you've got your picture about right – so that it looks like real life, and one you'd like to have – work backwards from it.* For example, if you dream of being some kind of executive, what are the steps between where you are now and where you want to be? If you've got children and a wife or husband in the dream, what kinds of things do you like to do with them? Did you do those things with your parents when you were a child, or will you have to learn more about being close to people than you now know?

The message here is that you're more likely to get to where you want if you know what it looks like – you'll be able to adjust your road map to the future if you know where it is, and you won't get lost if you run into detours or have to make side-trips.

Remember, you're not aiming at a perfect picture, but at an effective process.

CALVIN AND HOBBES © 1992 Bill Watterson. Dist. by UNIVERSAL PRESS SYNDICATE. Reprinted with permission. All rights reserved.

FIND YOUR VALUES

College is a major transition in most students' lives: If you're going to make good choices for yourself in college, start by finding out what's important to you – what you choose when you have a choice. Here are some questions you'll want to ask yourself. In looking for your own answers to these questions, think about what you've found enjoyable, useful, or otherwise positive in the past, and what you want for the future.

◆ What kinds of friends and activities are important to you?

◆ Do you want mostly social friends, or people you can talk with seriously?

◆ If you have a family, do they come first?

◆ Are sports important to you? As a participant or as an observer?

◆ Do you exercise? Hike, walk, or go to the gym?

◆ Is sitting and talking with someone you like very important to you?

◆ Are you an "ideas" or an "action" person? Is your game chess or football?

◆ Do you like working in groups? Belonging to clubs or starting group activities?

◆ Are there issues you feel strongly about? Politics? Religion? Sports?

◆ Would you rather play a game of Trivial Pursuit or spend a night on the town?

◆ Do you feel good when you help someone out of a jam – either by offering a solution or pitching in and helping?

◆ Do you like to eat lunch alone, or would you rather chat with others?

◆ Do you enjoy sharing thoughts and feelings with one or two other people?

◆ Do you work out personal problems by yourself, or share your feelings with others?

◆ How would you rank family, academics, work, sports, social friendships? In which areas of your life do you feel you must achieve?

◆ Do you work better when you compete or cooperate with others?

◆ What kind of humor do you like? Practical jokes, or more subtle humor?

◆ Do you need to learn how to trust people more, or are you too trusting and easily taken advantage of?

◆ Are you a detail or a "big picture" person?

◆ Do you feel that most situations can be best dealt with by "thinking on your feet," or by careful preparation?

◆ Do you like to listen to interesting stories – or tell them?

◆ Do you often take others' wishes into account, or feel held back by others?

◆ When do you feel most pressured? Is the pressure from external sources, or does it have internal sources? In other words, how much pressure do you place on yourself?

◆ Are you a good negotiator in a conflict? Do you see others' points of view?

In Your Words:
Examining Your Values

Working with another student, write some other questions that would be helpful to examine in getting to know yourself and your values.

1. _____
2. _____
3 _____
4. _____
5. _____
6. _____
7. _____
8. _____
9. _____
10. _____
11. _____
12. _____
13. _____
14. _____
15. _____

There are no "right" answers to these questions. Look at your life, the choices you seem to be making. What seems to work best? Do you feel "stuck?" in certain areas of your life? Are there choices you're making right now that you'd like to change?

When you work through the answers to these questions, keep a private journal of what's important to you. Not just what you *think* is important to you, but what you actually *do*. Look back in a month and compare your actions to your values. Examine the differences. What do they tell you about yourself – who you are and where you're going?

Values influence not only your goals, but also *how* you achieve them. For example, because of your values, there are certain things you won't do in order to achieve a particular goal. The Values Clarification game on the next page will help you think through this issue.

In Your Words:
Values Clarification

Complete this exercise with a group of students in your LTL class.

Wrecked on Mars*

You're a member of a space crew that will meet a mother ship on the lighted surface of Mars. Due to mechanical difficulties, however, your ship was forced to land at a spot some 200 miles from the meeting point. During re-entry and landing, equipment was damaged. Since survival depends on reaching the mother ship, the most important items must be chosen for the trip.

Game One

Fifteen items left intact and undamaged after the landing are listed below. Your task is to rank them in order. How necessary is each one if you and your crew are to reach your destination?

Place the number 1 by the most crucial item, the number 2 by the second most crucial and so on...

_____	Box of matches
_____	5 gallons of water
_____	Signal flares
_____	First-aid kit
_____	Food concentrate
_____	Life raft
_____	50 feet of rope
_____	Magnetic compass
_____	Portable heating unit
_____	Parachute silk
_____	Case of dehydrated milk
_____	Two 45-caliber pistols
_____	Two 100-pound tanks of oxygen
_____	Stellar map (on the moon's constellation)
_____	Solar-powered FM receiver transmitter

Game Two

You're expecting a rescue mission that might have a similar fate as yours. How will that change your decisions? How will you share the resources with the people in that group? Discuss the scenario and possible outcomes for both groups.

---

*This simulation exercise was devised by the Office of the Dean for Student Development at Boston College, and reprinted with their permission.

Using Your Fears Creatively

How can I harness my fears to create a positive outcome?

The only imagination worth having is the one that can see how things can be better. You'll increase your chances of success by assuming an *active* role. Don't ignore your fears, but don't get "bogged down" by them.

◆ Express them explicitly, either verbally or in writing. Be clear about what you're afraid of.

◆ Ask yourself what's the worst possible result and what's the best possible result. If you're emotionally prepared to deal with the worst, you're ready for the best. Most of our fears exist only in our minds.

◆ Act on your plan. If you find the activity exciting, you'll forget your fears.

In Your Words:
Using Your Fears Creatively

Fear is usually seen as a negative, because it tends to paralyze action and feels bad. However, the cause of fear can be analyzed and dealt with. Fear is a sign. A sign is neither good or bad; it's value comes from what you do with it. First, what do your fears tell you? Are they acting as a warning signal to slow down and rationally assess the situation?

Take your most recent fear to your Private Lab. What does this fear spring from? What is reasonable about it? Translate your fear into what can really happen. Be concrete and explicit.

_____

_____

_____

_____

_____

You might say to yourself, "I wish the situation were different." Or, believing you're not strong enough, you might tell yourself, "I wish I could handle this situation." If you could, what changes would you make in the situation? In yourself?

_____

_____

_____

_____

_____

Now take action. Look for *alternatives* to head-off the fearful consequence at the end of the road.

SELF-DISCOVERY GAMES

A Private Detective in the House

Pretend you're a private detective going into your own room. Look at the clothes, shoes, where and how items are placed. What kind of music is available? Books? Personal items? What do you see?

What's important to this person?

Try this game on your own and with a friend.

What do your actions tell you?

Make a list of 20 things you enjoy doing.

Are they free, or do they cost money?

Are they things you do alone, or with others?

What part of you does each of these use? (physical/intellectual/emotional/artistic/spiritual)

Then write the approximate date of the last time you did each of these activities.

Why has it been so long since you did some of the things you love to do?

What are the clues in how you live? Looking at these clues, do you both have a similar picture of who you are? Who your friend is?

Chapter 9:
RELATIONSHIPS

PERSONAL AND SOCIAL CHANGES IN COLLEGE

Recent High School Grads...

College is a lot more than school work. If you've just graduated from high school, you must be excited at the opportunity to make your own way. But if this is your first time away from home, you may find it hard to resist peer pressure to conform – even when it goes against your personal values and interests.

Adults Returning to School...

If you're an adult returning to school, you may have many responsibilities – home, spouse, children, a job. College is a way to build a better future, greater opportunities for you and your family. But at this stage, when you're just starting out, you may often feel as if you never have enough time for all the things you need to do.

Commuter Students...

As a commuter student, you're faced with two worlds. You still have the support of family and friends. But your experience in college may be very different from your daily life. And the pressure for you to succeed is strong, whether you're an adult returning to school or a recent high school grad: You may be the first person in your family to attend college, and you may not know where to turn when problems arise at college.

This is a lot to think about. Ask yourself this question:
How can the Four Thinking Tools help me solve these personal and social issues?

USING THE FOUR LTL THINKING TOOLS IN RELATIONSHIPS

Feeling Left Out
– How to "Connect" with People

If you find it hard to make friends, you may feel that you're the only one you know who feels insecure with others. You may sometimes "push" yourself to try to get to know people, but find that your efforts backfire. Here are some suggestions that can help:

◆ *Don't try to be the "life of the party" wherever you are.* People can't relax around "live wires." Also, they sense that something is not natural and will shy away from someone who tries too hard.

◆ *Don't worry about whether you said the "right" thing* or made the "right" impression. If you're that self-conscious, you won't have time and energy to pay attention to other people – to see what they need and who they are.

◆ *Join an activity group* in something that interests you. It doesn't matter what it is. If you become involved in something outside yourself and focus on what (not how) you're doing, the natural, "real" side of you will come out – the part that others can see and relate to.

◆ *Take a deep breath.* If you're finishing other people's sentences, you might be viewed as anxious. People reciprocate: If you're a good listener and speak when you have something to say, others will respond in kind.

◆ *Stand tall.* Keep a good posture and maintain eye contact with others when you talk with them. If you act self-confident, others will begin to treat you as if you are – and you will be, because self-image is often shaped by other people's responses.

◆ *You're not alone.* Remember that even the head cheerleader at your high school was worried about the same things you are.

How would you use the Four LTL Thinking Tools to solve problems you have in this area? If this is an area where you'd like to make some changes, turn to the Four LTL Thinking Tools exercise at the end of this chapter.

Ethics in Relationships with Others

Going to college means preparing yourself for the rest of your life. If you're just out of high school, college may mean living away from home for the first time. If you're an adult returning to school, college may bring an important shift in your responsibilities. You're preparing yourself for challenges that will require a higher level of decision-making.

This is a good time to re-examine your values. Your sense of ethics is your moral philosophy. To most people, being ethical means *doing the right thing*.

How will you know if you're relating to others in an ethical way? You'll know. Your intuition will tell you. Treat others as you would have them treat you. Try a thought experiment. Apply that concept to a situation you consider a "gray" area. (But remember that not everyone shares your likes and dislikes.) Put yourself in the other person's place. Even your body will tell you if you're on the "wrong" path. (For example, you may get a funny feeling in your stomach.)

So you know if you're doing the right thing. Like everyone else on the planet, you're continually making choices between doing what you consider right – or not. An ethical problem is not a matter of ignorance – it's ignoring danger signs, the voice of conscience. Your ethical intuition can tell when things are done out of love, friendship, indifference, or anger.

Why should you act ethically in your relationships with others? Because it's right. And because the best thing you can do for *yourself* is to care about others and treat them well: Thinking only of yourself will eventually bring bitterness and a narrowness of feeling that will not let you experience real emotion, real sharing, real satisfaction in life.

There's also the issue of *doing the right thing* as a student. College is a time to acquire skills that will help you reach your goals in life. It's true, you won't have to remember the terms of the Treaty of Versailles or write a paper on *Moby Dick* on the job. But you're limiting your career options if you don't learn to work towards a goal; learn what's needed; test yourself; reach for something "extra" – under pressure, under time limits. You're limiting your resources if you "cheat" on exams or papers. Taking the time to learn these skills in college will help you prepare for the challenges life will bring.

How do you feel when you do your best at something and achieve beyond your expectations? How large do you want your dreams to be? You're learning to use tools for success, and you have the necessary intelligence. It's just a matter of application. By doing your own work in school, you'll aim higher, your goals will be clearer, and you'll *make yourself proud* through real achievement.

---

*How would you use the **Four LTL Thinking Tools** to solve problems you have in this area? If this is an area where you'd like to make some changes, turn to the Four LTL Thinking Tools exercise at the end of this chapter.*

Developing Leadership Skills

When you become involved in group activities, it's important to know how to use leadership skills – how to be assertive in a positive way and resolve conflict situations when they arise.

Learning to be Assertive

People often confuse assertiveness with aggressiveness. They don't make their wishes clear to others because they don't want to start a fight. Assertiveness is not about starting fights. It's about communicating clearly and openly to others. Many people don't know how to present their ideas in a positive way: Whenever they step out of a passive role, they come on too strong. They use hostile words and actions in self-defense, anticipating resistance – assuming that others will challenge them.

Here are some guidelines for letting others know your wishes clearly – without making them react negatively:

◆ Start by describing the problem you're concerned about, without placing blame. Be specific. State when and how often the problem occurs.
e.g., *"It seems to me that the apartment only gets cleaned when we have visitors."* Or, *"You've only gotten three articles for the school paper on time this term. Let's explore ways to make that different."*

◆ Say how you feel about this – personalize the situation, and avoid dramatic words. e.g., *"That makes me feel ___ because..."* (angry/uncomfortable/ upset)

◆ Specify the changes you would like. State your wishes in terms of specific behaviors, not attitudes. e.g., *"I want ..."* (your solution)

◆ Ask a question that can't be answered by "yes" or "no," and that asks for the other person's solution to the problem.e.g., *"What do you think we can do to solve the problem?"*

You don't want to provoke an emotional response, but to initiate action to resolve the issue. So keep asking questions, and try to get yourself and the other person to be specific about possible solutions. If you can't agree, choose a middle ground and offer to experiment with it for a week, taking data on how well it works for both of you. You've at least made a start.

A good leader is one who is neither domineering nor passive. Good leaders set the stage for action by stating the problem clearly and allowing others to offer their contributions. They monitor progress; stay on top of the situation; make changes when needed. If you make it clear that the goal is worthwhile, that chances of succeeding are good, and that efforts won't be wasted, you've arranged the environment for action and placed yourself in the position of a manager and coordinator of the available resources – and thus a natural leader.

How would you use the Four LTL Thinking Tools to solve problems you have in this area? If this is an area where you'd like to make some changes, turn to the Four LTL Thinking Tools exercise at the end of this chapter.

FRIENDS:
People You Can Count On

Friends are more than people you spend time with. While it's important to know people with whom you can go out and see a movie or share a pizza, friendship is more than time spent in another person's presence. Friends are people you can share with in these ways:

◆ You and your friend enjoy each other's company, even when you're not doing anything or going anywhere special.

◆ You don't feel embarrassed about discussing a problem with your friend. (Of course, some friends are closer to you than others. If the problem is really personal, you may find that there are only one or two people you can talk with about it.)

◆ You feel comfortable with your friend, and don't try to be something you're not in order to impress him/her.

◆ There's a serious side to your friendship. If you're always just kidding around, you have access to only half of the potential of friendship. Neither of you trusts the other – or yourselves – enough to be natural.

◆ You see each other as resources in times of trouble.

◆ You don't feel in competition with your friend. You feel pretty good when something good happens to him/her – and you get the same feeling in return because you *belong*.

◆ You share past experiences with each other. For example, you talk about your childhood and your families with each other.

Examine your relationships. Do you have a friendship like this?
If not, you may have to work on filling in some gaps in your life:

◆ You haven't yet learned that you can be yourself without a "cover." You're operating on the surface, not yet able to let your personal side be seen by others.

◆ The people you know are also "under cover." You haven't yet found people who are comfortable sharing on a deeper level.

If you'd like to change this part of your life, try this:

◆ Working on a project with someone you'd like to get to know better will give you new opportunities for friendship. If you're trying to achieve common goals, you'll share lots of ideas – which is a beginning.

◆ Once you and the other person feel comfortable with each other, talk about how you both react to different things and people. Start with safe areas – how you like/dislike a certain TV show, for example. When you hear yourself or your friend say something strongly – with emotion – about one of these areas, you're off to a good start.

◆ If you find that this person shies away from "really" talking, give him/her time, but explore other possibilities for friendship. You *can* find a few people who are ready, like you, to begin to open up to others.

Questions about not closing yourself off from others:

◆ Is it a good idea to make new friends in college when I have so many old ones from high school days – or, (if you're an adult returning to school) from my neighborhood?

◆ What new activities should I look for on campus? Off campus?

◆ If you're an adult returning to school: Can other adult students provide a support network?

◆ Are any of my old friends enrolled in my college or at nearby schools?

◆ Can new friends become close friends? Will I have time for both new and old friends?

◆ When is assertiveness helpful in making new friends?

◆ What should I do when a relationship seems to be one-sided?

◆ What if my values are different from those of many other students at my school?

◆ What should I look for in a friend? What are some things mutually expected in friendships? What can my friends expect of me?

◆ How much time should I spend with my friends, as opposed to time with family, studying, working, etc.?

How would you use the Four LTL Thinking Tools to solve problems you have in this area? If this is an area where you'd like to make some changes, turn to the Four LTL Thinking Tools exercise at the end of this chapter.

BEING A COMMUTER STUDENT

Relationships at Home and at School

As a commuter student you live a kind of "double life." You're living in your old environment – which means you don't have to adjust to a totally new life. You can easily stay in touch with your old friends from the neighborhood. And your family can provide support.

But there are also difficulties. As a commuter student you may feel somewhat isolated – a stranger in both worlds. You may find it hard to make new friends and establish new alliances at school. And you may find that you have less in common with your old buddies if you're in college – and they are not.

As you make the transition to college life, you need a support network – people you have something in common with. Find out if your campus has a special group or club that deals with issues of commuter students. Or become involved in other ways. Are there activities that interest you on campus? Can you become involved in them as a commuter student? Or, if their schedule and yours do not mesh, is there a local civic group you might join that would give you the ability to grow, work informally with others, and assume responsibility as you learn?

In Your Words:
Making New Alliances

Give yourself the following assignment: Go to the Student Affairs Office at your college; look at your local newspaper; call your local Chamber of Commerce. List the activities and/or groups where you might find people whose experiences and dreams are like yours.

Write your ideas/list of places and activities in the space below:

_____
_____
_____
_____
_____
_____
_____

---

*How would you use the **Four LTL Thinking Tools** to solve problems you have in this area? If this is an area where you'd like to make some changes, turn to the Four LTL Thinking Tools exercise at the end of this chapter.*

DATING

Dating relationships can be very intense, with both parties expressing very powerful emotions. Here are some guidelines that can help you both grow:

◆ If you care about this person, show a basic acceptance of him/her. Don't try to change a romantic partner into someone more "acceptable" to you.

◆ Beginning a dating relationship with a person who has been your friend can be particularly difficult. If you start to become romantically interested in your friend, find ways (non-verbal if possible) to get clues about whether or not your interest would be reciprocated. And if you see that your friend wants to remain at the friendship level, continue to value that. Accept and respect your friend's decision. Don't daydream about ways to "make" him/her think of you romantically.

◆ If a friend shows more romantic interest than you have towards him/her, find ways (preferably non-verbal) to express how much you value him/her as a friend – but within your limits.

◆ Someone you are close to cares about your welfare, and vice versa. Don't force someone to be close to you; and don't be forced into uncomfortable situations. You can't "prove" you love someone by giving into something you're not prepared for. Anyone who requires this of you is not acting out of love.

◆ A person you date seriously should make you feel appreciated and secure – should raise, not lower, your self-esteem. If you continually feel put-upon, it's not love.

◆ Serious dating should be based on personal qualities and mutual caring. To choose someone because he/she is popular or good-looking is to risk feeling lonely in a relationship.

◆ If you're newly divorced, a return to dating can be very disorienting. The rules have changed since you were young. Intimacy of all kinds is expected sooner than it was the last time you were single. The most important rule is to be open, aware of your own needs and limitations, and communicate them clearly. Regardless of the norm, you are entitled to your own feelings and your own style.

◆ If you're a recent high school graduate, you're old enough for long-term relationships – but you're still growing and maturing. That can place stresses on a romance. Remember that you're both young, and have not yet grown to be all of what you will be. Your interests and life styles will change, and you may grow apart, as you go out into the world. Right now, look for mutual caring and growth, not necessarily permanence.

◆ Don't make a romance into a struggle or a "power" game, with one person dominating the other. Good relationships are balanced, with each person giving caring and support, and neither running the other's life.

How would you use the **Four LTL Thinking Tools** *to solve problems you have in this area? If this is an area where you'd like to make some changes, turn to the Four LTL Thinking Tools exercise at the end of this chapter.*

DIVERSITY:

RELATING TO OTHER GROUPS

We live in a society where much of the struggle over civil rights has moved from the courtroom to the classroom and the workplace. The concept of rights for non-traditional groups is an issue we all face daily, whatever groups we belong to. And the term "non-traditional" has acquired a wider meaning: It encompasses not only people of different cultures and ethnic or religious backgrounds, but also women, older persons, and the handicapped.

American society is experiencing a profound change. More than ever before, it is crucial that we call on and develop the skills of all of our people. Rapidly changing technology and a global marketplace mean that our industries must rely more on the skills and awareness of their workforce. At the same time, over the next decade the traditional mainstream majority employee, white males, will account for only 15% of the new entrants to our workforce.

Perhaps even more than the legal struggle for civil rights, these new economic realities may finally move this nation towards an appreciation and celebration of our differences. At the present time, these issues are here, today, on our college campuses.

If you are a member of a non-traditional group, college is a place where you may become more sensitized to your position as an "outsider." As a woman or member of an ethnic minority, you may be saddened or angered by words or behavior that exclude you. Even slights that are unintentional can hurt. If you attend a primarily majority-culture college, there are experiences which can make you feel isolated. For example, being the only African American in a large class of whites is not an easy situation. If you do well or badly, you feel – not unreasonably – that others will judge you by their assumptions about African Americans, or that they may later judge other African Americans by your behavior.

Facing issues raised by diversity may also challenge students who belong to the majority culture. In college, perhaps for the first time, these students may be "called" on their words or behaviors which suggest deep-seated prejudices. The initial denial of such prejudices may be followed by guilt, then anger: After all, you tell yourself, it's not your fault that injustice has been done by other members of your group or your sex.

There are prejudices – incorrect, biased assumptions – on all sides of this picture. At first, it may be hard to grasp that you have such prejudices. But you do; we all do. Awareness is the first step towards a larger, more inclusive humanity.

To be more aware of your own prejudices, take some data on yourself, and try the following thought experiments:

◆ If you're with members of your group, do you make jokes about people who are not in your group? Would you feel uncomfortable if you knew that others were joking about you in a similar way?

◆ If you're in a group that includes a person in a wheelchair, do you talk to, or about, that person? Do you meet that person's eyes in conversation?

◆ If you woke up tomorrow and you were a member of another group, how would you feel? How would you react to others' apparent displays of exclusivity?

◆ If you woke up tomorrow in a culture where women were the dominant group, which of your daily behaviors would you change? (Do the same thought experiment picturing African Americans and Hispanics as the dominant groups.)

◆ When members of a minority group, women, or handicapped persons display competence, do you find yourself thinking that they are exceptions to their group?

◆ As a woman or a member of a minority group, do you generally expect all men or members of the majority group to be insensitive to your situation?

◆ When you are in a conflict situation with someone who is not a member of your group, do you disregard this person's views? Do you tell yourself that this person's opinions are invalid, just a reflection of his/her group? (As in: "He's a man. What can you expect?")

To be more aware of your own potential for unfair bias, try the following exercise in class.

Classroom Simulation

Your teacher will divide the class into two groups. For example, Group A students wear clothing that contains red; members of Group B are not wearing any red clothing. Your teacher will then ask you to work together in sub-groups of 5–6 students – each containing members of both large groups. The sub-groups will work together on a common problem – like making suggestions about how to use a paper clip. Members of Group A are ignored; they are given no eye contact by members of Group B; their comments or suggestions are not acknowledged. Group B members also make disparaging remarks about the appearance of Group A members.

After 20–30 minutes, the situation is reversed: Group A members are privileged, while Group B members are ignored, etc.

This second section is followed by a debriefing, where all students discuss their experiences with this exercise. Your instructor will help you see the parallels between your experience in these groups and your daily experience with members of diverse groups.

Assignment

Apply the Four LTL Thinking Tools to your experiences with members of diverse groups. Ask yourself **questions** about your assumptions about and reactions to others; look at the **parts** of your interactions, and place yourself in the other person's shoes; if your contact with members of other groups is limited, set **goals** for yourself to broaden these contacts; take **feedback** on the changes you undergo as part of this process.

Don't stay isolated in your group. In an academic class, begin conversations with a person sitting next to you who is not a member of your group. (Try raising a neutral issue – something about the homework, the professor, or the course textbook.) At lunch, be courageous – don't always sit with people you know. Take risks: Make friends with people you've considered the "other." You'll find you have a lot in common with each other, and you'll begin to build a bridge to a better life.

SEXISM AND SEXUAL HARASSMENT

Sexism directed at women by men is very real. You have only to look at history books that fail to mention women's contributions in the professions and the arts – or the stifling social practices and active discrimination which long prevented women from realizing their talents. While women now make up the majority of college freshmen, sexism can still be found on American campuses: Women may be discouraged from careers in the sciences and mathematics; adult women returning to school may be told that they have too many responsibilities at home to attend college; women may be ignored in class, both by professors and by male classmates; women's ideas may not be taken as seriously as men's in seminar classes.

Sexual harassment is also a factor in society and on college campuses. While most sexual harassment is directed against women, men can also be the object of such treatment. What is sexual harassment? At it's most blatant level, it is the request that sexual favors be exchanged for something else – like a higher grade in class. More subtle sexual harassment can take many forms – a male looking at a woman's breasts while engaged in conversation; deliberately making provocative suggestions designed to make the object of harassment uncomfortable, etc.

Sexual harassment is against the law; there are also laws against deliberate discrimination on the basis of sex. If you feel that you have been the object of either sexual harassment or sexism, tell a friend or a counselor about the incident immediately. They will help you think through the issues, decide how you should respond. Should you talk directly to the person offending you? Is the matter serious enough to bring to authorities? The fact that you discussed the problem with others immediately after it occurred will provide support for your position if you decide to take formal action – indicating that what happened truly did offend you.

Applying LTL Thinking Tools
Relationships

Writing questions
Choose a personal relationship topic from this chapter. Write questions which the written material raised for you – either questions directly reflecting ideas we discussed – or questions that were not answered, but are important to you.

_____

_____

_____

_____

Focusing on goals
After writing your questions, you should be ready to focus on your goals in this area. What kinds of changes would you like to make in this area?

_____

_____

_____

_____

Breaking large tasks into manageable parts
Now that you're clearer about your goals, how do you want to break down the problem? What comes first? Write the order of changes that you think you can make in order of importance and/or how easily the changes might be made. Set some short-term goals.

_____

_____

_____

_____

Assessing your progress
How will you know if you're closer to meeting your short-term goals? Write down your short-term goals and take data on developments in this area.

_____

_____

_____

_____

Internet Exercise
Explore the Internet for websites related to "relationships."

1. Go to Yahoo! and click on a search engine like Webcrawler or Infoseek.
2. When you get to that search engine, click on "relationships."

For books on relationships, search "relationships" under Amazon.com or BarnesandNoble.com

A GAME OF IMAGINATION:

THE DINNER PARTY

We've talked about your relationships with others – and with yourself. And we've asked you to use the Four Thinking Tools to examine these relationships.

Here's another way to discover who you are – or want to be – with other people. Imagine yourself walking into a room filled with your heroes. They can be people in your life or from history – Alexander the Great, Henry David Thoreau, Clark Gable – anyone who you want to have in your room, at your dinner party.

What do you want to talk about with these people? What do you want them to say to each other? Ask each one of them to describe you. What characteristics do you hope they see in you?

Assignment

Think of a problem – personal, social, academic – that you might solve by applying the Four Thinking Tools. How can you apply them to your solve problem? Bring your example to class next time.

The LTL Journal

Continue your journal of your thoughts and feelings. How can the information in this chapter help you establish improved personal relationships?

Chapter 10:
BEING HEALTHY

You can't do your best at school if you're in poor shape physically and psychologically. There is increasing evidence that the connections between the body and the mind are very real. If you're under stress mentally, physically, or emotionally, you won't be able to think and learn well.

In this chapter you'll look at these areas and find ways to keep yourself healthy. You'll learn relaxation exercises to reduce stress. And you'll find ways to improve your eating habits and identify a useful exercise plan.

Treating yourself with care also relates to how you handle sex – emotionally and otherwise. You'll think through health issues related to sexual activity. You'll also read about the dangers of addictions: Alcohol, drugs, and cigarettes can all ruin your health and end your dreams. Finally, you'll learn to identify signs of depression and suicidal tendencies in those around you – and find out what you can do to help.

These are all important issues. We want you to take care of yourself – to be healthy and strong for the challenges ahead.

REDUCING STRESS

Stress is a fact of life for college students. Almost every aspect of your life is new. You're being continually tested, both formally and informally; you may have multiple responsibilities – at school, home, and work; and you're making decisions which may affect the rest of your life.

You may not always recognize when you're under stress. Especially in situations where there are no dramatic changes in your life, stress can slowly become a normal-seeming part of your life. Here's a checklist to determine if there's too much stress in your life:

◆ Are you sleeping poorly?

◆ Do you eat irregularly without enjoying your food?

◆ Do you engage in "binge" eating?

◆ Are you often irritable?

◆ Do you feel that you never have enough time to do what you have to do?

If any of these problems occur frequently, there's too much stress in your life.

What can be done to reduce stress?

If your stress is school-related, the LTL methods will solve much of that problem for you. You'll do better in college and feel better about yourself as a student. In particular, the LTL Task Management and Exam Preparation skills will help you reduce stress in daily life.

If you can't identify the source of your stress, you can help yourself deal with whatever seems to be the problem by doing short, frequent, relaxation exercises and physical workouts. We've included a detailed relaxation exercise on the next page. This exercise will help you deal more calmly with any anxiety-producing situation.

RELAXATION TECHNIQUES

A busy schedule can be very stressful – and the stress can make it harder for you to get things done. Here's a technique that will help you handle stress:

The 30-Second Stress Reduction Exercise

1. For practice at home and in public – while waiting for the instructor to pass out an exam, or just before making a presentation:

    ◆ Sit comfortably, with both feet on the floor and your hands resting on your thighs. You should have no bodily tension resulting from sitting at an angle, holding on to a pen, etc.

    ◆ Close your eyes and count backwards from 30 to 1. Breath very deeply from the abdomen, and count only when you let your breath out.

    ◆ Practice this skill at home until you can use it easily to relax.

◆ *Important:* During this practice, put your hands on your knees, each hand relaxed, but lightly touch the middle finger of each hand with the thumb. (Use one of the middle fingers, not the index finger which you use all the time whenever you pick up something. We're trying to establish a new response, so we need something – like touching a middle finger to your thumb – which is a little unusual. Your body will learn to pair this gesture with a relaxed state. Later, if you repeat this gesture in a stressed situation, you'll immediately feel more relaxed.)

If you do this exercise once a day, you'll feel more relaxed. You'll develop a conditioned response to relaxation, which you'll have access to during stressful times by touching your fingers together in the same way you do during your practice exercise.

The 15-Minute Stress Reduction Exercise

If you need more than a simple count to relax, take 10–15 minutes and practice the following method:

◆ Recall a pleasant time when you were feeling very relaxed, such as sunbathing on the beach, walking through the woods, petting your cat. Try to imagine how you felt then, hearing and "seeing" in your mind what you heard and saw. Relive the experience in full detail – color, sensations, smells.

◆ Take time with this, then carry the feeling into the future. Imagine yourself taking the exam the way you want to feel, feeling confident, using the LTL skills you practiced at home. Notice that your thoughts are clear, that you easily recall what you need to know. You can clearly "see" your Question Charts and Key Word Diagrams.

◆ Conclude with a slow count backwards from 5 to 1, gradually bringing the feeling to the present, feeling refreshed and ready.

Assignment

Practice these relaxation skills at home. Even ten minutes of daily practice will reduce your stress and help you move towards achieving your goals.

A STRESS MANAGEMENT EXERCISE

If you want to practice stress management on a regular basis, you may wish to record the following on an audio cassette:

Sit in a comfortable chair in a quiet, darkened room. Put both feet on the floor and rest your hands on your thighs. Close your eyes, and feel your body relax.

Take a slow, relaxed, deep breath for every count.

Imagine you are opening a door, and will descend a flight of stairs. As you walk down the stairs, your body gets heavier and heavier.

You're walking down the stairs now.
10... 9... 8... 7... 6... 5... 4... 3... 2... 1

At the bottom of the stairs is a small door. Open the door, and you will see a lovely garden. There is a small pond in the middle of the garden, and tall trees surround it. The air is light, the sky is blue. Flowers are everywhere, in all colors. You sit down in the garden and feel wonderful. Look around. Feel the sun on your shoulders. Feel the relaxation spread through your body.

Slowly raise your left hand: 1... 2... 3... 4... 5...
Now let your hand drop on your thigh.

When you awake, whenever you're beginning to feel tense, lift your hand and let it drop on your thigh. You will immediately feel calm and relaxed.

For special situations, add the following:

When preparing for exams
You will clearly visualize your Question Charts and Key Word Diagrams during the exam.

If you're anxious about seeing an old boyfriend/girlfriend:

You will feel confident and relaxed when you see ___ .

If you're preparing to give a talk
You will talk clearly and confidently, remembering everything in your Key Word Diagram as you talk.

Now you're going to leave the garden for awhile. Remember: You can come back to it whenever you want.

See yourself standing up and moving towards the door of the garden. The door is open, and you will walk up the stairs. As you walk up the stairs, you will feel lighter and lighter.

1... 2... 3... 4... 5... 6... 7... 8... 9... 10

Now open your eyes. You feel calm and relaxed. Sit for a moment and relax.

Student Voices
Eddie Smith

Learning to Learn helped me a lot. Because of LTL, my grades are a whole lot higher.

I went to Old Miss just out of high school. I got up there and I partied too much, so I couldn't stay in school. Then I went to East Central Community College. I did the work, but I found out that I didn't know how to study. My GPA was only about 2.3.

I took LTL when I came to Meridian, and it made a big difference. My GPA is a letter grade higher – about 3.5 on a 4-point scale. And it's more than just grades. I notice in class that I'm a better listener now. When the teacher's talking, I'm thinking about what she's saying and asking questions in my head. I'm going to continue using LTL. I'm not going to give up something that most definitely has worked so well for me.

Assignment

Use this tape once or twice a day to begin with. You may find that your increased calmness helps you sort out what's bothering you. If you're still feeling stressed – especially if you have answered "yes" to several of the signs of stress we noted above – make an appointment with a counselor at your school's Counseling Office.

Physical exercise is also a great way to get rid of stress. Do stretch exercises. Put on your sneakers and run around the block. Go to the gym and shoot baskets or slam a ball against the wall with a tennis racket. Take a bike ride, or swim a couple of laps in the local YMCA pool. Just a small amount of time engaging in vigorous activity does wonders for getting rid of tension.

Applying LTL Thinking Tools
Managing Stress

Writing questions

Write some questions that the previous material raised for you – either questions directly reflecting the material (perhaps building on our questions), or questions which were not addressed, but are important to you.

_____

_____

_____

Focusing on goals

After writing your questions, you should be ready to focus on your goals in this area. What changes would you like to make related to reducing stress in your daily life?

_____

_____

_____

Dividing large tasks into smaller parts

What comes first? Write the order of changes that you think you can make in order of importance and/or how easily the changes might be made. Set some short-term goals.

_____

_____

_____

Assessing your progress

How will you know if you're closer to meeting your short-term goals? Write down your short-term goals and take data on developments in this area.

_____

_____

_____

Empower Yourself
Taking Control of Your Life

The problem: You may be very clear about your goal, but the process of getting there looks too hard. So you decide to give up your goal – and drift without a plan, seeing where things will lead you. For example, imagine you'd like to be an accountant, but you hate studying. Ask yourself: *"What don't I like about studying?"* Your answers might be, *"I'd rather be out on the basketball court. And just studying is hard. I want to be out doing things with other people, period."*

Solving problems with LTL. You'll break down a complex task – like studying for an accounting exam – into *smaller parts* – and play basketball as a reward during a *break*. You'll find other students with similar goals – and socialize by *testing each other* on exam questions you and the others predict. That is, you'll find ways to make the *means* to your goals both exciting and rewarding.

In Your Words:

Working with another student, examine a non-academic goal that you think might be very hard to reach.

Try this:
◆ Break up the goal into sub-goals: What comes first? Next?

◆ Find a way to have fun and reward yourself for achieving each sub-goal (either by promising yourself something you'd like when it's done, or by making it into an LTL "prediction" game, where the "game" part interests you).

◆ Don't try to achieve perfection, but when you've reached a sub-goal, try to figure out how you'd make the process of getting there more enjoyable next time.

◆ Don't forget to take breaks and reward yourself.

◆ Don't get stuck with one plan. Continue to look for what's working and take feedback on how to achieve what you're after – while having a sense of fun and progress.

◆ Remember that no pre-planned, prescription for action will last over time. No static structure is correct forever. You'll need a *dynamic* structure – one that can be changed when you have new information. The basic idea here is that you're more likely to stick to a long-range, hard-to-achieve goal if you not only break it up into parts, but also find ways to enjoy the *process* of getting there.

THE FOOD YOU EAT

Nutritional research has shown that there's a relationship between diet and the risk of getting cancer, heart disease, and diabetes. Since at college you may be on your own for the first time, setting habits of a lifetime, we'd like you to know about some of our suggestions:

◆ Reduce total fat and calorie intake. For example, avoid lots of red meat, sugar rich foods, and fast foods.

◆ Eat more complex carbohydrates, both starch and fiber. (Beans, peas, carrots, broccoli, and bran foods are in these categories.)

◆ Eat plenty of fruits, greens, and yellow vegetables.

◆ Don't let your diet become monotonous. Experiment with different combinations of foods and different spices. Find ways to enjoy foods that are good for you. Recipes from exotic countries can make good food taste terrific. Try cooking up some of these at a friend's apartment or a dorm kitchen. If you're eating institutional food, develop a taste for fruits and interesting salad combinations. It will pay off in more energy now and a healthier, longer life.

An Easy, Fad-Free Diet

Americans are often obsessed by dieting. They're concerned with overeating, but they overeat. They gain too much weight and become worried enough to try crash or fad diets. However, an extreme reduction in calories will not result in maintained weight loss, and may undermine the metabolism, causing a more rapid weight gain when normal eating is resumed. *The key to a healthy weight-control plan is to develop an interest in foods that are fun to eat and that are good for you.* Lots of different spices and unusual combinations of tastes and textures will help you love healthy food.

We've suggested some of the foods that are good for you in the section above.

Here's a way of eating that will help you stay healthy:

◆ Don't eat too little. In fact, stuff yourself with soups, salads, protein (lean meat, chicken, fish), and vegetables. You'll be so full that you won't have room for dessert. And you'll never feel food-deprived, the feeling which leads to dramatic diet-breaking and resumed weight-gain.

◆ Reduce your consumption of breads, high fat-content fried foods, and sugar-laden foods.

◆ Try it. What do you have to lose?

Eating Disorders

In this society importance has been placed on getting and keeping slim. When this becomes an obsession, and for people who are perfectionists by nature, eating disorders can occur. The most common of these are anorexia and bulimia. Anorexia is a form of self-starvation characterized by the person's inability to recognize that unhealthy weight loss is taking place. Even a severely malnourished, 80-pound woman (most anorectics are women) will often deny that she has an eating problem. A bulimic person binges on foods, often high calorie foods, then purges herself (again, most are women) by vomiting. If you recognize these symptoms in yourself or in someone close to you, it's important for you to know the medical consequences of these behaviors. Tooth enamel loss, damaged esophagus and salivary glands can result from frequent vomiting. Even more seriously, both bulimia and anorexia can lead to interrupted menstrual cycles, muscle weakening, and damaged internal organs, including the liver, kidneys, and digestive organs. Death may result from irregular heart rhythms caused by the body's fluid imbalance.

If you or a friend of yours is a victim of an eating disorder, contact your school's counseling office. These disorders are serious but treatable.

EXERCISING FOR YOUR HEALTH

Do you have any regular exercise program? Do you swim, jog, play tennis, use whatever sports facilities your college has? Here are some of the benefits of such a program:

◆ You'll have more energy to do everything, and you'll feel more positive.

◆ You'll be more relaxed, less stressed. You'll sleep better, digest your food better, and feel irritable less often. So you'll have fewer fights with your roommate, boy/girlfriend, and parents.

◆ When you begin to feel angry or frustrated, you'll have an outlet for getting rid of the negative energy and be better able to sort through what's really bothering you.

In Your Words:
An Exercise Plan

In the space below, list exercise activities that you enjoy – and that you'd have time for, now that you're at college. How could you fit these activities into your life?

_____

_____

_____

_____

_____

What's My Best Weight For Good Health and a Long Life?

Statistics compiled by life insurance companies show that the following weights are most likely to be associated with longevity. The weights shown are measured in pounds, and are for different heights and body frames, when dressed in indoor clothing.

MEN			
Height	Small Frame	Medium Frame	Large Frame
5'2"	128-134	131-141	138-150
5'3"	130-136	133-143	140-153
5'4"	132-138	135-145	142-156
5'5"	134-140	137-148	144-160
5'6"	136-142	139-151	146-164
5'7"	138-145	142-154	149-168
5'8"	140-148	145-157	152-172
5'9"	142-151	148-160	155-176
5'10"	144-154	151-163	158-180
5'11"	146-157	154-166	161-184
6'0"	149-160	157-170	164-188
6'1"	152-164	160-174	168-192
6'2"	155-168	164-178	172-197
6'3"	158-172	167-182	176-202
6'4"	162-176	171-187	181-207

WOMEN			
Height	Small Frame	Medium Frame	Large Frame
4'10"	102-111	109-121	118-131
4'11"	103-113	111-123	120-134
5'0"	104-115	113-126	122-137
5'1"	106-118	115-129	125-140
5'2"	108-121	118-132	128-143
5'3"	111-124	121-135	131-147
5'4"	114-127	124-138	134-151
5'5"	117-130	127-141	137-155
5'6"	120-133	130-144	140-159
5'7"	123-136	133-147	143-163
5'8"	126-139	136-150	146-167
5'9"	129-142	139-153	149-170
5'10"	132-145	142-156	152-173
5'11"	135-148	145-159	155-176
6'0"	138-151	148-162	158-179

Applying LTL Thinking Tools
Food and Fitness

Writing questions
Write some questions which the previous material raised for you – either questions directly reflecting the material (perhaps building on our questions), or questions which were not addressed, but are important to you.

_____

_____

_____

_____

Focusing on goals
After writing your questions, you should be ready to focus on your goals in this area. What changes would you like to make related to reducing stress in your daily life?

_____

_____

_____

_____

Dividing large tasks into smaller parts
What comes first? Write the order of changes that you think you can make in order of importance and/or how easily the changes might be made. Set some short-term goals in this area.

_____

_____

_____

_____

Assessing your progress
How will you know if you're closer to meeting your short-term goals?

_____

_____

_____

_____

THE QUESTION OF SEX

Should you or shouldn't you? It seems from all the media hype that everyone over the age of seventeen is sexually active. But this is not so, and should only be so for you at the *time* and in the *way* you want it to be. Here are some things to consider:

Sex is more than two bodies meeting. It's all the good things you've read and heard about only when it's an expression of shared intimacy and caring. Otherwise, it's a pretty lonely business.

◆ Do you feel close enough to your partner to share your deepest feelings? Does he/she share equally with you?

◆ Can you talk about anything with that person – especially including birth control methods?

◆ Would you – do you – feel close to and happy with that person in non-sexual settings?

◆ Do you feel pressured into physical situations? Do you feel that, as a "macho" guy, you ought to place pressure on your partner? Or that as a woman, you have to prove your "sophistication?"

◆ Do you use sex to "punish" yourself? Many young people feel insecure about their social place, and express their insecurity through "sleeping around." That's really a call for help. If you're in that situation, make an appointment with someone from your campus Counseling Center to help you feel more comfortable with yourself and others.

A Special Caution

If you're at a residential school, it's probably the first time you've lived away from home. As we've said, people in that situation often feel they have to "prove" something to themselves and others about their new status. Be aware. Don't let yourself get pressed into something you don't want to do.

If you've taken these issues into account, and shared them in open discussion with your partner, there are some additional matters to consider on the following pages: birth control, sexually transmitted diseases, what you should know about AIDS, and how to protect yourself from sexual assault.

Birth Control
Did you know that:

◆ 20% of all children born in this country are raised by teenagers.

◆ Most teen marriages don't survive more than five years.

◆ Pregnancy is the most frequently given reason for women dropping out of school.

◆ Prematurity and low birth rate are substantially increased when the mothers are teenagers.

◆ College-aged young women are approaching their most fertile period in life. Since the time of ovulation is not easy to pin-point accurately, and sperm can live for up to three days, unprotected sex is a recipe for pregnancy.

If you're close enough to be sexually intimate, then you should be close enough to talk about the possible consequences of your intimacy.

Birth control is the responsibility of both men and women – neither should assume that the issue is "taken care of." If you decide to be sexually active, and have a partner you feel close to, you might consider visiting a birth control center together. Here are some of the most commonly used birth control methods:

◆ *Condoms and foam* can be purchased at any drug store, and are 98% effective when used together every time you have intercourse. They are significantly less effective when used separately. For maximal effectiveness, carefully follow the written instructions on their use.

◆ *I.U.D.s or Intrauterine Devices* must be fitted by a doctor. They are 95–97% effective in preventing pregnancy. They're not for everyone. Your doctor will be able to tell you if you're a good candidate for this form of birth control.

◆ *Diaphragms* must be fitted by a physician or nurse practitioner, and carefully placed each time they are used. Also, diaphragms must be used with spermicidal jelly. If a diaphragm is not used every time, a woman runs a 10-fold risk of becoming pregnant.

◆ *Birth control pills* are synthetic hormones. Taken as prescribed by a physician, they are 99% effective. However, the pill is only effective if it is taken every day of a 21-day cycle. If one or two days are missed, you should consider the pill ineffective for the remainder of that cycle, and use other birth control methods.

Sexually Transmitted Diseases

Serious sexually transmitted diseases (STDs) range from the potentially devastating but usually treatable – like chlamydia, gonorrhea or syphilis, to the incurable – like herpes, or fatal – like AIDS. It's important to realize that although you may be a "nice" person, no one is immune to these diseases. *One exposure is all that's needed.*

Here are some things you need to know about the most common treatable STDs, chlamydia, syphilis, and gonorrhea. At present, chlamydia is the nation's most common venereal disease: Several surveys indicate that one in six sexually active teenage girls has the disease. Moreover, teenage girls are most at risk for developing serious complications from the disease. A single untreated bout with chlamydia can lead to infertility in women. The symptoms of syphilis and gonorrhea will disappear over time. But untreated syphilis can irreversibly damage your brain, internal organs, and nervous system; untreated gonorrhea can result in permanent sterility.

At the present time, there is no cure for genital herpes, which is related to cancer of the cervix. Genital herpes may also be transmitted through oral sex with a person having an outbreak of oral herpes.

The most effective ways of protecting yourself against any form of venereal disease are:

◆ Using condoms during sex, even during foreplay.

◆ Reducing the number of your sexual partners. Monogamous relationships are helpful for both emotional and physical well-being.

While there are often genital symptoms for STDs, you may be infected but symptom-free. So if you've been sexually active with people who are active with others, get yourself checked out at your campus or local health center.

In Your Words:
A Heathly Approach

Imagine that you're about to talk with a young person you care about – a younger brother, sister, or cousin – about having a responsible approach to sexual activity. In your own words, what would you say to this young person to help him or her be appropriately careful in this area?

_____

_____

_____

_____

_____

What Every College Student Should Know About AIDS

> *"Unless it is possible to know with absolute certainty that your sex partner is not infected with AIDS, through sex or through drug use, you're taking a chance of becoming infected."*
> Former U.S. Surgeon General C. Everett Koop
>
> *"Everyone, particularly sexually active youngsters, should know that having sex without a condom and/or spermicidal jelly (which can help prevent a woman from being infected) is risking your life."*
> Robert Bazell, NBC Science Correspondent

Acquired Immune Deficiency Syndrome (AIDS) is a breakdown of the body's immune system which appears to be invariably fatal and which is presently incurable. The panic created in the press about AIDS has led many people to disregard the most important fact about the disease: It is not casually contracted. *Not a single case of AIDS has been attributed to non-intimate contact with an infected person.* You can't contract the disease by going to dinner with, sitting next to, or sharing a swimming pool with an AIDS victim.

AIDS is transmitted through exchanges of bodily fluids – through dirty needles used by intravenous drug users, and through sexual intercourse. AIDS may be transmitted through sex with both men and women. If you have unprotected sex with someone who has had other unprotected sexual contacts, you may be at risk.

You can decrease your risk of getting AIDS by

◆ Reducing your number of different sexual partners.
◆ Using condoms during sex, including foreplay.
◆ Knowing about the lifestyle of your partner and avoiding sexual contact with people who place themselves at risk (intravenous drug users, and people who have had contact with prostitutes, are bisexual or are otherwise promiscuous).
◆ Asking about the health status of your partners.
◆ Eliminating your use of illegal drugs and reducing your alcohol intake – both of these can weaken your body's resistance to infection. Especially eliminate use of inhalants and intravenous drugs.
◆ Not sharing toothbrushes, razors, or other objects that might be contaminated with infected blood.

If you think you might have contracted an STD, get tested immediately at your college or local health center. Early treatment can provide a complete cure for most STDs – and there are new, increasingly effective, treatments for AIDS. For the latest information on STDs and AIDS, call
◆ National STD Hotline (800) 227-8922
◆ National AIDS Hotline (800) 342-2437

Or visit the website of the Center for Disease Control at http://www.cdc.gov/

Protecting Yourself From Sexual Assault

Here are some things you should keep in mind to help reduce your chances of becoming the victim of a sexual attack:

Attacks by Strangers

◆ Avoid dark secluded places.

◆ If you must go out late at night, be sure you are accompanied by a friend.

◆ Keep your car door locked when driving at night, and always park in a well-lit area.

◆ Always stay alert when you're alone. Walk purposefully and with direction. People who look like they're daydreaming appear more vulnerable to a potential attacker.

◆ Report suspicious activities to your campus police.

Date Rape

In most sexual attacks, the victim knows the attacker. Some people justify "date rape" to themselves in a variety of ways – "She was asking for it," "She should have known what to expect," "She's a big girl now." This is wrong. Forcing another person to engage in sexual behavior is a crime, punishable by jail. *There is no excuse for attacking another person.*

Take "No" for an answer. Do not give yourself an excuse for violating another human being.

To minimize the chance of being a victim of date rape:

◆ Avoid being alone with a person who is intoxicated by liquor or drugs. People in these situations cannot be reasoned with.

◆ If you do not want to have sex with a date, (one who is not drunk or stoned, whom you can talk with), let him know firmly. Tell him that this is something you do not want, that you will report him to campus authorities and the police. Say "No" – and also give clear non-verbal cues. You'll rarely be attacked by a friend whose mind is clear of liquor and drugs and who knows that you mean no.

◆ Practice saying "no" in your head before a date, if that is what you want. Rehearse what you'd say or do if pressured to have unwanted sex.

A person who places you under strong pressure to have sex is disregarding your interests – and you. And a person who you know relatively casually may have had numerous sexual partners. Unprotected sex with that person can place you at risk for an STD – including AIDS.

ADDICTIONS 1: ALCOHOL

A Dozen Myths About Drinking

Myth 1 *Drugs are the real substance abuse problem in this country.*
Truth: True. And the biggest drug problem is alcohol abuse. Alcohol is a drug that acts as a depressant on the central nervous system. About 300,000 Americans are addicted to heroin. But 9,000,000 are addicted to alcohol.

Myth 2 *People get sick or drunk from switching drinks.*
Truth: Switching drinks doesn't matter too much. The usual cause of these problems is drinking too much.

Myth 3 *You can't get drunk or become alcoholic if you stick to beer.*
Truth: The effect may be a little slower, and you may need to drink more beer or wine than hard liquor, but the effect is the same. If you drink the same amount of alcohol, whatever the source, the level of alcohol in your blood will be the same.

Myth 4 *Only 25% of fatal highway accidents are related to alcohol consumption.*
Truth: 50% of all fatal highway accidents are alcohol-related. And an even greater percentage of non-fatal accidents are linked to alcohol.

Myth 5 *Women usually do not become alcoholic.*
Truth: Today almost 30% of alcoholics are women.

Myth 6 *Alcohol will keep you warm. It's good insulation at football games.*
Truth: No. Alcohol makes your blood vessels expand and your body loses its natural heat.

Myth 7 *"Social" drinkers don't become alcoholic.*
Truth: Not true. You can become just as drunk and just as dependent on drink whether you drink alone or with others.

Myth 8 *People are more enjoyable when they've had something to drink.*
Truth: Drunkenness is not any funnier than any other illness or disability. And people who are drunk are often more hostile and dangerous than they are sober: Half of all murders and one-third of all suicides are alcohol-related.

Myth 9 *A few drinks won't damage an unborn child.*
Truth: Wrong. Research shows that as few as 2–4 drinks on any one day in a 9-month pregnancy carries a 10% risk of fetal abnormality. Ten drinks on any day of a pregnancy results in a 75% risk of delivering an abnormal child. Fetal alcohol syndrome is the third leading cause of mental retardation.

Myth 10 *Drinking coffee or taking a cold shower will sober you up quickly.*
Truth: Your body oxidizes alcohol at a constant rate; the liver burns alcohol at a rate of 1/2 ounce of alcohol (one can of beer or one mixed drink) an hour. Time is the only thing that matters in getting sober.

Myth 11 *People are more relaxed and drive better after a few drinks.*
Truth Alcohol affects judgment. Studies have shown that even professional drivers' abilities diminish after 2–4 drinks.

Myth 12 *A Bloody Mary in the morning is a great cure for a hangover.*
Truth: There is no "cure" for a hangover. And drinking in the morning is more likely to produce intoxication later in the day, since there's less food in the stomach to slow down absorption.

Questions and Answers About Drinking

How can you tell if you're a problem drinker?
◆ Do you drink often to the point of getting drunk?
◆ Do you drink more than your friends?
◆ Do you feel that you "need a drink" whenever you're under pressure?
◆ Do you drink alone?
◆ Do you skip classes because of drinking?
◆ Have you ever had a problem with the police related to your drinking?
◆ Do you often feel embarrassed by what you did when you were drinking?
◆ Do you have drinking-related blackouts?
◆ Do you have difficulty putting a limit on your drinking or find that you get drunk even when you try to stay sober?
◆ Do your friends tell you that you drink too much?

What about drinking and driving?
If you're drunk, don't drive. Someone in your group should be the "designated driver" – someone who has *not* been drinking. If you have no designated driver, spend the night on a friend's couch. Or call someone you know or a taxi to get home if you're drunk.
◆ 50% of all fatal highway accidents are alcohol-related.
◆ 75% of all all-terrain vehicle fatalities are alcohol-related.
◆ 20–37% of all emergency-room trauma victims involve alcohol.

You'll even have difficulty with sports activities. For example:
◆ 40% of all drowning accidents involve alcohol.
◆ 40%–50% of youth diving injuries involve alcohol.

How can you help a friend who drinks too much?
◆ Don't be judgmental. Show that you care, expect resistance and denial, and offer specific suggestions about where to go for help.
◆ Before mentioning this topic with your friend, find out who can help. (e.g., Call your local Alcoholics Anonymous chapter.)

What if there's an alcohol-related medical emergency?

◆ Keep calm. Being too anxious can make the problem worse.

◆ Don't give your friend food, drink, or medication that might induce vomiting, which could result in choking.

◆ Keep the person still, and get immediate medical help.

◆ Call your school's infirmary, police, or a local hospital.

◆ Monitor your friend's breathing; don't put the person in a cold shower. The shock might cause him/her to pass out.

◆ Do not provoke the person. Keep your distance and act calmly. Intoxicated people are often dangerous to themselves and others.

What if you're giving a party but don't want people to get drunk?

◆ Perrier with a twist of lime looks just as sophisticated as an alcoholic drink and causes a lot less damage. Try serving non-alcoholic beverages, and don't stock hard liquor. Most people really don't want to get drunk.

◆ Have lots of small things to eat — trays of cheese and peanuts are especially good, since they're high in protein. For some people, food can be a substitute for drinking.

◆ Clear the floor for dancing. It's hard to get drunk when you're busy doing something else. And, if people dance at your party, it will be more important to dance well — and to keep dancing — than to stand around fading out into an alcoholic haze.

ADDICTIONS 2: DRUGS

The most widely used drugs today are marijuana ("pot," "grass") and cocaine ("coke"). You know that the use of drugs is illegal. If you know about these drugs' physical and psychological effects, you'll understand how they can affect your health.

Marijuana appears to slow down the world around the user. It slows down the user's reactions and coordination, so it's really dangerous to use when driving. Unfortunately, the effects of the drug can last 10-12 hours after the initial "high," so the user remains at risk as a driver long after the drug's effects seem to have disappeared. Studies show that marijuana damages lungs. Marijuana tars contain 50% more carcinogens than do high-tar cigarettes.

Marijuana affects sex hormone levels, which is especially dangerous for adolescents. It can strain the heart, since the drug results in an increase in heart rate up to 160 beats per minute.

Cocaine results in a high which is quickly followed by severe depression. There's a danger of overdose when coke is injected or smoked (in the form of rock cocaine, or "crack").

Cocaine can short-circuit the body's electrical system, resulting in sudden death. There is no antidote to the direct stimulation to the brain produced by this effect of cocaine. For example, if the basketball player Len Bias had suffered this effect of cocaine in a hospital emergency room, nothing could have been done to save him.

"Designer drugs" are chemical alterations of illegal drugs. They're tailor-made to have effects similar to those of illegal drugs. Making designer drugs is a way that people in the underground drug trade have of staying one step ahead of the law: If a particular drug is illegal, they make a similar one, different enough chemically so that there's a time lapse between the drug's manufacture and its classification as illegal. But legal or not, one dose of a drug with the "wrong" manageable parts can cause irreparable damage to the brain.

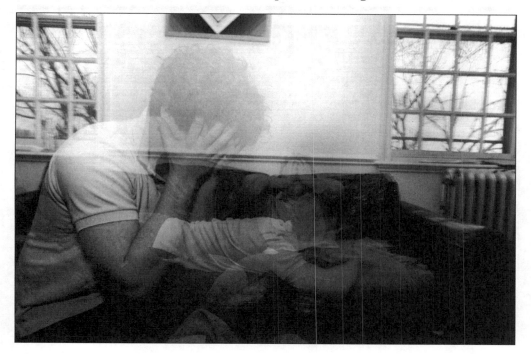

Myth: *If you've taken cocaine without ill effects, you won't have a problem with it.*

Truth: For a first-time or a 100th time cocaine user, the sudden-death syndrome may occur.

Myth: *Cocaine is not addictive.*

Truth: Because of the drug's direct effect on the pleasure center of the brain, it is the most highly addictive drug known to man. In an experiment with monkeys given the choice between cocaine and food, the monkeys chose to starve to death rather than give up cocaine.

IF YOU NEED HELP TO BEAT ALCOHOL OR DRUGS. . .

Go to your school's counseling office or call your local telephone information for the number of one of the following treatment centers in your area. We've listed the national number where available:

Alcohol 24-hour Hot Line:	(800) 252-6465
Cocaine Anonymous:	(213) 839-1141
Tough Love:	(800) 333-1069
Alcoholics Anonymous World Services:	(212) 870-3400
Local chapter of Alcoholics Anonymous:	See your Yellow Pages
Narcotics Anonymous:	See your Yellow Pages

ADDICTIONS 3: CIGARETTES
– You're dying for a smoke

Millions of Americans have quit smoking for some very good reasons:

◆ Men who smoke less than 1/2 pack a day have a death rate 60% higher than non-smokers. The rate increases with the number of cigarettes smoked: 2 or more packs a day means a death rate 120% above normal.

◆ The lung cancer rate of women has doubled in ten years due to increases in women smoking cigarettes over the last 20 years.

◆ The major health risks for smokers are heart disease (cigarette smokers have 70% more heart attacks than nonsmokers) and lung cancer (which is almost entirely caused by cigarette smoking).

If you're impressed by these facts, and want to stop smoking, here are some tips on quitting from the American Cancer Society:

◆ 50% of successful quitters did it cold turkey; the other 50% quit gradually. The first 48 hours are critical for most people. Once you pass them, it will be easier each day. So pick the tips that suit you.

◆ Smoke one less cigarette each day.

◆ Make each cigarette a special decision – and put off making the decision.

◆ Don't give up cigarettes completely. Carry one with you in case of need. You'll find you're saving it permanently.

◆ Don't tell yourself you're quitting "forever." Stop for a day. Then try quitting for another day – and the next day, and the next day.

◆ Tell your friends and family you're quitting. A public commitment bolsters will-power.

◆ Pick Q (Quit) Day and quit.

◆ When you stop smoking, get rid of all cigarettes, ashtrays, matches, etc.

◆ Keep a supply of chewing gum, cough drops, carrot sticks, etc.

◆ Nervousness, hunger, etc. are signs of the body's readjustment. If you find these side effects hard to manage, ask your doctor or your college's health service for help.

Join the 33,000,000 Americans who have quit. You can too!

Controlling Addictions

Writing questions

Write some questions which the previous material raised for you – either questions directly reflecting the material (perhaps building on our questions), or questions which were not addressed, but are important to you.

_____

_____

_____

_____

Focusing on goals

After writing your questions, you should be ready to focus on your goals in this area. What changes would you like to make related to controlling addictions in your daily life?

_____

_____

_____

_____

Breaking large tasks into manageable parts

What comes first? Write the order of changes that you think you can make in order of importance and/or how easily the changes might be made. Set some short-term goals in this area.

_____

_____

_____

_____

Assessing your progress

How will you know if you're closer to meeting your short-term goals?

_____

_____

_____

_____

Internet Exercise

Explore the Internet for websites related to "health."

1. Go to Yahoo! and click on a search engine like Webcrawler or Infoseek.
2. When you get to that search engine, click on "health."

LENDING A HELPING HAND

Good mental health also means helping others. In this section, we'll talk about some methods you can use to help others who are in trouble.

What Are the Signs of Depression or Suicidal Tendencies?

If a friend is showing some of these symptoms, he or she may be going through a major depression. Since suicide is the third leading cause of death among teenagers, it's important to be aware of these signs in others:

◆ Noticeable change in eating and sleeping habits
◆ Withdrawal from friends and family
◆ Persistent boredom
◆ Decline in quality of school work
◆ Violent or rebellious behavior
◆ Running away
◆ Drug and alcohol abuse
◆ Sudden shifts in mood from euphoric to depressed
◆ Unusual neglect of personal appearance
◆ Difficulty concentrating in conversation and work
◆ Radical personality change
◆ Psychosomatic complaints
◆ Conversation about suicide, either personal or in the abstract
◆ Evidence of mental confusion – disoriented in time or place, delusional, bewildered, responding inappropriately to conversation or events.

Depression is a both a physical and psychological state. It may be caused by purely physical factors, such as anemia, or psychological factors, such as personal loss (the death of a friend, the end of a romance or marriage), feelings of failure (poor academic or athletic performance), or a combination of these. Depression is almost always curable and suicide is usually preventable. But you are not a professional, and cannot improve the situation by yourself. If you notice the signs of depression we have noted above, seek out someone at your school's Counseling Office and make a referral for your friend. Your friend may not be willing to seek help on his/her own, but the Counseling Office people will have good ideas about how to "reach" him or her. Finally, be aware of warning signals: You're starting to avoid your friend (perhaps because his/her depression is beginning to "get to you"), or you're trying too hard to help your friend. In these cases, the situation is getting risky. Seek professional help as soon as you recognize this pattern.

The LTL Journal

Continue your journal of your thoughts and feelings. How can the information in this chapter help you have more control over your life?

Chapter 11:
GOING BACK TO SCHOOL

You're returning to school with life experience – and with a certain amount of baggage. How will all of that fit into what's needed for success in college?

Do You Belong in College?

Going back to school is scary. Will you be out of place among mostly young adults just out of high school? Will you be able to take tests, write papers, study new information – especially if you hated school before? Will college just take too long – and is it worth it?

Let's look at these issues one at a time.

Changing Student Populations

The face of the "average" college student is changing. According to the Census Bureau and the Department of Education, 40% of all college students are over 25 years old. This number will increase to 50% by the year 2000. More than 70% of part-time college students are 25 or older; and 80% of all college students are commuters. So you have plenty of company.

Succeeding in College

You may have done poorly in school before. Maybe you put off studying; didn't do assigned readings; completed writing assignments only at the last minute; and hated taking exams.

But you're in luck. You're using the Learning to Learn® system, which the U.S. Department of Education found is the most effective learning improvement program for college students. LTL is the *only* student success program that has a strong, long-term impact on college students' grades and retention through graduation.

For example, if you're a community college student, by taking LTL you're ***twice as likely to graduate from college*** than you would be if you used another learning improvement system.

Also, studies show that adults returning to school often perform *better* than students just out of high school. Why? Because adults come to college with a background of experiences. They often take crises in stride better than young students do. They look for solutions to problems, and apply what they learn beyond school – to personal problems and workplace problems. Adults have learned to be more independent. They question authority – and what they're learning – from a stronger, more realistic base. Adults returning to school also tend to be highly motivated: They have high expectations of themselves and their instructors. For all of these reasons, many college teachers find that teaching adult learners is more interesting and more rewarding than is teaching young students just out of high school.

Will College Take Too Long?

Many traditional and nontraditional college students now take more than four years to complete college. Lots of students work, take time off from college, and take reduced college loads. Many colleges accommodate these students by introducing accelerated courses, where students learn a semester's worth of information in a shorter, but more academically intense, time period.

You may also be able to get college credit for knowledge you bring to school. Many colleges accept college credit through **prior learning assessment**. Through this process, you may find that you've completed degree requirements through learning on the job. For example, you might get credit in sociology, social work, or psychology for work you've done in a human service agency, or your on-the-job training in computers might result in three academic credits in computer science.

Or, you may get college credit by taking tests which show your mastery of one or more subjects. So if you've been reading widely in a particular subject-matter – for example, if you're kind of a history "buff"– you can earn college credits by passing tests in the **College Level Examination Program** (CLEP). In fact, you can earn as much as 30 semester hours – one full academic year – by passing several of these subject-area CLEP tests.

Anyway, what do you mean by "too long?" If you put off going back to school because you think it will take too long, you'll be further away from your eventual goal in 2–3 years than you are now.

Is College Worth The Effort?

Are you happy at work now? Is the work itself satisfying? Do you have job security? Are you in line for advancement? Are you making a good living?

If you can answer "Yes" to all of these questions, college may fulfill your personal goals – but you may not need college for *practical* reasons.

But in today's changing economy, where more jobs require more skills, you probably can't answer "Yes" to all of these questions. Some studies indicate that most jobs will require at least 2 years of post-secondary education by the year 2000 – which is just around the corner. There are new technologies, and newly created jobs to meet the needs of these technologies. And with frequent company restructuring, the "survivors" are usually those with the most skills. Further, you're more likely to be considered for promotions if you have a college degree.

Can you afford college? The cost of a 4-year degree ranges from about $22,000 (full-time; public, non-residential institution) to as much as $120,000 (private, residential institution). But college graduates earn an average of **$60,000** more than high school graduates for ***every five years they are in the workforce***. Can you afford *not* to go to college?

Student Voices

Cheryl Thompson

I went back to school this year, at the age of 38, a month after my husband and I were separated. I could have just gotten a job, but I have a child to raise. The only way I could see raising my child in the lifestyle we'd been accustomed to was to go back to school and further my education.

I was terrified when my classes started. Not only had I been out of school for 20 years; I'd also been a homemaker, so I really hadn't been out of the house for years.

I took LTL the first semester at college, and it was a lifesaver. In high school, I never had to study, so I didn't know how to do it. With LTL, I learned how to study, and how to fit everything into the available time I had. LTL really paid off. I'm getting all A's, and I really enjoy school.

This summer, I entered a state and national competition in marketing, which is my major. My area was competency-based events. Fifty per cent of the grade was a test; the rest was role-play, where you were given a situation and then had a few minutes to figure out how you'd handle it. I used my LTL skills for both parts. The question-generating and exam strategies were invaluable, and the reasoning strategies helped me zero in on what was important. Since I just started in college this year, there's a lot that I don't know about marketing. But I did so well that I placed second in the state!

How would I have done without LTL? If I hadn't had the LTL skills, I wouldn't have made it through my first year of college, much less gotten A's. Going back to school was a major change in my life. And with LTL, I made it through the hardest part, and I know I'm going to continue to do well.

Campus Services for Adults Returning to School

With increasing numbers of adults returning to school, many colleges have made special accommodations to serve the needs of these students. Does your college have these services? If not, can you work with a dean or counselor to find some creative alternatives?

◆ *Registration*. Are students required to register for courses in person? Can you register for courses by telephone, mail, computer, or fax?

◆ *Parking*. Is free parking available to commuter students? If cars must be registered for on-campus parking, can this be done by telephone, mail, computer, or fax? Is the parking lot well-lit for students taking classes in the evening?

◆ *Office hours*. Are there evening office hours for important services like financial aid? If not, can assistance be provided by telephone, mail, computer, or fax?

◆ *Off-campus student facilities and services*. Do special offices provide services to commuter students – especially students taking evening classes? Does your college have study areas for off-campus students? Is there a lounge with food vending machines for off-campus students?

◆ *Library services*. Is the library open at convenient hours? If you are taking courses at a remote location, is there an interlibrary agreement between the main campus library and your local library?

◆ *Career services*. Does your college's career center provide services to adults who are making mid-career changes, or whose jobs have been eliminated through downsizing?

In Your Words:
Using Campus Resources for Adults

In the space below, write about how you can use these resources on your campus *this year*.

_____

_____

_____

_____

_____

_____

_____

RELATIONSHIPS AT HOME AND WORK

If you're an adult returning to school, you've got a lot on your mind. You may have many responsibilities: to children and to a spouse; perhaps also to aged parents and to an employer. There never seems to be enough time.

Also, you may feel at a disadvantage in comparison to college-aged students whose only responsibility is to do well in school. Not only do these young students have less to worry about and take care of – but also they've been in school all along. They may seem to you quicker, less subject to the very real responsibilities of an adult. And they're used to the discipline of studying.

Building From Experience

But there are very real advantages to returning to school as an adult. Because college is not a game or a party to you, you're probably more goal-oriented than younger students are. You know that you don't have time to waste, and you'll be selective about the courses you're taking. You're also used to thinking independently, you don't bend to authority because it is authority – and your opinions are likely to be more interesting in the classroom, and more valued by your professors, as a result.

As an adult, coming to new fields with a background of your own experiences, you have a context within which to fit much of what you're learning. So even if you may not have the "freshness" of youth, your learning may be richer, and your need to memorize less, because you have a wider understanding – and may be able to see many ways to apply what you're learning.

And if you have an academic setback, your world won't fall apart, as it might for a younger student. The fact that you've returned to school marks you as a determined person who knows how to overcome barriers.

Student Voices

Gregory Herman
Computer Programming

I took the Learning to Learn course the first semester of my freshman year at State. I was just beginning a two-year college program, and I had been out of school for 15 years.

Well, Learning to Learn helped me tremendously. I came out of school with a 3.81. As a result, I'm in two honor societies, and in the National Dean's Register. It felt great going back go school and doing so well. But I don't think that there was anything special about me. I did well because I was using the LTL methods, and it would definitely work for anyone who really used this system.

Now that I'm out of school, I'm still using LTL methods. I could go on and on. Basically, I'd like to say that the Learning to Learn system has given me a gift that I can carry with me throughout my life.

PERSONAL RELATIONSHIPS

There's often a certain amount of stress in returning to school as an adult. You need a supportive environment. In many cases, family members are proud when an adult in the family returns to school. But your family may not welcome your return to school – especially if you've been seen mostly as a care-giver, and your family still wants the same amount of care you gave before you returned to school.

RELATIONSHIPS WITH YOUR SPOUSE

Starting college marks an important transition in your life. If you're married, you and your spouse may have been through a lot together – growing through job changes, making a home together, perhaps raising a family. *Don't* keep your spouse out of this part of your life. Involve him or her in as many ways as possible. For example:

◆ Keep open lines of communication. Share your course planning with your spouse – including what courses you plan to take, and when you plan to take them. Listen to his or her feelings, and share your own.

◆ Understand that your spouse may resent your plans – feeling that your dreams will be realized, while he/she only gets more daily-task drudgery. Plan practical changes in household chores; be flexible with each other; make compromises with each other. Your spouse, your family are your top priorities. Let them know that, by what you say and what you do.

◆ Let your spouse know when you'll be most busy – say, at exam time. Planning ahead can save lots of headaches later.

◆ Find time for short walks with your spouse, for occasional evenings at the movies.

◆ Discuss your spouse's dreams, and how you can help them come true.

In Your Words:
Relationships With Your Spouse

Write some questions you'll want to answer – with your spouse – about the changes your college career will bring to your relationship:

_____

_____

_____

_____

_____

RELATIONSHIPS WITH YOUR CHILDREN

Let your children know what your plans are. Help them understand what changes will happen at home.

◆ Tell your children how important their help will be.

◆ Decide with them which chores they will undertake. (And, as with your spouse, be tolerant about the standards. Learn to accept a "pretty good" job of doing the laundry, folding towels, etc.)

◆ Let them know which activities you'll be available for, and which not. (You'll see them in the school play, but won't be able to make the costumes.)

◆ Tell them you need a quiet time and place to study – and that you're not going to be available to them during your study time. (You may find that setting up such a time and place provides a good model for your children – and helps them copy your example.)

◆ Take them to your college. Younger children will be more comfortable understanding where you are when you're away from home. And older children may be interested in the campus student center, the library, or campus events, like a film series.

In Your Words:
Relationships With Your Children

Write some questions you'll want to answer – for your children – about the changes your college career will bring to your responsibilities at home:

_____

_____

_____

_____

_____

_____

_____

_____

_____

_____

_____

_____

_____

Child Care

Child care is an issue of great concern to a parent returning to school. You want to be sure that your child is happy and safe, that he/she is eating good food, having a good time, being well cared-for. If you feel comfortable about your child care situation, you'll have the emotional energy you need to focus on school. Remember, in all child care situations, you have the right to ask any questions you want to – and the right to stop in at any time to see if your child is happy and involved.

Can you arrange for child care *before* you begin school? If you're working during the day, and going to school at night, available child care may be hard to find. Can you find a responsible teen-ager who will take care of your child at home? Can you "trade" child care nights with a friend who is also going to school at night, but taking courses on nights when you're at home?

You may find that there is day care on campus. If you're at a university, the day care may be part of an internship program for students at the school of education – and may be free of charge.

Can you form a day care cooperative with other parents, where you hire a professional together to care for your children? If you have school-aged children, are there after-school programs your child can be part of? If you have teen-aged children, let them know how to reach you; let them know where you'll be and what you'll be doing. Try to arrange after-school work or activities for them. Busy teen-agers are less likely to get into trouble.

What about emergencies? Snow days or sick-child days? Can you arrange a back-up system to take care of these unplanned events?

Above all, keep open the lines of communication between you and your children around child care, your school, and all other issues. Good communication helps people respect and take care of each other.

In Your Words:
Child Care Options

Working with another student, brainstorm some child care options that may be available to you:

_____

_____

_____

_____

_____

_____

_____

_____

RELATIONSHIPS WITH YOUR FRIENDS

Your friends may support your efforts to return to school. They may offer to help in a variety of ways. Find ways to accept their help: As the song says, "That's what friends are for."

But some of your friends may resent the changes in your life. They may not understand the new demands on your life and time. They may be threatened, feeling that you're moving into a new world, with new interests. If these are close friends, reassure them that you can still share confidences; but that you need to set limits on your time, so you don't wear yourself out. If your friends are mature, they will understand.

It's helpful to have all the support you can get. Arrange for your own cheerleaders. You'll make new friends at school – people in your classes, or students who work on projects with you. Find others at your college who are in a similar situation. Meet them for coffee between classes. Share experiences, and perhaps some responsibilities – like carpooling.

In Your Words:
Relationships With Your Friends

Write some questions you'll want to ask your friends – and yourself. What kinds of support can you expect from them? How available will you be to them?

_____

_____

_____

_____

_____

_____

What kind of support can you expect from new friends – those you meet at school, who are having similar experiences? Realistically, how can you be helpful to them?

_____

_____

_____

_____

_____

_____

RELATIONSHIPS AT WORK

Many employers encourage, and even pay for, continued education for their employees. As with your family, the best policy is to keep the lines of communication open.

◆ Discuss your plans with your employer. Find ways that your return to school can have the least interference with your work.

◆ If your work has seasonal peaks, try to schedule a reduced school load for periods when your work load is most heavy.

◆ Get started early on large academic projects and term papers, so you don't find yourself too stressed by work/academic requirements.

◆ Testing yourself 10 minutes a day on your lecture-note and reading questions will prevent you from having to "crash" study during exam times.

◆ Whenever possible, relate academic projects to your work. Let your employer know when you're doing this. You'll get more support for your academic efforts if you find ways to relate what you're learning to your performance on the job.

◆ Let your employer know if you must leave work for a class. Don't just leave.

◆ When planning your courses next semester, take your work schedule into account. For example, if your work requires travel, check this out with your future professors. If frequent classroom participation is required, you might choose a different course or arrange to do an extra project to make up for time out of class.

In Your Words:
Relationships With Your Employer

Write some questions your employer may want to ask you about how your return to school will impact your performance on the job.

_____

_____

_____

_____

_____

_____

_____

_____

RELATIONSHIPS WITH YOUR CO-WORKERS

People you work with may have a wide range of reactions to your going back to school.

◆ Some may support your efforts, and find ways to be helpful to you.

◆ Others may resent your attempts to make a better life for yourself, and – consciously or not – put some obstacles in your way.

The best way to deal with your co-workers on the issue of your going back to school is to make an effort not to get special treatment. For example, if you must leave early for some classes, make up the time later. Be aware of continuing to do your share of the work. And find ways to give back attention, care, and help to those who help you.

In Your Words:
Relationships With Co-Workers

Write some questions your co-workers may want to ask you about how your return to school will impact your working relations with them.

_____

_____

_____

_____

_____

_____

_____

_____

_____

_____

_____

_____

_____

_____

_____

_____

LEARNING TO LEARN® AT WORK

There are many ways you can use LTL skills to improve your workplace performance. For example:

◆ Generate questions (Chapter 3) in your attempts to solve workplace problems.

◆ Use Question Charts and Key Word Diagrams from Chapter 6 to create graphic displays and effectively use complex workplace information.

◆ Task Management (Chapter 5) can help you get work done on the job.

Empower Yourself
Using LTL at Work

Can you think of some workplace problems that might be solved with LTL? Are there specific ways you can use LTL skills on the job?

_____

_____

_____

_____

_____

_____

_____

_____

_____

_____

_____

_____

_____

_____

_____

_____

_____

_____

_____

USING LTL SKILLS IN DAILY LIFE

Daily living applications of LTL skills can be very useful to you as an adult returning to school.

◆ *The Four LTL Thinking Tools* (Chapter 2) can help you solve a wide range of personal problems.

◆ *Task Management* (Chapter 5) can help you arrange your priorities and break complex tasks into manageable parts.

◆ *Stress management and relaxation methods* (Chapter 10) will help you through the tough spots.

◆ *Question Charts* (Chapter 6) can help you assess the costs and benefits of the decisions you'll have to make.

◆ *Key Word Diagrams* (Chapter 6) can help you picture the results of certain actions. And asking questions can help you think through your day and predict and solve problems as you work towards a more successful future.

In Your Words:
LTL Skills in Daily Life

What other ways do you think the LTL skills can help you solve problems related to returning to school?

_____

_____

_____

_____

_____

_____

_____

_____

_____

_____

_____

Applying LTL Thinking Tools
Returning to School as an Adult

Writing questions

Write some questions which the material on returning to school as an adult raised – either questions directly reflecting the material, or questions that were not addressed, but are important to you.

_____

_____

_____

_____

Focusing on goals

After writing your questions, you should be ready to focus on your goals in this area. What changes would you like to make as an adult returning to school?

_____

_____

_____

_____

Breaking large tasks into manageable parts

What comes first? Write the order of changes that you think you can make in order of importance and/or how easily the changes might be made. Set yourself some short-term goals in this area.

_____

_____

_____

_____

Assessing your progress

How will you know if you're closer to meeting your short-term goals? Write down your own short-term goals and take data on your behavior for the next 2 months. Are you achieving your goals?

_____

_____

_____

_____

Internet Exercise

Find a chat group for adult students returning to school.

1. Go to Yahoo! and click on the Webcrawler search engine.
2. When you get to that search engine, click on "Older returning students" under "Message boards."

THE RETURNING TO SCHOOL GAME

Going back to school as an adult is an exciting challenge – but full of hurdles. Working in pairs, make up situations that might be faced by an adult returning to school.

Write your situations on 3″ x 5″ cards.

The 3″x 5″ cards are shuffled, and the class forms 2 teams.

Each round of the game has two contestants. A card is selected by the game leader, and read aloud. The contestants then have 3 minutes to figure out a solution to the "situation." (Only responses with key points on 3″ x 5″ cards are counted. This will minimize the 2nd contestant's advantage.) The contestant whose answer gets the loudest applause wins the round. (You can score the answers in any way you want – the most humorous answer; the most practical answer, etc.)

The team with the most points wins the game.

The LTL Journal

Continue your journal of your thoughts and feelings. How can the information in this chapter help you be successful as an adult returning to school?

Chapter 12:
PRACTICAL MATTERS

In many ways, your college experience is framed by two very practical matters – paying for college and the rewards of the career that a college degree can help you attain. We'll look at some issues related to both of these matters in this chapter.

With college tuitions skyrocketing, how to pay for college is important to the career of every college student. You'll learn to think through living on a budget, as well as the positive and negative aspects of using credit. You'll learn about federal and private financial aid programs, and you'll assess all of this information through the lens of the Four LTL Thinking Tools.

You'll probably have more than one career in your life. In the career section of this chapter, you'll discover that many skills you'll acquire at college are central to success in a wide variety of careers. We'll suggest ways that you can establish a network of contacts and use information-seeking interviews to find out more about your career goals The Four LTL Thinking Tools will help you find practical uses for this new look at career planning.

HANDLING YOUR FINANCES:
LIVING ON A BUDGET

At college you may have your first encounter with living on a budget. If you're a recent high school graduate, you may have been given an allowance or held down a part-time job for weekly entertainment activities in high school. But at college you're responsible for keeping all financial aspects of your life together – having enough money for both essentials and non-essentials. Here's a way to guide yourself through this process.

Start with your available money for the year (anticipated through your job; provided by a grant or scholarship; earned last summer; supplied by relatives). Write down the total amount of money you're sure to have this academic year. Now make up two lists of expenses: those you can predict and those which are less clear-cut.

✔ **THINK ABOUT THIS**

If you're an adult with added responsibilities, like children or aging parents, your list may be different from the one that follows. The key idea of this section is to obtain a specific, realistic view of your overall needs at the start of your academic career, so you can be better prepared when emergencies arise.

Anticipated Expenses
How much will it cost to:

◆ Buy textbooks and school supplies for the year?

◆ Travel to and from school and work?

◆ Go to the movies?

◆ Eat off campus?

◆ Take your annual vacation?

◆ If you're a parent: Provide for your children?

◆ buy Christmas or Chanukah and birthday presents?

◆ etc.

When you add up these items, and subtract them from the total amount of money you'll have for the year, you'll have a better idea how to budget for daily living expenses.

Less Predictable Expenses

Take data on yourself for a week early in the fall term, and look for the following kinds of weekly expenses:

◆ "Junk food" from dispensing machines

◆ Toiletry supplies, facial tissues, cold remedies, etc.

◆ Week-end entertainment

We're not asking you to keep to a rigid accounting of everything you buy all year. But if you keep track of what you spend for a week, you'll have a pretty good idea of what you're going to be spending for the year. Use the chart on the next page to keep track of these expenses.

Once you've looked at how these two expense lists add up against the amount of money you'll have this year, you'll have a better idea of what your financial picture really is. At this point, ask yourself the following questions:

◆ Can you get an extra part-time job or one which pays better than your current job?

◆ Can you plan a cheaper vacation?

◆ What can you cut out of your weekly budget on a regular basis? (It's important not to kid yourself here: You *will* get a cold, you *will* go to the movies, etc.)

If all of this doesn't add up, see the people at your school's counseling office. They'll help you set priorities so that you'll have resources when you really need them.

WEEKLY EXPENSE RECORD

	Food & Drink	Transportation	Telephone	Movies, etc.	Toiletries	Misc.
Monday						
Tuesday						
Wednesday						
Thursday						
Friday						
Saturday						
Sunday						

Student Voices

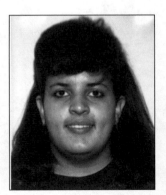

Rosie Herrera

I had a poor feeling towards school when I was in high school. I did what I had to do to get by. I just didn't read things, because I knew that I wouldn't understand them.

I took the Learning to Learn course in my freshman year. It helped my grades, but the most important thing was that it changed my attitude towards school. Using LTL meant a big improvement in my schoolwork. When I entered college, I was put in the Bridge Program because of my poor high school grades. I've used the LTL skills for two semesters now, and my grades are good enough so that I've been accepted into the nursing program.

USING CREDIT

If you've never used credit cards, you'll have a lot of opportunity to obtain credit cards as a college student. For example, some credit card companies provide credit card applications in college bookstores.

There are positive and negative effects of using credit.

On the positive side,

◆ *Establish a good credit history.*
If you use credit cards moderately and pay your bills on time, you can establish a good credit history. There are agencies like TRW which track people's credit history and provide the information to loan institutions. So if you'd like to buy a car or a home in the future, building a good credit history is an important place to start.

◆ *Take care of emergencies.*
Leaving an available balance on your credit cards can help you in an emergency – when you need to get home in a hurry, or if you get unexpectedly stuck in a strange place without a roof over your head.

◆ *Keep track of expenses.*
Credit cards keep a written record of all purchases, so it's easy to see where your money is going by looking at your monthly credit card statement.

◆ *Qualify for credit card bonuses.*
Many credit card companies offer bonuses – like free airline miles or other travel discounts – and some have tie-ins to related goods and services.

On the negative side,

◆ *Using a credit card means taking out a high-interest loan.*
Credit card interest is much higher than interest on a bank loan: It can be as high as 15 – 23%. That means that you're losing a significant amount of money every month you don't pay off your credit card loan.

◆ *Living on credit can be addictive.*
If you keep telling yourself that you'll pay off your credit cards next month, and you keep on acquiring new credit cards, you can get yourself into a deep financial hole. Living on credit can be a very hard habit to break. There are even support groups for people who get "hooked" on credit.

◆ *You can ruin your credit history.*
A bad credit rating can stay with you for years, making it difficult or impossible to get a car loan or a home mortgage. Once you get a poor credit rating, it's very hard to re-build good credit. Agencies like TRW keep instances of poor credit – like unpaid bills or credit card defaults – on their books for several years.

OBTAINING FINANCIAL AID

Most students and their families cannot privately finance a college education. For this reason, there's a system of grants, jobs, and loans, mostly under the direction of the federal government. In addition to federally sponsored programs, there may be local or school-based grants. In this section, we'll give you a general introduction to these sources of funds.

Federally Sponsored Programs

◆ **Pell Grants**. These are need-based federal grants where eligibility is determined by a standard formula relating to family income. As grants, these funds do not have to be repaid.

◆ **Supplemental Educational Opportunity Grants** *(SEOG)*. This grant is awarded on the basis of need, the availability of the grant at your campus, and the other aid received. Since the amount of these funds is limited, it's important to apply for them early.

◆ **College Work Study** *(CWS)*. The CWS Program provides jobs to college students who qualify for financial aid. The amount of aid and types of jobs will vary on different college campuses. In addition, at some schools there are both on-campus and off-campus CWS jobs. Off-campus jobs might be at a local non-profit organization which has arranged placements through your college. It's important to check out this option if you plan to go into a human service profession, since you may find that you can build your résumé while working at a CWS position. Again, deadlines for these CWS positions vary with each college.

◆ **Federal Direct Student Loans** *(FDSL)*. Available at low interest rates, the amount of the loan is based on need and the amount of FDSL funds at your college.

◆ **Other Loan Programs**. The federal government administers or supervises additional student loan programs, including the *Perkins Loans, Stafford Loans,* and *Plus Loans.*

◆ **Military Commissioning and Scholarship Programs**. Your college may maintain connections with branches of the military service and may be able to provide you with information if you would like to pursue training and a career in the military. You may be eligible for full or partial scholarships. If you're interested in these programs, see your Dean of Students or Financial Aid Office for more information.

To find out more about these financial aid programs:

◆ Obtain a copy of *The Student Guide* from the U.S. Department of Education, Office of Financial Assistance, Washington, DC 20202-5464.

◆ Contact the Federal Student Aid Information Center, P.O. Box 84, Washington, DC 20044, (800) 433-3243.

Private Loans and Grants

◆ **Guaranteed Student Loans** *(GSL)*. This loan is not school-based. It may be obtained through a bank, credit union, or savings and loan association. Because it is a loan, it must be repaid; interest on these loans is generally 7–9%. The cost of obtaining a loan may be steep: Look carefully at all your resources before you decide to obtain a bank loan to finance your college education.

Here is an example of some typical monthly payments for paying off a loan with an 8% interest rate:

Total Amount of Loan	Monthly Payment (if paid in 5 years)	Total Interest & Principal Repaid	Monthly Payment (if paid in 10 years)	Total Interest & Principal Repaid
$5000.00	$230.00	$12,180.00	$121.00	$14,520

◆ **Special-Case Scholarships.** You may find that your community or local fraternal groups have scholarship funds for students like you. Check your local Chamber of Commerce for information on local scholarship funds. In addition, your college may have little-known scholarships for people with specific characteristics (e.g., students from a particular area of the country, with a particular name, etc.). Check your college's Financial Aid and Development Offices to see if you fit any of the criteria for unusual, little-known scholarships.

Internet Exercise

For answers to frequently asked questions about financial aid – including private scolarships – check out this Internet address:

`http://www.finaid.com`

Applying LTL Thinking Tools
Financial Matters

Writing questions
Write questions which the previous material raised for you – either questions directly reflecting the material, or questions which were not answered, but are important to you.

_____

_____

_____

_____

Focusing on goals
After writing your questions, you should be ready to focus on your goals in this area. What kind of changes would you like to make related to your management of money?

_____

_____

_____

_____

Breaking large tasks into manageable parts
What comes first? Write the order of changes that you think you can make in order of importance and/or how easily the changes might be made. Set some short-term goals in this area.

_____

_____

_____

_____

Assessing your progress
How will you know if you're closer to meeting your short-term goals? Write down your own short-term goals and take data on your spending patterns for the next 2 months. If you're achieving your goals, reward yourself with a gift which results from your savings. If you've planned well, there should be something you'd like that you can now afford.

_____

_____

_____

_____

YOUR CAREER: CHOICES FOR THE FUTURE

Three things are important to remember when you're thinking about a career in relation to your life as a student:

◆ As a student trained in Learning to Learn®, you may have an open door not readily available to non-LTL students. For example, many companies are now training their employees in Learning to Learn®. Since employee training is expensive, new employees already trained in LTL may have an initial advantage in the hiring process.

◆ This is your life. The choices you make, for majors, electives, and later for a career, should be your choices. Only you will experience the highs and lows of daily life resulting from these choices.

◆ You will probably have more than one career in your life. The choices you make now will change over time, depending on your experiences.

All this means that, even after you've chosen a major, you're *not* locked in for life to the choices you are making now. Besides preparing yourself in your major field, you'll be developing your *transferable skills* and finding out more about yourself and who you are becoming.

Self-Assessment

In order to look intelligently at what you want to do, it's important to find out about what and who you are. The **values clarification** exercises mentioned in Chapter 8 should help with this. Also, it's a good idea to look at yourself from the perspective of the career-related aspects of your personality. Asking yourself the following questions should help:

◆ What are your interests and hobbies? Do they involve working with others or working alone? Solving particular kinds of problems? Contributing to a worthwhile cause?

◆ Have you ever known anyone who worked at something that interested you? What aspect of their work did you find exciting?

◆ In the jobs you have had thus far, which aspects of the work did you most enjoy? Which did you like the least?

◆ Picture yourself in 10 years' time. What do you want to be doing with your life? Put as much detail into the picture as possible. Try to imagine what an average day would be like. What kinds of responsibilities would you like to have in your work?

Course Selection
and Transferable Skills

You don't need to have a vocationally specific major, like accounting or nursing, to be successful in many careers. The transferable skills you develop in college will help you do well in a wide variety of careers:

Speaking

Good public speaking and thinking quickly on your feet are skills which need practice, both in and out of classrooms. Join organizations, and practice the question-writing methods until you find yourself able to volunteer questions and ideas in class and in the organizations you join.

Writing

Take courses which require good writing skills, and practice writing in a variety of formal and informal situations: Write letters to the editor or columns in your school newspaper. Don't always call home – write. Keep a diary – a journal of personal ideas, or of important events – whatever works for you.

Supervising

Take responsibility for projects in organizations you join, group assignments, etc. Learn how to give and take orders and advice from people who supervise you and whom you supervise. You might gain experience by becoming a Big Brother or Big Sister in a local community service organization.

Teaching

Find a skill you have and look for chances – formal or informal – to teach it to others. Teaching will help you learn to organize your ideas and will give you valuable practice in public speaking and supervising others. Look for a teaching assistant position; teach an adult education course; work as a tutor in a local community service organization.

Interviewing

Whenever you're going into an interview situation — whether it's an information-gathering or a job interview – write questions first, make up key word answers, and practice the interview informally at home. It's just like the predicting questions and exam preparation skills you learned earlier in this book: *Practice the activity which you'll later be expected to perform under pressure.*

Coping with Deadlines

Use LTL Task Management methods for non-academic as well as academic aspects of your life. When you begin to break large tasks into smaller parts as part of the way you think, you'll be better at dealing with deadline pressures. Test this – put yourself in situations where you have artificial (i.e., constructed by you) deadlines. How well does the task management system work? In what ways, if any, will you change this system to help you with non-academic deadline pressures?

Public Relations

Put yourself in situations where you have to greet visitors, answer the phone, explain programs to clients, etc. In these situations, how well do you respond to other people's questions and needs? Do you try to be aware of their questions, or do you just reel off information you think they probably need to know?

Negotiating

In your personal life, as well as in dealings you have with instructors, employers, and co-workers, learn how to see both sides of a question and find ways to negotiate between warring parties – to state each side's position to each other.

Organizing

Take responsibility for events – organizing a party, a school conference, a meeting. Through these kinds of activities, you'll learn the relationship between planning and achieving goals. You'll see that deciding the step size of an activity – breaking a large task into sub-tasks – can be as important as your choice of the direction to meet a given goal.

Managing a Budget

We talked about managing your personal budget earlier in this chapter. If you can, get involved in planning and budget management for a group or organization.

Whenever you apply for a position – either during college or after graduation – be sure to mention your transferable skills, and talk about how you feel these skills will be helpful to an employer. Make changes in emphasis as needed: Organization and planning skills will be more important than budget management for some positions, for example. Include mention of these transferable skills both on résumés and in interviews. Also, your list of questions and answers for interviews and the content of your résumé should vary according to the positions you're applying for.

In Your Words:
Gaining Experience

How can informal experience in these areas help you attain your career goals?

_____

_____

_____

_____

_____

_____

INFORMATION-SEEKING INTERVIEWS

In choosing a career, you'll want to know more than flyers or brochures — and even the most skilled person at your school's Career Center – can tell you. You'll want to know what a particular job is like from people who currently hold that type of job. Make appointments with people at lower, middle, and higher level positions in fields which interest you. Here are some questions you'll want to ask:

◆ *What is the daily job like?*

◆ *What kind of academic and/or job experience was necessary for that person to obtain his/her current position?*

◆ *What are the best and worst aspects of the position?*

◆ *How much and what kind of responsibility does the position call for?*

◆ *How easy is it to assume greater levels of responsibility and to rise in the ranks of that career?*

◆ *(What are some other questions you might ask?)*

We would not suggest that you ask people how much they are paid – you can get this kind of information elsewhere. Nor is this a job-seeking interview. You want to know the daily details and general picture of the job and its related career – and whether the activities interest you and would call for your skills.

ESTABLISHING A CONTACT NETWORK

This is often an important aspect of obtaining the "right" entry-level position. Here are some suggestions for making contacts in your chosen field:

◆ Use the alumni network for your college, if your school's career center has organized such a network.

◆ Brainstorm which personal contacts may be useful to you – friends, relations, previous employers and instructors, etc.

◆ Take advantage of internship opportunities in your intended career area. Internship programs have important benefits for your future: They help you gain experience, which you should put on your résumé; they help you make personal connections with people in your area of interest who may later be able to help you; and, they give you a chance to find out if you really like the area you've been interested in.

Applying LTL Thinking Tools
Career Planning

Writing questions
Write some questions which the material on careers raised – either questions directly reflecting the material or questions that were not addressed, but are important to you.

_____

_____

_____

_____

Focusing on goals
After writing your questions, you should be ready to focus on your goals in this area. What kind of changes would you like to make related to your career planning?

_____

_____

_____

_____

Breaking large tasks into manageable parts
What comes first? Write the order of changes that you think you can make in order of importance and/or how easily the changes might be made. Set some short-term goals.

_____

_____

_____

_____

Assessing your progress
How will you know if you're closer to meeting your short-term goals? Write down your own short-term goals and take data on your career-related activities for the next 2 months.

Internet Exercise

Explore the Internet for websites related to "careers".

1. Go to Yahoo! and click on a search engine like Webcrawler or Infoseek.

2. When you get to that search engine, click on "careers."

CAREERS GAME

Divide the class into 2 teams. Each player draws from a deck of cards. He/she is the only member of his/her team to see the card. Each card contains the name of a career and words commonly used describing that career. (e.g., nurse: sick, hospital, doctor, medicine). The player must describe the career *without* using any of the words on the card. To receive a point for the round, members of the player's team must call out the correct career name within 3 minutes. (A player from the other team watches to ensure that the player does not use a taboo word. If a taboo word is used, the point goes to the other team.)

Needed: A stopwatch or egg timer. A deck of prepared cards.

The LTL Journal

Continue your journal of your thoughts and feelings. How can the information in this chapter help you plan your finances for school and reach your career goals?

REACHING FOR THE TOP 2
ASSESSING YOUR PROGRESS

Now that you've completed this course, rate yourself again on a *Reaching For The Top* chart. Rate yourself from 1–5 on each category below, with 1 = lowest and 5 = highest.

How We Learn
1. I know when and where I study best, and use this information to plan my study time.
2. I know if I'm a "big picture" or a "detail focus" learner, and have found ways to make up for what I'm missing.
3. I know if I'm a left- or right-brain learner, and use this information to study most effectively.
4. I know how messy or neat my optimal work environment is, and have set up my work environment to match my needs.
5. I know what the key barriers to my learning are, and have found ways to overcome them.

Generating Questions From Lecture Notes
1. I write my notes to the left of a 3-inch margin.
2. I record as much as possible, inserting * when I'm confused.
3. I generate questions from my lecture notes, making sure that I'm writing enough higher-level questions.
4. I write "What if...?" and Creative Questions about information I'd like to know about that was *not* mentioned in lectures.
5. I test myself on my lecture-note questions for 5 minutes every night.

Reading to Answer Questions
1. I write pre-reading questions and read to answer my questions.
2. I use my reading for self-testing.
3. I concentrate on math problem-solving questions when reading math-based material.
4. I use effective speed reading techniques.
5. I look for the distinctive "voice" when reading literature and poetry.

Time/Task Management
1. I have a good estimate of how long it will take me to do my school work and other work.
2. I break up complex tasks into manageable parts.
3. I take short, creative breaks.
4. I monitor my progress in completing major projects.
5. I map out a large task, and work backwards, ensuring that I have enough time to complete the task.

Preparing for Exams
1. I generate exam-type questions to prepare for exams.
2. I use visual organizers to prepare for exams.
3. I test myself when preparing for exams.
4. I have an effective strategy for taking objective tests.
5. I have an effective strategy for taking essay exams.

Writing, Research, & the Internet
1. I write well-constructed paragraphs.
2. I have an effective strategy for writing term papers.
3. I back up my written ideas with evidence.
3. I know how to do research using the Internet.
4. I know how to do research using an electronic card catalogue.

Being All That You Can Be
1. I am good at taking initiative.
2. I can see the positive side of things.
3. My self-esteem is good.
4. I have effective ways of helping myself overcome self-doubts.
5. I act in accordance with my values.

Relationships
1. I am good at making and keeping friends.
2. I feel confident in a romantic relationship.
3. My relationships are free of racism.
4. My relationships are free of sexism.
5. I act in an ethical way in my relationships with others.

Being Healthy
1. I use effective methods to reduce stress.
2. I eat in a healthy way.
3. I get enough exercise.
4. I have a responsible approach to sexual activity.
5. I am free from addictions.

For Adult Students: Going Back to School
1. I know where to find campus resources for adult students.
2. I balance school and work well.
3. I have an effective way to balance my responsibilities to school and my responsibilities to my spouse.
4. I have an effective way to balance my responsibilities to school and my responsibilities to my children.
5. I have an effective way to balance my responsibilities to school and my responsibilities to my employer.

Practical Matters
1. I know how to live on a budget.
2. I have an effective way to finance college.
3. When choosing my courses and extra-curricular activities, I take into account transferable skills.
4. I have a plan to establish a contact network.
5. I have clear career goals.

Where are you now?

Add up your total score. Your score on each category has a possible range of 5 (if you rated yourself 1 on each item) to 25 (if you rated yourself 5 on each item). Fill in the bar graph below, and compare your graph to your Pre-Course Assessment on pages 13-15.

Assessing Your Progress

Chart the results of your self-assessment here:

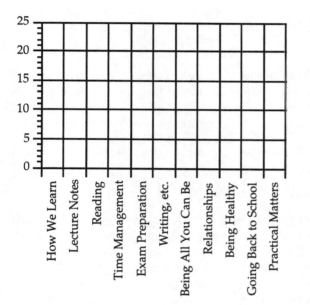

CONCLUSION

If we've achieved the task we set out to achieve, you are now an independent learner. You'll continue to raise questions about what you read and hear – and these questions will go beyond reflecting information to evaluating its meaning and its place in your task-oriented thinking. When you find a difficult problem in or out of school, you'll break it into smaller, more manageable, parts; you'll talk your work out loud to yourself (or to a trusted friend) when you get stuck; you'll draw pictures and diagrams to construct the meaning behind initially obscure information and ideas. And all of this will become almost like a game for you – exciting because you can see where you're going, and what you need to know to get there. You're playing a kind of video-arcade game of the mind, where you get immediate feedback.

You'll learn to question "finished" products in your courses – to ask yourself *why* and *how,* and not just memorize steps in accounting or symptoms of an illness for nursing. *(Why is this item where it is? Why did this happen when it did? How does this information relate to the rest of the course?)* You'll become an active thinker, less dependent on others for ideas and solutions to problems, both in school and out. You'll be goal-oriented: When you do research for a paper, you won't spend time chasing down facts you don't need. You'll move confidently in your new environment, achieving the results you need to succeed.

When you explore the concepts in this book, you'll find things possible that were not so before. We know from the experience of many students that you'll reach your goals if you apply these techniques to your academic and non-academic life – even if you happen to face obstacles along the way. This new ability will give your life a clearer direction, greater purpose, important achievements and satisfaction. You'll spend your time more productively, knowing that you can do what's needed to get where you want to be.

Index

Photo credits

Cover photograph by Asia Kepka
All students in the cover photograph attend the Boston Conservatory
1st row: Marisa Geary
2nd row, left to right: Julian Reyes Epstein, Amanda Brasher, Daniella Rossy
3rd row, left to right: Preston Morris, Chris O'Hara

Chapter 1 facing page: Boston College
Chapter 2 facing page (page 16): Boston College
Chapter 3 facing page (page 44): Fayetteville State University
Chapter 4 facing page (page 70): Boston College
Chapter 5 facing page (page 98): Savannah State University
Chapter 6 facing page (page 114): Boston College
Chapter 7 facing page (page 152): Benedict College
Chapter 8 facing page (page 184): Boston College
Chapter 9 facing page (page 206): Boston College
Chapter 10 facing page (page 220): Boston College
Chapter 11 facing page (page 244): Boston College
Chapter 12 facing page (page 260): Fayetteville State University
Page 10: Harvard Crimson
Page 22: Boston College
Page 37: Boston College
Page 64: Boston College
Page 79: Howard University
Page 100: Boston College
Page 106: Boston College
Page 111: Boston College
Page 127: Hampton University
Page 134: Boston College
Page 150: Boston College
Page 159: Boston College
Page 161: Marcia Heiman
Page 164: Boston College
Page 199: Marcia Heiman
Page 208: Marcia Heiman
Page 213: Harvard Crimson
Page 239: Boston College
Page 241: Boston College
Page 274: Kirkwood
Page 278: Boston College